Psycholinguistics

Introductory Perspectives

Psycholinguistics

Introductory Perspectives

Joseph F. Kess

University of Victoria

Academic Press New York San Francisco London

A Subsidiary of Harcourt Brace Jovanovich, Publishers

ACADEMIC PRESS, INC.
111 Fifth Avenue, New York, New York 10003

United Kingdom Edition published by
ACADEMIC PRESS, INC. (LONDON) LTD.
24/28 Oval Road, London NW1

Library of Congress Cataloging in Publication Data

Kess, Joseph F
    Psycholinguistics.

    Bibliography: p.
    Includes index.
    1.   Languages–Psychology.   2.   Language and
languages.   I.   Title.
P37.K47   401'.9   75-13076
ISBN 0–12–405250–9

**For Cathy,
and Mom and Dad**

1972160

Contents

10

Preface

This book is intended as a general, but readable and practical introduction to some of the main themes in the field of psycholinguistics. The field of psycholinguistics is a relatively new one, and has blossomed into countless publications and research techniques in the past several decades. Psycholinguistics is many things to many people, depending upon one's specific training and research interests. However, it is certainly safe to say that whatever has to do with the fuller understanding of language behavior is the proper subject matter of psycholinguistics.

The scope of psycholinguistics includes the investigation of the abilities involved in the human capacity called language and the investigation of the actual use of language by human beings. Man, it seems, must know whereof and wherefore he speaks, and as a result men have always been interested in the qualifiable side of language. How is it that language arises? How is it that language is maintained? What is the part played by language in acculturation to a given society and culture? Can it be that thought and language have some secret and powerful relationship that we are not entirely aware of in everyday conversation? Do we really say what we mean, and mean what we say? The questions are many, and the answers equally numerous.

Some may object that such questions are the special prerogative of specific disciplines. Still, the field of psycholinguistics is an interdisciplinary one and justly so, for after all, the questions one asks about language and those who speak languages are also relevant to the fields of anthropology, sociology, linguistics, psychology, philosophy, and education. In fact, the student of language finds himself in a complex web of relationships, which include not only those disciplines just mentioned but also the fields of communication engineering, political science, journalism, stylistic and literary analysis, aesthetics, advertising, and so forth—all of which depend on some facet of language behavior for their reason for being, or their inspiration, or both.

Since courses in psycholinguistics and language behavior are variously given in departments of psychology, linguistics, or various interdisciplinary programs, depending upon the college or university, and since students from various backgrounds often take these courses, I have tried to lay out some of the history of investigation into language activities and some of the approaches employed in doing so.

I have not attempted in this volume to go too far into the explanation of or promulgation of specific linguistic or psycholinguistic theories, and will trust that the interested reader will avail himself of the other detailed treatments on the subject. But I have tried to capture some of the more exciting topics, both traditional and current, in the field of language behavior, and have tried to give a general overview of what the direction of activity is or has been in those areas. This text can thus best serve as a first set of readings with which to orient oneself in the field of language behavior, and this is what the subtitle *Introductory Perspectives* was taken to imply.

Acknowledgments

I wish to acknowledge my debt to Howard McKaughan and M. H. Scargill for their support in the past. I am also indebted to Otfried Spreen and Gary Prideaux for having read and commented on substantial portions of the manuscript. I am particularly grateful to Ron Hoppe, not only for his review of the manuscript, but also for having been the ideal colleague to have shared a psycholinguistics course with. This work was supported by a sabbatical leave from the University of Victoria and a Canada Council Fellowship.

The Nature of Psycholinguistics

Language has been perhaps the most important influence on the directions in which man has developed. Although other members of the animal kingdom—for example, bees and dolphins—have highly developed communication systems, these systems are of a different order. The essence of human language, which distinguishes it from the communication systems of other animals, is the quality of abstraction. This quality allows man to use language for planning and reminiscing as well as for conversing. Man's development of written language systems has, of course, provided him with the means for a relatively unchanging and accurate external memory. Moreover, although the real world can be interpreted in many different ways, every human language, both written and spoken, does so in an extremely limited, relatively precise fashion. Thus, all the writers or speakers of a particular language have common points of reference.

The study of language as a characteristic behavior of the human species is embraced by the field of psycholinguistics. As the term implies, the field of psycholinguistics is essentially an outgrowth of two disciplines, psychology and linguistics, though theorists and experimenters in other fields continue to participate in the investigation of the psychology of language. The field still represents a variety of approaches that attempt to elucidate various facets of human language and of related behavior according to the model chosen and the investigation undertaken. As in most fields, there is, unfortunately, no single ultimate experimental question that, once answered, provides the answers to all the other questions.

Linguistics is the study of language as a system of highly patterned behavior. The purpose of most structural linguistic studies has been to describe a language itself—that is, to record, in the most precise and economical way possible, what is pertinent about that language. Such language descriptions are clearly taxonomic enterprises, consisting of highly ordered sets of rules that provide an accurate picture of how the language works.

The subject matter of psychology has traditionally been the study of human behavior in general, or, more specifically, the investigation of the general principles that underlie human behavior. A glance at any university catalog will quickly show the variety of interests in the field of psychology. Included as basic courses in a sound psychology curriculum are such topics as learning, motivation, perception, pathology, and social psychology. If the psychology of language, or psycholinguistics, does not appear as a separate course, then certainly it will appear as a subtopic in the larger field of social psychology. Looking at the catalog, one immediately grasps the difference between psychology and linguistics as they have been traditionally conceived of and practiced; psychologists are interested in the general laws governing human behavior, and linguists are interested in the specific laws governing a specific form of human behavior called language. Some generative transformational linguists, however, have suggested that the rigid separation between the disciplines is artificial and that linguistics is really a branch of cognitive psychology (N. Chomsky, 1968).

Interest in the psychology of language is by no means recent; psycholinguistic theory and research have had a long and fruitful history in both Europe and North America (Blumenthal, 1970). However, the current resurgence of widespread interest in psycholinguistic investigations is more the result of innovations in linguistic theory than in psychological theory. The following brief historical sketch should help to explain why.

In the past, some social scientists in other fields looked at the rigorous methodology developed in linguistics during its structuralist, or taxonomic, period and regarded both the method and the results with some envy. Here were a set of data whose boundaries seemed easily identifiable and a methodology that could be used to describe those data in a direct fashion. At several interdisciplinary meetings held under the auspices of the Social Science Research Council in the early 1950s, psychologists and linguists were provided with the formal opportunity to exchange views. The general consensus was that each discipline could profit from the other's perspective on language behavior.

Actually, as Maclay (1973) points out, the perspectives may not have been as dramatically different as the separation between the two disciplines implied. Both linguistics and psychology, at least those branches increasingly involved with psycholinguistic research, were committed to an operationalist, empiricist approach to scientific endeavor. Moreover, the very objects of their respective investigations were neatly separated. Osgood and Sebeok's definition (1954) of the field of psycholinguistics is illustrative:

> The rather new discipline coming to be known as psycholinguistics . . . is concerned in the broadest sense with relations between messages and the characteristics of human individuals who select and interpret them. In a narrower sense, psycholinguistics studies those processes whereby the intentions of speakers are transformed into signals in the culturally accepted code and whereby these signals are transformed in the interpretations of hearers. In other words, *psycholinguistics deals directly with the processes of encoding and decoding as they relate states of messages to states of communicators* [pp. 3-4].[1]

Thus, while linguists devoted themselves to the nature of the messages themselves, psychologists attempted to account for the communicators who produced and received those messages and for the way in which they did so.

This division of labor is very reminiscent of Morris's division (1938) of the primary relations of linguistic forms, as well as other signs, into pragmatics, semantics, and syntactics. Pragmatics encompassed the expressive aspects of a language, relating linguistic elements to their users; semantics had to do with those things or concepts that linguistic signs stood for or referred to; and syntactics dealt specifically with the formal relation of the linguistic signs to one another. The parallelism is highly suggestive, with psychology claiming pragmatics,

---

[1] From C. E. Osgood and T. A. Sebeok, Eds. *Psycholinguistics: A Survey of Theory and Research Problems.* Indiana University Publications in Anthropology and Linguistics, Memoir 10, 1954. Reprinted by permission of Indiana University Press, Bloomington, Indiana.

philosophy semantics, and linguistics syntactics, in this view. The same kind of division of labor was to characterize the relationship of psychology and linguistics in this period of psycholinguistics; so long as their empirical domains were well defined and their general mode of philosophies vaguely congruent, few differences arose.

The new hybrid term **psycholinguistics** began to appear with increasing frequency, and linguists and psychologists looked forward to increasingly profitable association in the years to come. However, the apparent unanimity that characterized the field of linguistics was soon rocked by the iconoclastic notions of N. Chomsky, whose *Syntactic Structures* (1957) changed the very outlook of the discipline. Among other things, Chomsky's claims about linguistics reoriented it from what he and his followers claimed was a taxonomic passion to a science more given to theory construction and rationalism. By **taxonomic,** Chomsky meant that linguistics was too obsessed with gathering and describing data and that little had actually been done in the realm of theory that might lead to a universal theory of language. It was as if linguistics were a verbal botany, tidily sorting, labeling, and classifying its specimens of language data. Linguistic theory was the methodology for discovering and labeling linguistic units in languages. In effect, linguistics consisted of a large number of small theories of individual languages, since a description of a given language is a theory of that language. Not enough attention was paid to the theory of language with a capital letter L—language as a universal grammatical theory of linguistic abilities. Whether this assertion was entirely warranted was hotly contested in both journal and conference, and the issue occasionally still arouses fierce debate.

Nevertheless, it would be unfair to say that what linguists did accomplish during the structuralist period was trivial or meaningless. They did develop a rigorous methodology that in practice was never taken to the extremes Chomsky claimed it was, and descriptions of language phenomena were certainly justifiable. Still, Chomsky's criticism of the direction that linguistics had taken since Bloomfield's primer, *Language,* was published in 1933 served to turn the discipline around in many quarters, initiated entirely new perspectives on language for many, and opened new avenues of research in general. This period, generative transformational grammar, named for the type of grammatical formulations used in the description of syntax, prevailed from 1957 until the late 1960s, when Chomsky's students in turn began to criticize the new direction and its methodologies and to initiate other theoretical concerns.

During the past two decades, the development of psycholinguistics has often paralleled that of linguistics. Although the research methods used in the two fields have not always been comparable, and the results have not always been translatable from one discipline to the other in a way that would allow the formulation of a composite theory of language, some of the recent trends in linguistic theory and method have had far-reaching ramifications in related areas of psycholinguistics. For example, as will be seen in the ensuing chapters, generative grammatical theory in linguistics is often reflected in psycholinguistics. Moreover, in a response to this interaction, some scholars are now studying the results of psycholinguistic investigations in the hope that a theory accounting for language behavior may serve as input to a theory of the essence of human language itself. Other social scientists, such as B. F. Skinner, the behavioral psychologist, and K. Pike, the linguist, would prefer a theory of language co-extensive with, or at least congruent with, a general theory of human behavior. In any case, the confluence of the two streams of investigation can only be productive, even if it does not result in the formulation of a complete model of language behavior.

However, there now seems to be a basic philosophical rift between older schools of investigation in psycholinguistics that exactly parallels the recent division in the field of linguistics. Many of the early contributions in linguistics, as well as in psycholinguistics, were derived largely from the seemingly objective and empirically based assumptions that guided so much of physical-science and behavioral-science activity in the West during the past several decades. These were the assumptions of the point of view most recently articulated as **logical positivism,** a philosophical movement holding that meaningful statements are either analytic and a priori or synthetic and a posteriori; the implication is that metaphysical and mentalistic theories are meaningless. This philosophy was elaborated into a methodological position in many sciences that called for rigor and objectivity in all taxonomic enterprises. According to many modern researchers, however, the use of this methodology sacrificed much of its insight to artificial rigor. The most influential recent critic of this methodology has obviously been Chomsky, who exchanged empiricism for rationalism in the description and analysis of linguistic behavior. This position, already reinforced by Chomsky's successes in the field of linguistic theory, has readily carried over into psycholinguistics, especially in discussions of language acquisition, semantics, and linguistic universals. Empirical approaches have, however, contributed substantially to our knowledge of language and are still being used in psycholinguistic research. Perhaps theoreticians are too single-minded in their concerns to admit or even realize that the interests served by one theory are not comparable to those served by another and that each contributes a great deal to our understanding. In the empirical, structuralist period of linguistics, theorists were not very interested in possible psychological correlates of many facets of their language descriptions. However, linguists did occasionally employ some measure of psychological reality in establishing their descriptions. For example, the establishment of the **phoneme** as the basic unit in the sound pattern of a language was based to some degree on speakers' recognition of functioning units in their respective languages. In eliciting speakers' responses that such words as *pit* and *bit* are different and thus establishing /p/ and /b/ as functioning phonemic units, one is at least indirectly testing recognition of the units. To assess whether the *p*-like sound in *pit, spit,* and *apt* or the *l*-like sound in *leap, full,* and *clip-clop* is the same is to assess speakers' categorical perceptions of the organization of sound patterns in the language. Accomplishing even such minor tasks by purely mechanical procedures is impossible; speakers' reality notions must be involved. Even Chomsky (1957, 1965) initially claimed that a model of generative transformational grammar does not represent a speaker–hearer in the sense of being a model or perfect analog of what goes on. But he later implies (1968) that there is a clear psychological interpretation for the linguist's theoretical and descriptive work in the study of universal and particular grammar. The task for the psycholinguist interested in verifying the psychological implications of linguistic models now is to discover to what extent the model accounts not merely for the language data but also for the possible processes whereby the actual language behavior is acquired and maintained. Much of modern psycholinguistics, like a good deal of modern linguistics, reflects Chomsky's theorizing about the structure of language and the nature of a theory of language. His theory of language, generative transformational grammatical theory, has provided the discipline of psycholinguistics with an integrated and relatively stable basis for the investigation of language. Equally important, it has provided for a new congruity of investigative concerns that makes discussion and evaluation possible.

One of the most important distinctions in Chomsky's theory of language that is reflected in psycholinguistics is the distinction between **competence** and **performance,** the deep-seated difference between a speaker's underlying abilities and knowledge of the language and his use of that language ability. The two are very different indeed, and they must be kept separate in an analysis of natural language. Natural language is not finite, but infinite. Speakers of natural languages can go on creating new sentences at will, and the chances of their repeating themselves in whole or in part are not all as great as one might think. As a result, a good many of the sentences that speakers utter are entirely novel. To verify this statement, you have only to examine the sentences on this page or in any other body of spoken or written language. Nevertheless, speakers are able to interpret such sentences, provided they are well-formed sentences, according to the rules of structure that govern the creation of sentences in the language. It is this ability to generate new structures, all well formed according to the grammatical core of the language, that lies at the heart of Chomsky's method of description and analysis, generative transformational grammar.

The term **grammar** as used here does not mean the kind of grammar that one associates with high school English classes and dry-as-dust afternoons spent parsing sentences. Nor does it refer to the notions of propriety that so often accompany the exposition of English grammar in certain school traditions. "Good grammar" and other prescriptive notions have little to do with the concept of grammar as described by linguists and the notions of grammaticality examined in psycholinguistic investigations. In this meaning of the term grammar, what is characteristic of a language—the various components that make it up and the rules that operate on each of those component levels—is its structure, and a description of such operations of the language is its grammatical description, or, in short, its grammar. Thus, a grammatical description is simply a catalog of information about the language and about speakers' abilities to form and interpret well-formed utterances, whether on the phonological (sound), the syntactic (sentence), or the semantic (meaning) level.

If the finite set of rules in a grammar is presented in a certain order and if following that order exactly can only result in or generate grammatically well-formed sentences, the grammar is a generative grammar. An analogy is a computer program. If the program has been correctly formulated, the computer, which has no native intelligence and less wit, can follow it and accomplish the desired end on the print-out or on other tasks. One would have the program of a language if he had somehow managed to list in the proper order native speakers' abilities to produce and interpret grammatical as opposed to ungrammatical sequences. First this, then that; if you take this path, this will follow; do this and then that. This is exactly the format of a generative description of a language.

Performance, on the other hand, is the actual manifestation of speakers' underlying competence. A speaker's performance, when measured over an hour, a day, a week, a year, even a lifetime, is only a small reflection of the infinite possibilities afforded by the creative power of language. But performance is what actually occurs, and it is influenced by an amazing number of factors—the place of language in social interaction, memory span, connotative value judgments, interplay with other, concurrent communicative systems, such as nonverbal behavior, and so forth. Still, the manifestation of language in its structural form as an ordered system is somewhat dependent on the underlying system of rules, or competence.

It is this competence that most modern grammatical descriptions try to account for, and for some psycholinguists competence is the central issue of the discipline, especially those grammatical features that can be said to be universals. Many others feel, perhaps rightly so, that the study of performance is equally important. Still others feel that the competence–performance distinction is no longer a valuable or even a viable one. Continuing debate over the exact meaning of the terms competence and performance likely accounts for a great deal of the controversy over which is the primary concern. Nevertheless, it seems clear that we should continue to investigate both.

Language use has been the subject of much investigation. For example, statistical models have long been applied to quantify the usages of speakers, and attempts have been made to extend such models to account for human language as nothing more than a set of frequency distributions. Similarly, some attempts have been made to regard language as simply an information-carrying system by quantifying the amount of uncertainty reduced and consequently the amount of technical information transmitted. Nonverbal communication is increasingly studied as a system complementary to language performance. The role of language in society is also an important topic in the current study of language behavior.

The theoretical models and practical methodologies used to investigate these different areas of concern are not always compatible, but then neither are the areas themselves. Each of these areas represents one of the many facets of language and communication, in which many different events occur and many different kinds of information are being transmitted at the same time. Thus, language is at its simplest a hugely complicated affair, and theories to deal with it have proliferated in the various disciplines. Moreover, numerous approaches may be taken to a single area of investigation within a particular discipline. Reber's characterization (1973) of the predominant approaches to psycholinguistic issues provides an example.

Reber's psycholinguistic paradigms are three, the **associationist** ori-

Table 1.1 The Association, Process, and Content Positions on Important Issues in Psycholinguistics[a]

Issue	Orientation		
	Association	Process	Content
1. Biological considerations			
a. Subsidiary level: defining scope and form of physical response	*		
b. Generalized structures: assumptions about processing of information		*	
c. Specific structures: assumptions about universal grammar			*
2. Uniqueness questions			
a. Language shares common base with other behaviors	*		
b. Language linked in general cognition		*	
c. Language independent from other behaviors			*
3. Acquisition			
a. S–R: associative linking and mediational processes	*		
b. Differentiation: abstractions derived from experience		*	
c. Enrichment: matching principles based on innate ideas			*
4. Competence–performance (knowledge–use)			
a. Performance: stress on observables (use)	*		
b. Competence: stress on a general representational mechanism (knowledge and use)		*	
c. Competence: stress on a formal axiomatic system (knowledge)			*
5. Mentalistic considerations			
a. Behavioristic: links to observables	*		
b. Mentalistic: links to general cognitive systems		*	
c. Mentalistic: links to linguistic systems			*
6. Reductionism			
a. Strong reductionism: S–R principles	*		
b. Weak reductionism: general cognitive operations		*	
c. Weak reductionism: sentences			*
7. General philosophical position			
a. Empiricism	*	*	
b. Rationalism			*
8. Description of language			
a. Markovian	*		
b. Generative		*	*

[a] From A. S. Reber, "On Psycho-linguistic Paradigms," *Journal of Psycholinguistic Research* 2 (1973): 289–319. Reprinted by permission of the author and the Plenum Publishing Corp., New York.

entation, the **process** orientation, and the **content** orientation. The associationist position (represented by Skinner, Osgood, and Staats) is linked to the behaviorist school of psychological thought. The fundamental operation in this position is the conditioned association between a stimulus and a response, and the primary emphasis is on learning and learning theory. The process orientation (represented by Bever) assumes that a set of general cognitive mechanisms, not an endowment of a species-specific language faculty, is responsible for the child's acquisition of the linguistic system. Thus, this cognitive ability is not necessarily linked only to language behavior; the regularities found in and hypothesized for languages are merely a reflection of these general process mechanisms. The content position (represented by N. Chomsky and McNeill), on the other hand, assumes a specific language-acquisition ability, complete with formal and substantive universals that are predictive of the underlying form any natural language can take. These formal and substantive universals also guide the child in developing hypotheses that will account for the language input he is experiencing; thus, although he is learning language, he is also assumed to know (that is, to be endowed with) something that guides him in his learning. Table 1.1 indicates the positions of the three approaches on key theoretical and methodological issues.

To examine the complex field of psycholinguistics more closely, we should first look at the theoretical foundations in linguistics and psychology that have contributed to its overall development. Chapter 2 begins with a review of some of the basic premises of linguistics in both the structuralist period and the generative transformational period. A review of psychological models of language follows, together with some commentary on how they have been viewed from the perspective of psycholinguistic investigations inspired by the generative grammatical period in linguistics. The rest of the chapters examine the problems and results of investigations in specific aspects of language behavior.

Theoretical Foundations

Structural Linguistics

In the structuralist view of language, description of the framework of a language is of paramount importance. A given language is considered a system, with rules that govern its operation. The task of the linguist is to discover these operations and the way in which they function. In this sense, the linguist's mode of operation is not unlike that of a skilled watchmaker or mechanic. Given this finely coordinated machine, what makes it tick? How does it operate? What are its component parts? How are they ordered and interrelated? In approaching the system called language, one takes it apart to find out what makes it operate, what makes the system what it is. To do so, one must inquire about the items that constitute the system, the arrangements in which they occur, and the rules that govern the use of both the items and the arrangements.

To use another analogy, suppose that the game of chess is unknown to a friend and that you want to teach him how to play it. Before you can introduce him to chess strategies, you must explain how the game works and what each piece can and cannot do. You must tell him that pawns can move only one space at a time, that the queen can move in any direction for any distance, and so on. And, of course, you must tell him about other rules, all of which must be observed if the game of chess is to make any sense at all as a game of chess and if it is to operate as the consistent system it is.

Note that chess was not characterized as logical: It is consistent but not necessarily logical. Like the rules of chess, the rules of language are arbitrary. But simply because there is no objective rationale for why language is the way it is does not mean that it works less efficiently. Rather, the arbitrariness may be the basis of the symbolic activity that language is.

Another feature of language is that it consists of different levels—the level of sound units, the level of intonational units, the level of word-building units, the level of sentence-building units, and the level of meaning-bearing units. Each of these levels interacts with and is dependent on the level immediately above it. Thus, sounds are built into the word-building units called **morphemes,** which are built into words, which are combined to form sentences. Although a number of other things, such as intonation and meaning, are happening at the same time, this is the kind of pattern that structural linguists established as the basis of their approach to language.

The level of **phonology,** or relevant sound units, is perhaps one of the most accessible and immediately noticeable aspects of language. Structural linguists usually began their analysis of a language at the level of sound units. They could not rely on writing systems as such for the fairly obvious reason that not all languages use the Latin alphabet, and for the sometimes less obvious reason that writing systems do not always accurately represent sound systems. As anyone who has learned to read and write English can testify, our writing system is particularly ill matched to our sound system.

Spoken language is what language is all about. Written languages, for those languages that employ writing systems, are only secondary systems intended in some way to make permanent the fleeting appearance of vocal communication. Children are already fluent speakers of their native language by the time they reach school age in the Western world; in school they learn the secondary, language-related skills of reading and writing.

Structural linguists developed a way to represent, on a consistent one-to-one basis, the sounds of a language. In this system, each sound is represented by one and only one symbol, and each phonetic symbol stands for one and only one sound. Each language, according to this system, has a small number of sound units, or **phonemes,** that are relevant points of contrast in that language. These units are particular to one and only one language system, and the first step in a descriptive analysis was usually, to isolate and describe these phonemic units.

The usual method of deciding on whether a particular sound was a relevant unit was to establish whether the sound contrasted in a meaningful way with other sound units in the language. For example, the first parts of the words *pie* and *buy* or *pit* and *bit* contrast, so we can say that /p/ and /b/ are phonemes in English. The convention has been to represent phonemic transcriptions and individual phonemes between slanted lines (/x/) to signal them as distinct from orthographic symbols.

Extending the principle of contrast further, we find that the initial sounds of *fie, sigh, rye, lie, guy, tie, die, thigh,* and *thy* all contrast. As a result, we can postulate that the initial sound of each of these words is a phonemic unit in English. Some of the symbols used in rewriting, or transcribing, the words according to their phonemic shape are quite familiar from the Roman alphabet (/p, b, f, s, r, l, g, t, d/); others are not so familiar (the /θ/ initially in *thigh* and the /ð/ in *thy*). These symbols present the sounds of the language in a straightforward manner, without ambiguity and without overlap. The phonology is not distorted by a writing system which may no longer reflect the sound patterning of the language. The development of a system of phonological description and transcription was a major step in reorienting the study of language to a more scientific outlook.

The phoneme is actually an abstraction in speakers' minds to account for a range of similar sounds that occur under highly restricted, and often predictable, conditions. Take /p/, for example, which is not the same in words like *pit* as it is in words like *spit*, where it appears after /s/. In the former word it appears accompanied by a puff of breath, in the latter without. Such variants of a phoneme are called **allophones.** A similar contrast is that between the initial /l/ in *lie* and the final /l/ in *full*. To English-speaking people, both are instances of the same /l/ because they are accustomed to considering them as the same.

A close look at the two variants, or allophones, of /p/ reveals that they occur in predictable conditions; the initial sound in *pit*, where the puff of breath occurs only initially, and the one without the puff of breath occurs only after /s/. Similarly, the allophone of /l/ that appears in *lie* occurs only initially, and the variant of /l/ in *full* occurs only at the end of a word. The point is that the units of one level always seem to fit neatly into the next, as allophones do into phonemes. Thus, hearers immediately group the stream of speech sounds into rough categories that include a number of similar types of sound.

Since language is orderly in this system, it is not surprising that

phonemes are patterned into **morphemes,** just as raw sound is patterned into phonemic categories. The unit we call **word** is a bit too big
to consider at this point, for many words are composed of building
blocks smaller than words. These units, or morphemes, occur over and
over again and are the key materials in the building of words. Consider, for example, the sentence *John's ungentlemanly behavior caused dis-
belief among his friends.* The sentence is composed of eight words, but
it can be further broken down into at least 16 morphemes, as follows:
*John, 's, un-, gentle, man, -ly, behav-, -ior, cause, -ed, dis-, belief, among,
his, friend, -s.* In word building some units are used in definite patterns. The possessive ending, or affix, after *John* occurs after the noun
John—not before, not in the middle, not as a change in the pitch of the
voice, not as anything other than an affix after the noun—because this
is the rule of how possessive affixes appear in English.

Morphemes also have variants under specific conditions. Such morphemic variants, or **allomorphs,** are highly patterned and thus predictable. In *friends,* for example, *-s* stands for plurality. The sound
system of English would have us write /z/ for the plural of *friend,* or
/frɛndz/. If the word had been *cat,* the plural morpheme would have
been an /s/ so that the word would have been transcribed as /kæts/. If
the word had been *roses,* the plural would have been /ɪz/. So morphemes, like phonemes, have variants. But the allomorph variants are
conditioned as well, since the choice of allomorph variant to show the
plural is automatically (and unconsciously) selected by native speakers
of English on the basis of the last sound of the noun. Thus, if the last
phoneme of the noun is transcribed as /s, z, š, ž, č, ǰ/ (*kiss, fez, rush,
loge, witch,* and *bridge*), the plural morpheme is /ɪz/. If the last
phoneme of the noun is voiceless—that is, articulated without any vi-
bration in the vocal cords—as with /p, t, k, f, θ/, then the plural morpheme is /s/. If there is accompanying voicing in the production of the
sound, then the plural is /z/. The /z/ turns up after all sounds other than
those mentioned.

Test these rules for yourself by determining the plurals of such
newly coined nouns as *gronk, blib,* and *griz.* Native speakers of English
will invariably use an /s/ for *gronk,* a /z/ for *blib,* and an /ɪz/ for *griz.*
Children quickly assimilate these rules in their acquisition of English
morphology, as pointed out in a classic study by Berko (1958). They
also tend to generalize the majority rules to the exceptions, such as
feet, teeth, oxen, geese, and *mice.* Children exhibit a rule-oriented language behavior, and it is maintained in adulthood.

This kind of patterning is characteristic for other morphemes as
well. Take, for example, the past tense of *cause* in our sentence. It is

different from the past tense of such verbs as *help* and *wait*, but only according to certain highly restricted patterns. Such patterns also apply to newly coined verbs as well as to verb forms borrowed from other languages. This patterned rule behavior in the pronunciation of such inflected words occurs throughout the English language system, though the changes that do occur are different.

The important point here is that patterning occurs on the level of morphology as well as on the preceding level of phonology, so that one begins to expect this kind of congruent patterning throughout the structure of language. The units are so neatly labeled and their patterning so congruent that the method has been used in other investigations that are language-oriented as well as some that are not. One descriptive framework closely modeled on the **etic–emic** distinctions inherent in the allophone–phoneme and the allomorph–morpheme relationships is Birdwhistell's theory (1952) of **kinesics,** or the study of body motion as nonverbal communicative behavior. Thus, we have the **phone,** or raw sound, as the basic unit in prelinguistic study and the phone as allophone, or etic variant, of the relevant emic unit of sound on the phonological level, the phoneme. Similarly, we have morphs as allomorphs of specific morphemic units. These are then arranged into the larger units of words and sentences. In Birdwhistell's theory the **kine** is the unit of raw body motion, and in the analysis of the nonverbal communicative aspects of such activity, the kine is an **allokine** variant of a specific **kineme** unit. Kinemes, like phonemes, are also a part of larger constructions called **kinemorphemes,** and these in turn are patterned into kinemorphemic constructions. A well-formulated methodology often comes to be used in other areas of study, and the taxonomic methodology of structural linguistics was adapted in a number of interesting ways.

In the linguistic hierarchy, the next level of sentence building is **syntax,** or sentence structure. This level was not studied with the same flurry of excitement as the preceding levels, but sentences do have structure, and much of their meaning comes from the patterning of the words, not the sum of their semantic value. The sentence *John loves Mary* is not the equivalent of *Mary loves John.* Why not? For the same reason that we know who gave what to whom in sentences like *John gave the boy the dog* and *John gave the dog the bone.* This distinction between structural meaning and lexical meaning was the basis for the separation of syntax from semantics in structural analysis.

The method used to analyze sentence structure was usually the immediate constituent type. The linguist using this method assumed that sentences are constructions—that is, two or more units sharing a grammatical relationship—and then broke such constructions into their relevant parts by a binary type of procedure. Each level of construction was considered to have two constituents on the level immediately below it (hence the term immediate constituent analysis). For example, the construction *old man* has two constituents, *old* and *man*; the construction *the old white house on the corner* has the two constituents *the old white house* and *on the corner*. For a sentence, this binary form of analysis can be carried right down to the last possible break, showing all the relationships in a ladder-like arrangement, proceeding from the highest-level relationships to the lowest and labeling them along the way. For example, the sentence *Fat cats like warm milk* can be broken into *fat cats* and *like warm milk; fat cats* into *fat* and *cats; like warm milk* into *like* and *warm milk;* and *warm milk* into *warm* and *milk*. The first break can be labeled the relationship between a subject and its predicate; the break between *like* and *warm milk* the relationship between a transitive verb and its noun-phrase object; and the breaks between *fat—cats* and *warm—milk* the relationship between a noun and its modifier.

Immediate constituent analysis can also be used to analyze certain kinds of sentence ambiguity. For example, without accompanying intonational and stress patterns, the sentence *They are cooking apples* is ambiguous. The ambiguity is quickly dispelled by marking the sentence unit to which cooking has the closer relationship: *They are— cooking apples* or *They —are cooking— apples*. Unfortunately, the complete method of immediate constituent diagraming is somewhat cumbersome, and it never had the elegant simplicity of analytic notions on the levels of phonology and morphology. Moreover, such analysis fails to show any kind of relationship between different sentences.

Structural linguistics is best characterized as an analytic approach for identifying the specific units of the structure of a language and describing how these units are interdependent. According to this approach, although each language has a unique structure, it always consists of units that can be classified and discussed in the same way, through the units, labels, and arrangement terminology glimpsed in the preceding discussion of phonology, morphology, and syntax. Moreover, since languages are limited in their potential combinations of phonemes, morphemes, words, and so on, the description of any language will also be a finite matter.

Such descriptions were usually derived from interviews or field work in which the help of native speakers, usually bilingual, was solicited to provide translations and to cue the linguist about which linguistic elements were functionally the same or different. Structural linguistics was direct in its approach to the data; it was inductive in general outlook and relied, in theory, exclusively on the mechanical discovery procedures that had been evolved to convert raw language data into a complete description of a language.

The one exception to the preceding statements may have been, or at least is often said to have been, the field of semantics. It is not necessarily true that structural linguists chose to ignore the field of meaning, but they obviously did not find semantics amenable to the same neatly patterned kinds of approaches that were being so successfully employed on other levels of linguistic analysis. Moreover, as it had seemed to Bloomfield (1933), a description of the semantic structure of a language would entail a description of all that the speakers of the language knew of their universe and its workings. Such a task would be impractical, not to mention uneconomical, and the endeavor was abandoned in lieu of more profitable activities. In not dealing directly with meaning, linguistics was not much different from some other behavioral science approaches to the study of man. Insistence on objective criteria and mechanical discovery procedures that would reveal the elemental structures of language was not consistent with an interest in the unwieldy world of meaning, which is elusive at best. It simply was not within the philosophy of science that linguistics had embraced.

Generative Transformational Linguistics

The 1957 publication of N. Chomsky's *Syntactic Structures* resulted in a new period in the history of linguistics. Some of Chomsky's suggestions dealt with the discipline as a whole. His feeling was that linguistics was not sufficiently concerned with the development of a theory of language in the sense of a universal theory. Too much attention was being paid to individual descriptions of individual languages and not enough to the nature of language itself. However, as some have observed, the absence of a universal theory of language was never an issue until Chomsky made one of it. Most linguists felt that what they did have constituted a satisfactory theory of language.

Because of the equal status of linguistics and psychology in psycholinguistics, any change in linguistic theory was bound to have some effect on psycholinguistics. But the revolution in linguistic theory that Chomsky initiated did not have just a casual influence on psycholinguistic theory and research. The net result was that the cornerstone philosophies of structuralism and behaviorism were severely damaged, if not destroyed, by Chomsky's book, his 1959 review of B. F. Skinner's *Verbal Behavior,* and his 1965 publication of *Aspects of the Theory of Syntax,* which expanded and somewhat altered his earlier theories. Moreover, psycholinguistics, which was previously characterized by an extraordinary diversity of activity and the lack of a single unifying paradigm, acquired a paradigm that is rather demanding in its theoretical postures and highly suggestive of research avenues. Chomsky's impact on linguistics, on the other hand, was the exchange of one paradigm for another. I do not mean to imply here, as Greene's title (1972) does, that Chomsky + Psychology = Psycholinguistics. This is simply not the case, for the discipline of psycholinguistics, broadly conceived, incorporates a good many fields unaffected substantially by this paradigm change in linguistics. Even among those who more narrowly conceive of psycholinguistics as experimental or theoretical psycholinguistics, the main task of which is to investigate experimental support for theoretical claims in linguistic theory or psychological theory, there would likely be vigorous and loud discussion of what the Chomsky + Psychology equation really means. Yet it is equally important to stress that the impact of Chomsky's work has been substantial in psycholinguistics.

Chomsky's concern with the nature of language has led to a shift from the rigidly empirical practices of linguistic structuralism to a rationalistic orientation in language analysis. The difference between rationalism and empiricism, again in the forefront of Western scholarly debate, has had some far-reaching ramifications in the underlying philosophy of analytic goals as well as in methodology. Some of the more obvious ramifications are discussed in the chapters dealing with language and thought and the acquisition of language. This new posture also means that linguists are no longer limited to the relations between linguistic signs but can entertain questions about the nature of cognition, first language learning, semantics, and, in general, the nature of verbal behavior. But note that this refers primarily to the competence of speakers and does not include specific instances of language behavior labeled as performance (though generative grammar proponents would maintain that competence grammars are a vital component of any performance theory).

Another of Chomsky's suggestions has more to do with the actual method of analysis. For Chomsky, the capacity to be described is an ideal speaker–listener's competence in the language. **Competence,** once again, is the term used by Chomsky to indicate the underlying abilities that enable speakers to produce infinite performance manifestations of language. Thus, instead of relying on a sample of a language usually taken from one or more native speakers of a language, as structural linguists did, generative transformational linguists insist on tapping the underlying abilities themselves. It is possible that no amount of sampling will bring out important or relevant distinctions, and, more important, speakers have certain abilities that cannot be adequately described by simply sampling language behavior without recourse to the speakers' intuitions. Sentences like *Flying planes can be dangerous* and *The shooting of the hunters was terrible* cannot be differentiated by simply applying the yardstick of immediate constituent analysis to sort out the surface relationships. Such sentences come from different underlying forms, and it is only with recourse to the speakers' intuitions that such differences can be sorted out. Similarly, with sentences like *John is easy to please* and *John is eager to please,* the underlying forms are different, and native speakers are aware of that; automatic sentence-parsing procedures would likely classify these sentences only as the same structural type.

This view means, of course, that the ideal analyst is a native speaker of the language, who can make explicit his abilities in and intuitions about sentence structures in that language. It also means that from a practical point of view the analysis of language starts at the syntactic level of sentence formation. Unlike structural linguistics, in which analysis was usually begun at the phonological level, generative analysis begins with syntactic units. Finally, this viewpoint means that a crucial distinction must be made between **grammatical** sentences and **ungrammatical** sentences. A language must be redefined as the set of its grammatical sentences, or those utterances that are well formed according to the rules for the formation of sentences and hence the object of analysis. A sentence like Chomsky's original *Colorless green ideas sleep furiously* makes little sense semantically (or at least it did not then), but native speakers of English will recognize it as being formed according to the same general principles that *Colorful red flames leaped viciously* and *Cute white kittens played happily* are. The point is that the grammatical rules for making sentences are finite in number, but the possible combinations that can be made according to the rules are infinite. And simply because a sentence does not have an easily definable meaning at the moment does not mean that it will not have. A century ago, sentences like *Light is both particle and wave* and *The astronauts completed their space walk as their space capsule orbited outside the earth's atmosphere* did not have an easily definable meaning, but they could have been generated by the underlying rules of formation.

Thus, sentences need not be acceptable semantically to be perfectly grammatical according to the yardstick of competence. Our interpretation of a sequence like *Colorless green ideas sleep furiously* or *Pork sausages and paper clips are the principal Serbian exports* attests to that. A grammatical description must account for both this type and grammatical and acceptable sequences, like *John met Mary in the park, The cuddly white kittens played endlessly,* and *I bumped into her in the supermarket.* A fully developed grammatical description would, however, contain context-sensitive semantic rules that would allow a sequence like *Pork sausages and paper clips are the principal Serbian exports* to be regarded as a conventional sentence but would make some commentary on sequences like *Colorless green ideas sleep furiously* and *The sleeping wastepaper basket snored excessively* to indicate that they violate the present rules of collocation in English. Although these sentences are grammatically well formed at the highest level of rule in the grammar, by certain other, lower-level rules they would become utterances that would perhaps appear only in modern poetry, fairy tales, rock music, and so forth.

Sentences that are both ungrammatical and unacceptable need not claim our attention at all, for they are not sentences in the language and hence are not part of the language as a system. Sequences like **Result both well if and fuzzy can universal* and **On and men maintenance own perhaps machine mortar engine* may look to some degree familiar because they consist of English words and not, say, Chinese, but they have no order and no structure, and, thus, no sentencehood. In reading these sequences, you will have used the same kind of intonation that you would use in enumerating random objects in a series, while you will have used a perfectly normal declarative-sentence intonation in reading the sentences in the previous paragraph. Acceptability may be the result of many judgmental factors related to the performance aspects of language behavior—appropriateness to the situation, familiarity, style, degree of deviation from grammatical and acceptable sequences, aesthetics, and a number of other criteria.

The sentences that do constitute the grammatical output of a language are the object of the analysis—or, more correctly, the competence that underlies their formation is. A collection of these rules is termed a grammar of the language, and because of the explicit, formulaic manner in which they are organized, the entire grammar is called a **generative grammar.** What speakers actually do say—their actual performance—is only a small reflection of what they can say, and by and large it is relegated to other kinds of study. In transformational grammar, language is strictly defined by its syntactic structure. In fact, Chomsky in his later writings leaned more and more toward the notion that the very syntactic structure of languages is a reflection of the universals of language and the innate mental properties that are brought to the acquisition of language.

Chomsky's earlier work, *Syntactic Structures,* is essentially concerned with the outline of a theory of syntactic analysis. Such a framework would allow a more complete description of syntactic structures, showing explicitly the relationships both within and among the sentences. His later *Aspects of the Theory of Syntax* is a full-blown linguistic theory, one that does indeed attempt to cope with the whole of language. Its ambitious goal is to explain the totality of language, to explain all the linguistic relationships from the level of the sound system right up to the meaning system of language. This, then, is a total grammar of language and a fully integrated theory that can be applied to the particular or the general.

The concept of the sentence as a central theme in Chomsky's exposition is dependent upon more than just its use as a point from which to begin linguistic analysis. The sentence is of crucial theoretical importance as well, for to Chomsky and others the syntactic structure of language may be the result of universal principles of learning and organization. The rules of syntactic structure can be indicated in two-dimensional fashion by tree diagrams, but it is important to remember what such rules may imply about the nature of language and its organization.

The term **rule** is perhaps a misnomer here because it has often been misinterpreted. In the sense used here, and usually in other linguistic, psychological, and psycholinguistic instances, a rule is simply a convenient summarization of the observations of a normal, or statistically frequent, type of behavior in a given situation. Given novel instances of the same situation, one looks for confirmation of the rule in new responses. An example is the use of regular allomorphic variants after nonsense words purporting to be English nouns or verbs. As was discussed, the plurals of such new nouns as *gronk, blib,* and *griz* are automatically and unhesitatingly given, although speakers generally cannot explain why the answers are correct. The reason is that the internalized rule has simply been generalized to these new instances. Rules are thus merely patterns that guide behavior, not rules that arise from logical necessity. There is no rhyme or reason for why things operate as they do—they just do. A summarization of the way they just do is a rule.

The rules themselves are not as forbidding as they have often seemed. They are called **rewrite rules** because symbols on the left-hand side of the arrow are rewritten as symbols on the right-hand side of the arrow. If a sentence is represented as S, and S is rewritten as a noun phrase, NP, and a verb phrase, VP, the rule is S → NP + VP. In sentences like *A man hit the dog, The cat chased a rat,* and *The boy loved the girl,* VP consists of a transitive verb, Vt, and its object, a noun phrase, NP. Thus, the second rule is VP → Vt + NP. So far, all NPs have consisted of a determiner (D), like *the,* and a noun (N). The third rule, then, is NP → D + N. In sequence, the rules look like this:

$$
\begin{aligned}
S &\to NP + VP \\
VP &\to Vt + NP \\
NP &\to D + N
\end{aligned}
$$

Such rules are called **phrase-structure rules,** since they indicate in graphic, rule-ordered form the structure of sentences and phrases.

The next step is a set of rules that translates the final symbols in the phrase-structure set into words. Such rules are called **lexical rules.** The following, which fill in the final category labels of Vt, D, and N, are examples:

$$
\begin{aligned}
Vt &\to \textit{hit, chased, loved, etc.} \\
D &\to \textit{a, the, etc.} \\
N &\to \textit{man, dog, cat, rat, boy, girl, etc.}
\end{aligned}
$$

The *etc.* means that such lexical rules apply to many more lexical items. The one phrase-structure rule S → NP + VP applies to thousands of sentences, and the lexical symbol N stands for the thousands of words that can occupy this particular position. Therefore, if the rules are ordered in the stipulated way, not only can the three sample sentences be reconstructed, but many more new ones can be generated as well. This quality of explicitness means that if what is relevant is covered in the rules and if they are properly sequenced in the analysis and properly followed throughout the description, only grammatical sequences will result. Such ungrammatical sequences as *A a man boy chased,* *Rat the loved go dog the,* and *Hit girl the a chased* will never result, since the rules are meant to reflect the patterns that underlie well-formed sentences in the language. In the computer analogy used earlier, if the program is correctly formulated, as the rules in the example were, the computer will generate those three grammatical sequences as well as many, many more. In this sense the program, or, in linguistic terms, the generative grammar, would account for some of the abilities of native speakers to generate grammatical sentences.

The computer analogy is a handy one because it sharpens our notion of just what kinds of abilities speakers of natural languages have. Perhaps equally important, it throws into focus some of the problems to be faced in making these abilities explicit. As the preceding sample rules indicate, our observations are to be cast in an explicit, easily available fashion, and yet in a manner that allows no deviations, questions, or false starts. Some of these difficulties are overcome by such rewrite rules, which develop categories step by step as the rules progress. Moreover, the rules are also ordered for maximum efficiency and explicitness. Such generative grammar formulaic notions bear some resemblance to, and were in fact influenced by, the methods of dealing with combinatorial systems in formal logic. (It should be noted that the format of the rules presented here is slightly old-fashioned, but it serves to illustrate the method of writing the rules and how they are developed.)

An alternative method of representing the structural hierarchy of sentences is a device called the **branching-tree diagram** or **tree.** One of our original sentences, *The cat chased a rat,* can be represented by the following branching-tree diagram, giving a labeled bracketing for each of the steps involved in the derivation of the sentence.

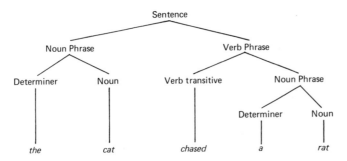

One advantage of branching-tree diagrams is that they provide immediate information about the hierarchy of relationships within the sentence. The ambiguous sentence *They are cooking apples* has two readings, each depending on the phrase-structure derivation of the sentence. The first diagram clearly labels *cooking* as adjectival and indicates its close relationship to *apples;* the second labels *cooking* as part of the verbal predicate and indicates its close relationship to *are.* Thus, the construction of the sentence on the various levels of syntactic formation is rather easily retrieved by this graphic representation of phrase-structure-rule applications.

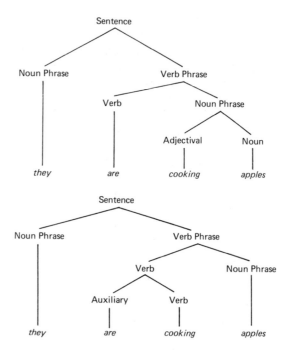

This particular form of generative grammar became known as generative transformational grammar because in its early stages one of the attractive innovations of the grammatical model was that it was able to show the relationship between obviously related sentences. Take, for example, our previous sample set of *A man hit the dog, The cat chased a rat,* and *The boy loved the girl.* In English there is a corresponding set of sentences, *The dog was hit by a man, A rat was chased by the cat,* and *The girl was loved by the boy.* The relationship between the first set of sentences and the second set is that of active sentence to passive sentence. This relationship turns up for all active-voice, transitive-verb sentences, so a rulelike observation should stipulate that such a relationship exists and that members of the second set of sentences can easily be derived from the first. If the simple, active, declarative sentences in a language like English are considered the kernel sentence types, as was done in early stages of the generative model, all other sentences can be considered alterations, or **transformations,** of that kernel set. Thus, members of the second set can easily be derived by a single transformational rule:

$$NP_1 + Vt + NP_2 \Longrightarrow NP_2 + was + Vt + by + NP_1$$

This transformational rule changes the ordering of our first and second NPs (NP_1 and NP_2, respectively) and produces the desired effect for all sentences that belong to the same structural pattern. Hence, the name generative transformational grammar was simply taken from the mechanisms employed in earlier stages of Chomsky's syntactic model. Although the model has not remained the same, transformational rules still perform tasks that phrase-structure rules cannot. Transformational rules are simply operational devices within the grammar that allow linguistic elements, larger or smaller, to be added, substituted, deleted, or permutated. Moreover, these rules are used to complete the operational manipulations necessary to account for natural language.

In later models discussed by Chomsky and others (Katz & Fodor, 1963; Katz & Postal, 1964; Chomsky, 1965; Chomsky & Halle, 1968), the phonological and semantic components of a grammar are integrated, in principle if not in fact, into Chomsky's early syntactic theory. The syntactic component itself is seemingly altered substantially in Chomsky's later discussion, in which both the phonological and the semantic components are seen as being amenable to analysis in terms of atom-like units that should account for the universals in phonology and meaning. Such phonological units, called **distinctive features,** had been used in linguistics before but were now grafted onto an integrated linguistic theory. The inclusion of semantics, on the other hand, was an innovation. According to this view, the rules governing the hierarchical organization of semantic units and the way in which they operate in syntactic strings can also be described. Unfortunately, the semantic-theory component of generative grammatical theory is not as well developed as are the components of phonology and syntax. But more on this topic appears in Chapter 7, which deals with meaning.

The important fact for the development of psycholinguistics is that Chomsky's theories presented refreshing new directions for research. In addition to structural linguistics, several major sources for possible horizons of research in psycholinguistics had been available in statistical models of language, information theory from the field of communication engineering, and learning theory in psychology. His claims also forced not only structural linguists but some psychologists and psycholinguists as well to re-evaluate their entire approach to language. Chomsky criticized information theory and learning theory as inadequate for explaining language. One of the major sources of criticism is that such models do not take into account all the possible grammatical sequences in a language, for they are potentially infinite. A statistical theory of probability operates within a bounded sample space, and its sample is necessarily assumed to be either a closed one or a highly representative one. Similarly, learning theory, with its emphasis on conditioning and reinforcement, cannot account for how the child learns language; the samples each child encounters are different indeed, yet all speakers of the same language come up with the same grammatical framework. Because it would take a child thousands of times his own age to encounter all the possible combinations used in the language, experimental learning does not seem to be a very likely explanation for the way in which children acquire language.

Chomsky's later discussions (1965, 1966) are in other ways not radically different from his early work. Essentially, his theory has been an expanding one, and in order to make his earlier position less prone to misinterpretation, he appears to have restated some of his earlier claims. Moreover, in later discussions Chomsky moves further afield in drawing psychological and philosophical conclusions about the implications of his theory of human language. It is these conclusions that have had far-reaching ramifications in fields beyond the realm of simple linguistic analysis. His model has changed somewhat, but major changes are more in the way in which the model is organized than in its basic philosophy. For example, in the 1957 model, with its phrase-structure rules and transformational rules, followed by a set of morphophonemic rules to cover the apparent exceptions to generalized rules, no attention was paid to semantics; in the 1965 version the syntactic component is still the keystone of the theory, but it is related to the phonological and semantic components.

Another distinction that has had some impact on psycholinguistic research is Chomsky's 1965 introduction of the notions of **deep structure** and **surface structure.** Numerous sentences have a single deep-structure origin but many different surface-structure manifestations. The sentences *John behaved recklessly, and this worried Sheila, What worried Sheila was John's behaving recklessly, That John had behaved recklessly worried Sheila, For John to have behaved recklessly worried Sheila, John's having behaved recklessly worried Sheila,* and *John's reckless behavior worried Sheila* all derive from the same deep-structure source of paired underlying strings—perhaps *Something worried Sheila* and *John behaved recklessly.* On the other hand, the two different readings of the ambiguous sentence *Visiting relatives can be a nuisance* have different deep structures; different phrase structures underlie their formation. Reading 1, *Visiting relatives can be a nuisance[1],* is derived from deep structures like *Someone visits relatives* and *Something is a nuisance,* while reading 2, *Visiting relatives can be a nuisance[2],* is derived from deep structures like *Relatives visit* and *Something is a nui-*

sance. The same is true for all such ambiguous sentences—*Flying planes can be dangerous, The shooting of the hunters was terrible,* and so forth. The appropriate transformation rules must be applied to embed these sentences in order to arrive at the actual surface-structure manifestation. Similarly, our knowledge of what marks sentences like *John is easy to please–John is eager to please, They are drinking companions–They are drinking highballs–They are drinking glasses,* and many others rests in our knowledge of their deep-structure origins and derivations. Thus, these sentences are not covered by the previous explanation of the ambiguity in *They are cooking apples.* Although the hierarchical breaks between the phrase segments in those sentences could be shown, understanding *Visiting relatives can be a nuisance*[1] and *Visiting relatives can be a nuisance*[2] demands recourse to deep-structure interpretations.

Ambiguity occurs in all languages, as do multiple surface structures for a single deep-structure set. This phenomenon is probably the result of a system's attempting to portray with finite means an infinitely large inventory of meanings, and gives one pause for thought on what the nature of artificially constructed languages can be in the face of this naturally and inevitably occurring ambiguity. Surface structures clearly do not provide all there is to know about sentences, their internal structures, and their relationships with other sentences. Speakers know a great deal more about sentence structures than what is actually showing in the outward form of a sentence. Indeed, surface structures are often misleading as to what the underlying relationships are, and our knowledge as speakers includes a great deal of abstract knowledge of how sentences are arranged and rearranged. Some of this knowledge is explained by the dichotomy between deep and surface structure.

The introduction of the notion of deep and surface structures immediately confused for many the notion of kernel and transformed sentences, which was commonly held to be the explanation of the two. However, the earlier obligatory transformations were taken to operate only on the strings underlying the kernel sentences, not on the kernel sentences themselves. This view is not unlike the later claim that every sentence has a deep and a surface structure, with certain transformations mapping deep structures onto surface structures of sentences. Moreover, instead of the earlier optional transformations leading to passives, negatives, passive negatives, questions, and so forth, underlying deep structures now contain a transformation marker for passive, negative, question, or whatever, and such transformational rules operate at the appropriate time in the grammar. Thus, at least some of the differences between the early generative framework and the later one are not as real as they might have seemed.

Operationally, the new format calls for the familiar set of phrase structures, but phrase-structure rules give the underlying deep structure of sentences. Sentences that are alterations of the basic theme have a negative, passive, question, or emphatic marker that is chosen as an optional item as the phrase-structure rules are developed. In such cases the appropriate transformation changes the sentence string to give the resultant sentence. For example, sentences like *The cat did not chase a rat, A rat was chased by the cat, Did the cat chase a rat?* and *The cat did chase a rat* are related by negative, passive, question, and emphatic markers and the appropriate transformational operations to the underlying sentence from which they are derived, *The cat chased a rat.*

Similarly, sentences that are the result of conjoining or embedding operations are handled by the introduction of an optional sentence marker (S) in the development of the rules. If the option is taken, a sentence can be developed according to the same basic structure rules, which again provide for an optional sentence marker. Theoretically, the recursive process can be repeated an unlimited number of times, and the observation that no theoretical limit can be set for a sentence generation is easily handled by the introduction of such a sentence marker (S) in the development of the rules. Because noun phrases usually can take another modifier, whether word or phrase, one place in which the optional sentence marker should be inserted is after the noun in noun phrases. Our base rules in the categorial component now look like the following:

$$S \rightarrow NP + VP$$
$$VP \rightarrow Vt + NP$$
$$NP \rightarrow D + N + (S)$$

Thus, sentences like *His father, a TWA pilot, wears a mustache, The snow on the ground is lovely,* and *Cathy is a beautiful girl* are seen as being the result of embedding operations involving simple sentence structures and the choice of the optional sentence marker in their development. For example, *His father, a TWA pilot, wears a mustache* can be interpreted as the result of embedding a constituent sentence,

His father is a TWA pilot, into the matrix sentence, *His father wears a mustache*. A simple rule deleting any repeated items in the result of such embedding operations would be applied to the string *His father, his father is a TWA pilot, wears a mustache* and *his father is* would be dropped, leaving *His father, a TWA pilot, wears a mustache*. Similar procedures would account for *The snow on the ground is lovely* from *The snow is on the ground* and *The snow is lovely*, as well as *Cathy is a beautiful girl* from *Cathy is beautiful* and *Cathy is a girl*.

Let us examine the same information through the alternative means of illustration, the branching-tree diagram. The base component of our grammatical description might generate the deep structure *the + snow + the + snow + Present + be + on the ground + Present + be + lovely* for *The snow on the ground is lovely*.

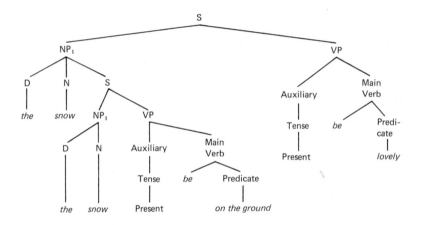

Now let us put the verbal forms back into the shape they have in the surface structure manifestation of the sentence. A transformation changes the sequences of *Present + be* into the appropriate form, *is*. Another transformation deletes repeated items, so that the sequence *the + snow + the + snow + is + on the ground + is + lovely* becomes the sequence *the + snow + on the ground + is + lovely*.

As we have already seen, transformations can perform a number of operations besides simply deletion; permutation, addition, as well as combinations of these activities, may also be the outcome of transformations. For example, the sentence *The boy who chased the dog loved the girl* might have the following deep structure:

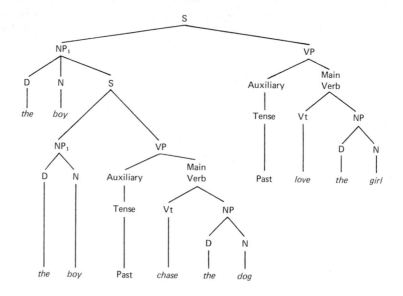

The application of the relative transformation will substitute *who* for the repeated noun phrase *the boy* in the following fashion:

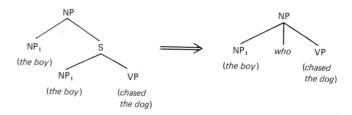

As can be seen, transformations affect only that part of the string that is explicitly given in the rule itself; all other elements remain the same unless otherwise specified. Thus, the syntactic section of the grammar consists of two major divisions, a base component and a transformational component. The base component generates deep structures, and the transformational component converts these deep structures into surface structures. These transformations change deep structures into surface structures by providing the correct shape for sequences of symbols within a given string (for example, Present + *be* becomes *is*) or for longer, embedded strings (for example, *the* +

snow + the + snow + is + on the ground + is + lovely becomes *the + snow + on the ground + is + lovely*).

In Chomsky's 1965 expansion of his theory, the base section of the grammar is divided into a categorial component, much like the 1957 phrase-structure rules, and a lexicon. The categorial section contains the ordered rewrite rules that underlie all sentences in the language. It also provides for, as was discussed, recursive power to encompass the theoretical possibility of infinitely long sentences, as well as the more realistic necessity of accounting for complex and compound sentences, which appear to be nothing more than conjoined or embedded simple sentences. The lexicon is like a list of dictionary entries in the language, except for the crucial difference that all items in the lexicon are coded for their operational equivalences in the grammar. A lexicon entry contains two types of information—the semantic features of the word and the selectional restrictions that indicate how the word is combined into meaningful sentences on the basis of grammar and collocational privileges. More discussion of selectional restrictions is provided in Chapter 7.

Thus, our rules dealing with the base syntax rules and lexicon rules might look something like the following in a grammatical theory more closely aligned with Chomsky's 1965 revisions. The **complex-symbol** notation indicates a symbol to be enlarged by the lexicon rules.

$$
\begin{aligned}
S &\rightarrow NP + VP \\
NP &\rightarrow D + N + (S) \\
VP &\rightarrow Vt + NP \\
N &\rightarrow \text{Complex Symbol} \\
D &\rightarrow \text{Complex Symbol} \\
V &\rightarrow \text{Complex Symbol}
\end{aligned}
$$

We can now see that although the machinery of linguistic description has changed somewhat, the underlying approach, in which a set of ordered rules generates all the grammatical sequences in the language, has not. The rules also provide an ordered sequence of steps that automatically give a full structural description of every grammatical sentence so generated. As branching-tree diagrams show, each part of the derived sentence is labeled, and the way in which each part has been combined to result in the sentence itself is indicated.

A specific grammar is seen as only a subset and thus only a representative of universal grammar. All languages have grammatical structures consisting of base components of both phrase-structure rules for generating the deep structures of sentences and general rules for generating undeveloped lexical categories. All languages also have a transformational component that operates from the highest appropriate levels in the grammar to the lowest until actual surface structures are generated. This basic schemata of grammatical description is not characteristic of English grammar alone; it should apply to Chinese, Apache, Russian, Swahili, or whatever. According to this theory, all languages have the same mechanisms, so a grammatical theory is, in effect, a universal theory of language organization.

In summary, one can best answer the question, "What do linguists do?" by saying that they make descriptions of the world's languages. They are also concerned with discovering what it is that constitutes the nature of language. To accomplish this, linguists, like all other scientists, must subscribe to a particular theory and corresponding methodology as to how to best go about accomplishing this task. Linguistics has seen two particular philosophies of language in the last several decades, structural linguistics and generative transformational linguistics, and it is hoped that the preceding discussion has given some general understanding of what each of these two theories of language are all about.

Behaviorism

Because behavioral psychology assumptions are so important in psycholinguistics and because learning theory represents one of the major threads running through a great deal of argumentative discussion in psycholinguistics past and present, some examination of the most influential models within this tradition is in order. Learning-theory proponents have been interested in constructing a model that will explain how man learns and uses language. Such psychological theories constitute a continuum of explanatory attempts that are, in effect, theories of the language user, not of language.

Behavioral psychology is in a way a reaction to certain aspects of psychological endeavor in the last century. At that time a great deal of the science of psychology rested on givens, and much speculation about what actually goes on in human behavior was based not on observed behavior but on notions of certain underlying and intangible mental faculties. Factors within the human organism were credited with this or that ability, and the proliferation of such faculties within the organism was largely the work of agile minds. Certain psychologists in this century decided to tighten the study of the relation between man's environment and his behavior by concentrating on strictly observable behavior. No attempt was to be made to explain behavior on the basis of what supposedly went on inside the human organism; everything was to be directly tied to specific stimuli experienced by the organism. Thus, these psychologists wanted observables at both ends of the behavioral process—the stimuli that serve as inputs to the organism and the organism's resultant outputs. If the relationships between stimuli and responses were direct, and they were assumed to be during this stage of behavioral psychology, then it was largely a matter of tying certain stimuli to certain responses. Presumably, if such relations do exist, once they have been adequately described, it should even be possible to predict behavior. If a specific stimulus is given, a specific type of behavioral response should result; if another type of stimulus is given, another behavioral response should result.

Although the straightforwardness and simplicity of this approach may seem rather one-sided in terms of the current rationalistic recourse to hypothesizing innate faculties, we must remember that the approach was a response to an era of hypothesizing gone astray. The behavioral school prohibited hypothesizing without explanation, and theoretical constructs were considered meaningless if they were not powerful explanatory devices. Much of the psychology at the turn of the century was dominated by the attention paid to states of consciousness and introspection. Theories abounded with constructs that included as part of their premises the postulation of ideas, images, instincts, thoughts, attitudes, and whatnot, all of which were intended to explain behavior but could never be tested and verified. The reaction was a swing back toward objectivism and a concentration on defining and explaining behavior simply on the basis of verifiable hypotheses. Watson's (1924) remarks may best sum up the tenor of the new age:

> The behaviorist asks: Why don't we make what we can **observe** the real field of psychology? Let us limit ourselves to things that can be observed, and formulate laws concerning only those things. Now what can we observe? Well, we can observe **behavior—what the organism does or says.** And let me make this fundamental point at once: that **saying** is doing—that is, **behaving.** Speaking overtly or to ourselves (thinking) is just as objective a type of behavior as baseball [p.6].[1]

---

[1] From J. B. Watson, *Behaviorism*, 1924. Reprinted by permission of W. W. Norton, New York.

The effect of Watson and the other early behaviorists upon the direction of psychological endeavor was undoubtedly substantial. Such concepts as consciousness and mental processes were rejected outright by many who followed; only physical reality could be trusted to provide some kind of objectivity. In such an extreme materialistic conception of behavior, language and thought are easily equatable, so that thinking became for Watson only a kind of implicit, veiled language behavior.

One of the more obvious manifestations of the switch from simply theorizing to basing conclusions on observed behavior was, of course, the appearance of such laboratory animals as the white rat. Accordingly, a popular conception has been that psychologists only teach rats to run mazes, press levers, and pull gadgets, and, in general, to comport themselves in an amazing number of ways. White rats may be much easier to handle, much cheaper, and far less troublesome than humans, but whether knowledge obtained from the observed behavior of laboratory animals is relevant to speculations about the acquisition and maintenance of human behavior has been heatedly argued.

The development of behaviorism inevitably resulted in the neglect of many topics. In the study of language behavior, many of the most interesting topics were ignored because they are unsuitable for this kind of approach. As in the development of automatic discovery procedures in structural linguistics, scholars were sometimes obliged to invent all manner of maneuvers and modes of investigation to preserve the illusive reality of an objective and scientifically rigorous approach.

This intellectual atmosphere probably led Bloomfield and his followers to reject the suggestion of mentalism in their approach to language. In psychology the rejection of the millenium-old idea of dualism, in which mind and body are separate and distinct entities, may have included a rejection of the psychological problem of dealing with subjective, unobservable behavior. Not only were soul, spirit, mind, and so on scrupulously avoided, but also any suggestion of dealing with implicit, internal, unobservable, but nevertheless real, behavior. The approach that emerged was one confidently engaged in the observable behavior of organisms, human and otherwise. This was empiricism in the social sciences at its apogee, and in both psychology and linguistics important and influential scholars promoted the approach. Certainly, in linguistics, the rejection of any suggestion of mentalism, never too clearly defined, continued to guide and limit language research until a new philosophical framework emerged. As Kuhn (1970) has pointed out, it is not until a new philosophical framework counters the almost religious hold of the previous one that new avenues of research can be developed with congruent methods of investigation. Bloomfield's observation that to study meaning is to study the entirety of man's knowledge of the universe was of course extreme, and not all subscribed to such an extreme view. Still, there was sufficient to occupy the linguist on the levels of phonology, intonation, morphology, and perhaps syntax, without rifling through the untidy mental drawers of the filing cabinet labeled "meaning."

Thus, those psychologists interested in the field of psycholinguistics were by and large behaviorists who were also interested only in observable data. Like the operational procedures in structural linguistics, behaviorist theoretical formulations came down to the question of deriving operational methods that could be readily linked to the real world of data. This may be one reason for the heavy emphasis on experimental design during this period as well as the great amount of attention paid to the statistical analysis of data.

For such psychologists, investigation is and can only be the study of behavior—no intangible constructs, no unobservable behaviors, no unprovable theories. If such concepts are allowed, they are seen as an extension of observation based on behavior output and thus an elaboration on the simpler theory of behavior. According to early behaviorists, a theory is sound to the degree that it predicts and controls the behavior being observed. If it provides an adequate explanation of the observed behavior simply in terms of observed variables as stimuli resulting in given responses, then the theory is a sound one; if it does not, then the theory is incomplete or incorrect. Moreover, if the theory depends on other intellectual machinations by the psychologist to account for the behavior, then the theory is metaphysically overweight. All one needs are the observables and the lawful, direct relationships between them.

Skinner and the Functional Analysis Approach

The most straightforward application of behaviorism on this continent is Skinner's attempts (1938, 1957) to explain the behavior of organisms, human and otherwise. His notions are reflected in novel form in *Walden II* (1948) and in essay form in *Beyond Freedom and Dignity* (1971). Skinner believes that society itself is generated on the basis of behavioristic principles and that society and the quality of life in it are determined by the particular philosophy of life being implemented. This fact of control is all-important, especially for the young as they acquire their individual and group personalities in the culture in which they live. Skinner has been severely criticized for such opinions, especially in egalitarian-minded America, but one wonders what, in effect, is controlling our aspirations and way of life. It need not be a single individual or group; it may be simply a random assortment of values that affects us all. Skinner has a point, and more time might be spent on deciding just which social forces that control our lives are destructive to individuals and society as a whole instead of on demolishing Skinner's arguments.

In language, behaviorism implies that a speaker's performance, or his responses, can be traced back to specific stimulus–response relationships. Thus, a simple behavior theory seeks to determine which of the stimuli present in the environment prompted an utterance and, further, whether it will be reinforced by the behavior of others. Say that a given set of responses, perhaps a half-dozen, is made and that one of these is rewarded and thus reinforced. The state that motivated the speaker has been satisfied, and obviously the response that has been satisfied will be conditioned as being the appropriate one if the same state of affairs arises again. If it does, it is extremely likely, according to this very simple behavioral model, that the same or a similar response will emerge again. If such a response in fact does and is again rewarded, it is obviously on its way to becoming ingrained as the appropriate response to such situations. Skinner might accord the development of one's entire verbal repertoire to this simple technique of reinforcement and conditioning.

There may be some wisdom in Skinner's early remark (1938) that the only major differences between rat behavior and human behavior are in verbal behavior. This remark, of course, discounts the tremendous difference in complexity between the behaviors of the two types of organisms. But regardless of one's views of the similarities to be posited between various animal behaviors and human behaviors, it is difficult to make many generalizations from the behavior of other creatures to the verbal behavior of humans.

Skinner's model is different from classical behaviorist stimulus–response views in that he admits two types of response behavior, respondent behavior and operant behavior. In a strict view of stimulus–response patterning, if there is no stimulus, there is no corresponding response. This theory is clearly lacking in view of much human behavior—especially language behavior. Skinner's solution is to admit a second kind of response, or operant behavior. **Operant behavior** is the type of behavior that results when no stimulus can be designated as the causal agent. Behavior that is elicited by causal agents is called **respondent behavior.**

Skinner's notion of respondent conditioning is thus not entirely unlike the earlier conception that resulted from classical-conditioning experimentation. If some sort of behavior can be considered as the specific response to a specific stimulus, then that is in fact a specific response that is clearly already associated with a specific stimulus. However, classical concepts like unconditioned stimulus and unconditioned response do not appear to explain the kind of learning that goes on in the learning of language. For behaviorists, language was obviously not present without some prior training, conditioning, or reinforcement. Language was not in the same class of stimulus–response relationships as a blink in response to a flashing light, salivation in response to the presentation of food, or an involuntary reflex movement in response to a falling sensation.

Viewed as response, language behavior appears to be more a response emitted without specific reference to any particular stimulus in the environment. As a result, operant behavior must figure heavily in Skinner's attempt (1957) to account for language behavior, or, as he terms it, verbal behavior. For Skinner, the matter of learning language takes place entirely according to the laws of operant conditioning. In fact, Skinner suggests that this kind of behavior is more typical of much of human behavior than respondent behavior anyhow.

The strength of such operant responses is directly related to the degree to which they have been linked to rewards. Language behavior implies a social reward arising from others' approval, or reinforcement. In the acquisition stages of language, certain operant behaviors that will become language behavior are conditioned on the basis of their results. Such results can be termed positively or negatively reinforcing for the child, and they create a pattern that then becomes habitual. If certain types of verbal behavior are positively reinforced, they will become appropriate responses in certain situations or in general; if they are sufficiently negatively reinforced, they will likely disappear. And, of course, if a particular response is conditioned in a particular situation, the same response is likely to appear in future situations that are seen as analogous when a similar need or stimulus exists.

In operant behavior there is, therefore, no directly identifiable stimulus that results in a specific response. The organism does learn to operate upon (hence the term **operant**) or make use of certain features of his environment, but these responses emerge on a trial-and-error basis more than on a predictable one. The organism simply emits a number of responses to the situation, and one of these is reinforced as the appropriate response. Because there is no way to control the actual response given until it occurs, one must await its appearance, if it appears at all. One can make the atmosphere conducive to certain kinds of responses, but there is no way to control them. Once the desired response has been emitted, reinforcement, if consistently applied, can result in the learning of that response set to given situations. Thus, learning takes place as the result of reinforcement rather than as direct and unconditioned responses to conditioned or unconditioned stimuli.

Not all verbal behavior is the same, however, and even Skinner has established a functional typology of language. His categories of **mand, tact, intraverbal operant, textual operant,** and **echoic operant** are intended to cover the various types of linguistic behavior and to explain their origins and maintenance in terms of operant conditioning. Simply stated, Skinner's verbal operants are defined in terms of the kinds of situations in which they occur.

An example of how Skinner puts such principles to use in his outline of a theory of verbal behavior is the notion of the mand. A term patterned on words like *demand* and *command,* the mand is not tied to a directly observable stimulus, though it serves to alleviate the drive state of the speaker. Such mands as *Food! Water! Get it!* and *Shut up!* arise from the unobservable internal state of the speaker and are likely to be reinforced by the listener, and so become fixed in the speaker's repertoire. The tact, on the other hand, results from those situations in which the child makes a verbal response in the presence of a given stimulus. If the child is rewarded for the response and if he continues to make the response whenever he comes into con*tact* with that stimulus, he can be said to have acquired a tact verbal response.

One question that does not seem completely answerable is why the organism responds to reinforcement at all. It is not trivial to question whether the organism wants the experience at all and, if the organism does, whether it is motivated by drive or deprivation states to accept the reinforcements that enable it to learn a specific kind of behavior. Although the notions of operant behavior and operant conditioning are attractive, one wonders why they seem to work at all. Rationalists arguing for the innateness of language constructs and the acquisition of language along maturationally defined chronological lines might find this observation a crucial one, and it is surprising that more have not added this argument to their arsenal.

Mands and tacts essentially are related to such concepts as reinforcement and the fulfilling of need states. Skinner's other functional categories—echoic operants, textual operants, and intraverbal operants—are linked to verbal behaviors themselves. Echoic operants are responses to the verbal stimuli of another speaker; they are simply echoes of what the other has said. For example, in Skinner's theory such behavior occurs when a child repeats a verbal stimulus emitted by his parents and is then appropriately rewarded. The textual operant is a response to a textual—that is, written or drawn—stimulus. Instead of echoing the words of another, as in *Say ahhh—OK, ahhh,* or the words themselves, as in the partially duplicated *Ping–Pong, fiddle–faddle, fuddle–duddle,* or *mishmash,* the speaker sees the written form of a word and then says it aloud. Thus, reading the words on this page aloud is a textual-operant response. The category of intraverbal operants is used to explain those instances in which one verbal stimulus prompts the production of another. Examples are *Jack* followed by *and Jill, bread* followed by *and butter,* and *Together we stand* followed by *Divided we fall.*

In attempting such a simple cause–effect explanation, behaviorists have, many claim, lost sight of the very linguistic data they are trying to explain. It is interesting to note that in the most complete published version of Skinner's views on language (1957), he cites little experimental evidence for his claims and takes little account of the extensive work done in the field of linguistics up to that time. These two facts have made Skinner's position untenable and have aroused a good deal of criticism by linguists. N. Chomsky's review (1959) of the book is particularly harsh. Certainly the most pointed criticism is Chomsky's admonition that instead of being based in reality, Skinner's approach is a retreat to mentalistic psychology. There has never been a reply as such, and the two continue to investigate those facets of language that are most important to them.

To Chomsky and most linguists, Skinner's model is simply not correct. Other psychologists, such as Osgood, have viewed the functional analysis model as being inadequate instead, and have attempted to refurbish the basic behavioral approach by broadening both its scope and its premises. One main reason linguists may reject Skinner's model is that it does not take into account the entirely novel character of the rule-behavior system the neophyte speaker of a language is learning. Skinner ignores the creativity of language as such; in viewing language as a fixed, bounded set of data to be acquired by conditioning and reinforcement, he leaves no room for the infinite, dynamic character of language. Psychologists may reject the model because of Skinner's obvious reluctance to deal with meaning or any other sort of intangible, but nevertheless necessary, mental construct in accounting for language. However, it should be pointed out that Skinner's work, past and present, contains much of value, and the failure of his model to account for the nature of language does not in any way detract from his contributions to our knowledge of learning and behavior. After all, no one else has proposed a model of language behavior that is unanimously accepted as the true explanation of how it all happens.

Osgood and the Mediational Approach

More tolerant and less puristic stimulus–response theories of language posit notions that had been automatically excluded from consideration. These neo-behaviorist approaches include the question of thought and mental processes in their analysis of human behavior and, consequently, the question of meaning in the explication of human language behavior. Such models unabashedly assume possible intermediate processes, functions, or steps occurring within the organism itself as connecting such events.

This dealing with stimulus–response relations by positing internal intermediate processes, functions, steps, or whatever has given the name of **mediational model** to the best known and perhaps most widely accepted of such positions. This model is most closely associated with Osgood, though other psychologists, such as Mowrer (1954) and Staats (1968, 1971), have used it. Osgood has consistently expanded the mediational position in an attempt to answer some of the more pressing criticisms of learning theory in order to manage an adequate explanation of language. His earlier models (1953, 1957) were simpler two-step mediational models, while his later publications (1963, for example) attempt to meet some of the major criticisms from transformationalists and others. With Skinner's functional analysis having been abandoned by most psycholinguists, Osgood's mediational model needs even more so to stand up to criticism from language researchers, if not from the point of view of accounting for language, certainly from the sheer number of critics who have turned their attention to Osgood's position.

In contrast to the behaviorist theories of language, mediational models postulate a mediating step that intervenes between the stimulus the human organism is responding to and its response. Thus, a mediational theory of language behavior would look for a stimulus–response sequence within the organism itself as a mediating stage between the external, observable stimulus and response. As such, the mediational approach is not entirely unlike the behavioristic model; some have characterized the former as a two-step learning-theory model and the latter as a one-step learning model. Moreover,

neo-behaviorist concepts are also stated in operational fashion and reflect empirical ultimates as the basis of their explanatory power.

Insofar as mediational models attempt to describe the meanings of
words as part of the total response repertoire of the organism to the
items that the words represent, the approach is somewhat reminiscent
of classical-conditioning concepts. In a mediational model like that of
Mowrer (1954), for example, the meaning of the word *thief* is an internalized part of the total repertoire of behavioral responses a person
may have to a thief. The internal response that constitutes the
meaning of the word *thief* is obviously not the same as the total behavioral pattern of responses to an actual thief but is representative of
some part of it. This concept is reminiscent of classical conditioning
where the conditioned response is only similar to, not identical with,
the kind of unconditioned response.

Similarly, such meanings in a mediational model can be conditioned
or switched to other word concepts in ways reminiscent of conditioning techniques. In the sentence *Tom is a thief,* the internalized
response that now constitutes the meaning of the word *thief* can be attached to the word *Tom.* Meaning is the mediator between the external
stimulus and the external response behavior. Although the connection
between stimulus and response is no longer a direct one, meanings
are not just there to begin with; they are acquired through conditioning just as other kinds of learning are. In the establishment of a
meaning for the word *thief* encountered in this paragraph, part of the
total repertoire of reaction to the real thing is internalized as the reaction to the word that stands for it in a symbolic, representative way.

The mediational nature of this explanation is graphically represented
in Figure 2.1. In Osgood's heavily behavioristic analysis (1957) of per-

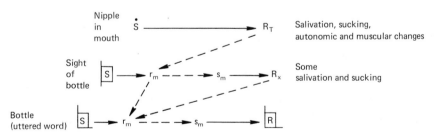

Figure 2.1 An example of the development of meaning in the mediational model. [Reprinted
by permission of the publishers from Charles E. Osgood, "A Behavioristic Analysis of Perception and Language as Cognitive Phenomena," in *Contemporary Approaches to Cognition, A
Symposium Held at the University of Colorado,* Cambridge, Massachusetts: Harvard University Press, © 1957 by the President and Fellows of Harvard College.]

ception and language as cognitive phenomena, a definite stimulus, such as a nipple in a baby's mouth, will produce a definite pattern of response behavior, such as salivation, sucking, and so forth. Thus, the unconditioned stimulus $\dot{S}$ gives rise to an unconditioned response set, the total behavior associated with that stimulus, Osgood's R_T. Next the conditioned stimulus, the sight of the bottle or breast nipple (Osgood's $\boxed{S}$), may come to produce response behavior reflective of the original total response behavior. Some of this behavior may be overt, R_X (salivation, sucking, and other autonomic and muscular changes), while some may be covert and unobservable, the mediating response r_m. If one accepts the argument thus far, it is a relatively simple matter to tie language concepts to the process of mediational conditioning already exhibited. The r_m has become the "meaning" of the actual physical reality, in this case the bottle or breast. Words can be assigned as the linguistic labels for these "meanings" derived from conditioning and be in effect derived from the R_T, the r_m, or the R_X aspects of the response behavior, or even from other words.

According to this theory, then, all meaning in language is ultimately derived from observable behavior, and language itself is produced by the operation of some set of classical behavioral principles, albeit through mediational stages. Viewing language in this way allows, of course, for the constant alteration and expansion of meanings. Osgood and his colleagues (1957) have also made attempts to measure meaning. The most widely known method they have used is the semantic differential, which is mentioned here because of its relationship to Osgood's position. The problem of meaning and the semantic differential are discussed in greater detail in Chapter 7.

In sum, the essence of the mediational model is that because of our inability to speak simply of stimuli and responses, a third variable is necessary to account for language behavior. Certain internal states, called meaning, are assumed to occur as responses to external stimuli. These internal states then become stimuli that in turn control overt external behavior, or the responses we observe. The mediational model is based on an explanation of the relationship between the external stimulus and its corresponding internal response and between this unobservable response and the organism's final observable response. This model does seem more attractive than Skinner's functional analysis because it admits some internal processes into the fact of language use and attempts to describe these processes. The mediational model is also in some ways a more viable position in that it admits the notion of meaning. In this view, words and sentences do have meaning, but the meaning ultimately stems from the association with the items or experiences for which they stand. However, the model is even harder to validate on the basis of external criteria than is Skinner's unless we assume concrete neurological correlatives to various aspects of the model. At present, of course, this assumption is unwarranted and perhaps somewhat optimistic.

The Cognitive Approach

Some comment should also be made about the school of cognitive psychology and its contribution to our understanding of language. The role of cognitive psychology may not have been as obvious as that of behavioral psychology for the simple reason that the latter has dominated North American psychological thought for the past few decades. Moreover, cognitive psychology is more difficult to pin down in terms of observable constructs; this school deals more in theoretical constructs to explain learning and language. The best known of the cognitive notions is the Gestalt approach, which suggests that humans perceive reality in terms of meaningful wholes and integrated units. The parts of a whole can be broken down and analyzed, but doing so is an artificial process; our preferred perceptual mode is the whole rather than the part. For example, when we see an incomplete figure, we unconsciously tend to fill it in to form a whole. Thus, instead of seeing four unjoined lines drawn at right angles to one another, we see a square.

There is a compelling analogy between this notion of conceptual wholes and the way in which psycholinguistic experiments of the click paradigm have shown that individuals tend to perceive sentences in terms of their constituent phrases. When clicks are superimposed on heard sentences, the tendency is to hear the clicks as coming at major constituent boundaries in the sentences even though they were actually superimposed at points before or after the boundaries. More on this topic appears in Chapter 9, which deals with experimental psycholinguistics.

An interesting account of the similarities between the structural concepts employed in modern linguistics and the Gestalt notions employed in the investigation of visual perception is offered by Neisser (1967). Neisser points out that the meaning of a sentence is not entirely dependent on the sum of its parts, the words in it, or even the sequence of the words. Rather, the meaning of a sentence is apparently related to the structure of the sentence and its hierarchical ordering of large constituent units. Neisser also draws attention to the similarity of this phenomenon to the study of visual perception by Gestaltists who called attention to the importance of perception along the lines of wholistic interpretations. Another similarity can be seen in the study of ambiguous sentences in generative grammar and the well-known study of ambiguous visual figures in Gestalt psychology. Neisser also notes that the old Gestalt psychology and recent linguistic theory both react negatively to behaviorism, take a nativistic approach to the innate principles underlying perceptual processes, and so forth.

The school of cognitive psychology and the emerging cognitive approach to psycholinguistics cannot be taken as exactly the same in all respects, however. A cognitive approach to language users concentrates on discovering those cognitive abilities that are a prerequisite for language behavior. Thus, the actual observation of actual language performance is secondary to the study of the knowledge, processes, and abilities that underlie this performance. Chomsky's work can even be seen in some ways as a precursor of the cognitive approach to language, but perhaps not in the way envisioned by Bever (1970) and others.

Some, like Maclay (1973), see in this the beginning of another period in psycholinguistics, one that can be loosely characterized as the cognitive approach. According to this point of view, language, particularly language acquisition, is merely one of the number of products generated by the underlying cognitive processes. Such a position obviates the demand that grammatical theory occupy a central place in our understanding of human cognition and characterizes linguistic competence as a reflection of the other cognitive and behavioral systems involved in the development of language. Thus, the very nature of language structure is derived from the more basic cognitive foundational structures, and the acquisition of language is affected by the interplay of this linguistic structure and other behavioral considerations. Generative transformational theory remains an important part of this approach, but not the central concern. This is obviously somewhat different from the way it was at the height of the primacy of grammar era.

Other than Bever's discussions (1970, 1971) of the cognitive basis for linguistic structures and a number of other presentations, a unanimous swing toward this point of view is not yet evident. But such an approach may in the future serve as the melding point for psycholinguists who have never completely agreed with the generative transformational approach and have not assimilated it into their idea of the fundamentals of psycholinguistic theory to the exclusion of all other approaches. If that happens, linguistic theory may no longer be seen as fundamental to psycholinguistics. Instead, such an approach may mean the beginning of a theoretical orientation that takes the best of both disciplines and melds them into a workable philosophy-of-science paradigm. Apparently, others also see this possibility as a viable one, and Reber (1973), in his discussion of psycholinguistic paradigms, implies that the discipline is tending to move in this direction (he calls this position the process orientation).

As a conclusion to this chapter, let us review the theoretical underpinnings of current psycholinguistics research—at least those influenced by the previously discussed linguistic and psychological viewpoints. Much work up to the time of generative transformational grammar was centered around statistical inferences gleaned from language data or the description of language as simply verbal responses. Perhaps the single most important contribution that Chomsky made to psycholinguistics was to call attention to the potentially infinite nature of language and the importance of linguistic creativity. Language is an immensely complicated activity, and no simple model of cause and effect will explain it adequately. Just a casual glance at any attempt to present certain aspects of the grammar of English in a generative transformational framework is sufficient to convince one of the inherent complexity of language behavior. Certainly, if the fervent activity during the past four decades has not been equal to the task of constructing a complete grammar of English, let alone other languages, simple cause-and-effect explanations are not likely to do the job satisfactorily either.

Still, many questions remain essentially unanswered, so that other psycholinguistic and sociolinguistic interests have blossomed. One point left unanswered in Chomsky's approach, for example, is the concept of performance and its relevance to the analysis of actual language manifestations. Even if an adequate grammatical description of language abilities existed, it would not explain why certain of these abilities are used in certain ways and on certain occasions in communication. The very important facet of language behavior, which cannot be overlooked in a purportedly complete treatment of human language, is being examined in research concerned with language as a social phenomenon, bilingualism, nonverbal communication, and so forth. The results have been both productive and promising. Nevertheless, any description of psycholinguistic concerns would fall far short if it did not include the contributions of Chomsky's linguistic theory and the ramifications it has had within its own discipline as well as in psycholinguistics.

Language
Acquisition

The Origin of Language

Most early speculation about the acquisition of language was hampered by a lack of serious interest in the origin of language. Trivialized by such names as the "yo-heave-ho theory," the "ding-dong theory," and the "bow-wow theory," notions of language origin assumed that a man imitated some facet of his environment. According to this view, the symbols we call language were connected with external stimuli and hence given meanings through some underlying principle of appropriateness. Such theories emphasized the representational side of language, flirted with notions of onomatopoeia, and, in general, failed to answer some of the most basic questions about this complex topic.

Nevertheless, the origin of language remains somewhat of a mystery, one enshrouded with many others in the dim recesses of man's evolutionary history. The notion of the origin of language itself enables us to view it in a manner congruent with our own beliefs about man, the universe, and his place in it. But whenever and however language did originate, it was one of the developments that helped to establish our identity as a species apart from all others. The place of prelinguistic man is somewhere between the apelike proto-hominids some choose to call our ancestors and *Homo sapiens,* modern man. The change must have been dramatic and is clearly one of the most important evolutionary or historical developments that have made us what we are today. A major portion of this chapter is concerned with the question of whether the development of language is to be tied to evolutionary development or simply to a historical development in cultural history.

Animal Communication and Communicative Chimps

Animals besides man communicate, since they actually exchange information. Although the communications are of various kinds, no animal of our acquaintance has ever developed language or acquired language, despite the work reported on dolphins by Lilly (1961), on chimpanzees by Hayes (1951), the Gardners (1969, 1972), and the Premacks (1972), on bees by von Frisch (1950, 1955), and so forth. With von Frisch's bees, for example, the communication system is frozen, good only to bees, and cannot be used to communicate information about anything except the quality, quantity, direction, and so on of nectar. The system is a closed one, and likely to remain so. Still, the ritualistic dancelike movements through which bees convey information (direction, distance, and quality of the nectar) about their favorite topic in the absence of the original stimulus are clearly communicative in function. The debate over whether this communication system and those of other animal forms should be classed as language seems irrelevant. If we choose to label our particular form of communication language, then so be it; other species have their own ways of conveying whatever type of information is important to them. Nothing more can be made of that.

There have, however, been some interesting investigations with some of our closer relatives in the animal world. Researchers have often toyed with the notion of teaching apes, monkeys, or chimpanzees human language, but have had little success. "Monkey see, monkey do" may have prompted some researchers to test the imitative and intellectual skills of some of our simian counterparts, but from the results it is readily apparent that the saying will not be changed to "Monkey hear, monkey talk." For example, Hayes (1951) was only able to get her chimp to produce a few wordlike utterances (*momma, poppa,* and *cup*) with any regularity, and even these were somewhat unintelligible, despite the considerable loving care and training she had lavished on the chimp. It would appear that the ability to reproduce human speech sounds is not within the motor-skills repertoire of such creatures.

Until recently, such efforts to teach animals language have been as futile as teaching fish to fry eggs and dogs to program computers. Talking and language-related activities do not depend on intelligence, imitative capacities, and so forth; they depend on simply being human. If one is human, one will develop a language. If one is not, one will not. In fact, Lenneberg (1964) and Chomsky (1968) claim that even the most elemental stages of human speech are quite beyond any nonhuman species.

Some interesting developments have taken place since Hayes reported on her simian houseguest. Hayes and most of the other researchers tried to teach human language to chimpanzees and the like through the same communicative channel that man uses, the aural–oral channel. The attempts failed because of obvious physiological differences, with the exception of faint successes in the same vein as Fido in talking-dog stories who can answer *rough, roof,* and *Ruth* to appropriate questions. The Gardners, however, translated the word portions of English into the American Sign Language for the deaf and have met with some success in training their chimpanzee, named Washoe.

The American Sign Language uses signs to represent objects or concepts, for example, rubbing the first finger against the teeth for *toothbrush,* tapping the head for *hat,* tapping the thigh for *dog,* and holding the hand in a fist, index finger extended, while rotating the arm at the elbow for *always.* The contrast between *always* and *hat* shows that some signs are arbitrary, while others are transparent in their function, shape, or relationship to spoken language. There is another form of sign language, which spells words out by the fingers running through the appropriate finger signs for the letters of the alphabet, but this was not selected for obvious reasons.

There can be little doubt that Washoe has learned something, perhaps a primitive form of language. She has learned a vocabulary of surprising proportions, and unlike what happened in the oral–aural attempts with chimpanzees, her vocabulary is expanding. The Gardner's first report (1969) lists Washoe's vocabulary as consisting of some 34 sign words. A later film report at the 1972 Toronto meeting of the American Anthropological Association shows her as having doubled, if not trebled, her inventory. At this point, she uses sign words and combines them into sequences containing several elements—for example, *gimme tickle, please open hurry,* and *gimme drink please.* That she occasionally uses sign words inventively and in novel, though primitive, combinations is of special interest, for part of the charisma of human language is this ability to innovate. Anyone who has seen the films presented by the Gardners at scholarly meetings cannot fail to be convinced that Washoe has indeed acquired something, though one may not wish to equate it with human language.

Similar findings were reported by the Premacks (1972) with a chimpanzee named Sarah. Sarah was trained with colored, differently shaped plastic figures on the kind of magnetic board that children play with. Each of the colored pieces of plastic represents a word, and she boasts a 130-word "reading and writing" vocabulary. She can recognize and use the appropriate symbols, can form simple sentences on the pattern of English syntax, can answer questions, and apparently can create new combinations to engender new sentences. Sarah's setting, however, is strictly an experimental one. This may not be a communicative system, but rather her repertoire of responses to a set of word games, which are highly suggestive of sentences.

One must remember that such chimp sentences are not like the endless James Joyce sentence in Molly's soliloquy in *Ulysses,* but usually simple three- or four-element affairs. Still, the process and the discovery of it are remarkable. The accomplishments of these two chimps suggest to researchers that perhaps it was only the wrong type of communication system that they were trying to coax the animals to acquire, while the rest of us are reminded that we are perhaps not so far removed from what we prefer to call the animal kingdom.

In an age of environmental consciousness, such research and other ethological studies of animal behavior may serve an excellent purpose in helping man to know himself as one of many who inhabit the earth. There are indeed striking differences between man and the animals, but one wonders whether the same would not be true if Japanese beetles were able to verbalize and congratulate themselves on their uniqueness. However, language is language and, as far as we know, man's alone. To this end, Hockett (1960, 1966) offers a lengthy list of defining criterial attributes of human language and Hockett and Ascher (1964) and Hewes (1973) both offer explanations as to how and possibly when this revolutionary development took place. But we still do not know enough about other forms of animal communication to make any sweeping generalizations except that other species do have communication systems appropriate to their uses but these systems are rather limited.

Rationalism versus Empiricism and the Biological Basis of Language

Regardless of what happens in other species, no healthy human being ever fails to learn language, and, congruently, no human society fails to have a language. And each language has the same functional kind of patterning, with each structural level built into the next level. Some see this omnipresence of language as a basis for regarding it as a species-specific endowment of man. This belief has some important ties with the basic assumptions one makes about the nature of knowledge and experience.

The contrasting sets of assumptions that have dominated Western thinking on this problem are classical empiricism and classical rationalism. Briefly, rationalist theories are characterized by an emphasis on intrinsic or innate principles in mental operations and learning. According to this view, organizing principles either directly guide man's perception and learning or at least indirectly do so by predisposing man to operate in a certain way. Empiricist theories, on the other hand, stress that experience and environmental factors condition the organism to specific modes of behavior. There is no innate organizing structure, and there are no innate ideas in the mind that are not themselves the product of environment and of admission and transferral by the senses. This is the view that has been prevalent in the development of modern behavioral science.

This contrast in points of view does not say much about the origin of language—a problem that is also insoluble, given the present state of our knowledge—but it is directly relevant to the problem of the acquisition of language. In a reflection of the current philosophy-of-science debate, scientists are asking whether language is acquired on the basis of reinforcement, conditioning, and experience or whether it is acquired according to some preconceived guiding set of principles. The latter view seems to have served as the impetus for a great deal of debate and research during the past decade.

Rationalism, in this sense, would attribute language to the store of common notions and innate organizational universals that guide much of human activity. The point is that the specific knowledge itself is not there, but the organizational principles for perceiving, organizing, and using such knowledge are. These innate universals are present not because of specific experiences but because of the nature of the mind. Even here, however, rationalists like N. Chomsky and his followers would certainly not deny the contribution of specific experiences to fill in the organizational grid the young human mind brings to language learning. The specific knowledge is in this way the reflection of what experiences and environmental factors the human organism has been exposed to; the innate factors provide the grid onto which these are mapped and given some substance and organization. In this light, language is a latent structure, present in the human mind, but needing specific experiential stimulation to activate the capacity. The capacity is innate and needs only to be activated by a specific language experience which follows set guidelines in its development. In fact, the guidelines seem to follow a path of maturational development, not unlike motor skills in human development.

A corollary of this point of view is that all languages will be found to be rather similar in their deep structures because the possibilities are fixed by the innate organizational structures. Languages may thus be extremely different in their surface structures, as any casual observation of different languages will indicate, but they should be very similar in their underlying principles. Such a notion is, of course, congruent with Chomsky's theory of generative transformational grammar; the set of data in which a theory of language is based must be the entire set of the world's languages, and these must be seen as having certain basic, inescapable similarities for the establishment of such a theoretical position.

As many have pointed out, that children acquire a language under the conditions they do is sufficient to arouse curiosity in the possibility of an innate acquisition capacity. Children usually manage this task in the absence of any overt or explicit instruction. Moreover, they do so at a time when other intellectual tasks are far beyond them—and even sometime in the absence of normal intelligence factors. Indeed, in view of the incredible structural complexity of language itself, it is astonishing that children can proceed with the learning of language at all.

Even though language is an enormously complex system of rules, as shown by generative transformational descriptions, children learn their native language in a relatively short time. Interestingly, their progress from the earliest period of random babblings to early-childhood mastery (not the complete mastery of adult speakers) is relatively smooth, despite differences in language stimulation and differences in practice. It would appear that the developmental schedules are more or less congruent from individual to individual and so almost analogous to a maturational schedule of development. In a discussion of how the child's apparently scheduled stages of linguistic development correlate with the milestones in his motor and intellectual development, Lenneberg (1967) implies that the parallels are too close in general terms not to warrant some speculation on what this may mean for our understanding of genetically based maturational development for the species. Language development appears to parallel such other developments as stance, bipedal locomotion, and hand, foot, and general muscular coordination. All seem to follow a programmed set of stages of development that is entirely independent of learning as a formal exercise. Moreover, the ability to learn language eventually reaches a plateau and then declines rapidly, just as other skills do.

The path of development appears to be much the same in normal, healthy children the world over, and culture seems to have little to do with the emergence and development of the stages of acquisition. Furthermore, children cannot be taught to speak language before a certain period, and once the process of acquisition has begun, arresting it seems to be difficult, if not impossible. If a child of the right age is placed in any linguistic community, he will immediately and with no difficulty whatsoever begin to acquire, and acquire perfectly, that language if adequate stimulation is provided. However, once he is past the age of puberty, and here the age varies somewhat from individual to individual, the ability deteriorates rapidly; much to our chagrin, language acquisition as adults often becomes a tedious, time-consuming intellectual exercise instead of the rapid and facile experience it is for young children.

Although the order of the language stages of acquisition seems to remain much the same, children may differ in their actual rate of language development within a given linguistic community, yet any differences that do occur are not enormous. Much the same thing can be said of differing linguistic communities when comparing acquisition of language across cultures. However, a word of caution is in order here. When applied to such situations, the concept of normality means a range of behavior. One cannot specify exactly when a certain linguistic behavior will begin to appear and exactly when it will mature. The development of such behaviors differs from individual to individual and lies on a continuum, with the median the point of departure for discussion purposes. Except in cases of abnormality, the slightly earlier or later appearance of certain linguistic behaviors is not a matter on which to make value judgments.

That children learn language at such an early age and arrive at exactly the same grammatical formulations from different sets of data experiences would lead one to shy away from behavioristic positions and consider the possibility that language learning must be controlled by a predisposition for such activity. If we assume that we are all fluent native speakers of English, we must wonder how it is that in spite of our having been exposed to different language experiences with the very same language, we all created essentially the same model to account for it—competency in the English language, or our grammar of English. One possible explanation for this seemingly incomprehensible state of affairs is that, as budding speakers of the language, we were directed in choosing among different explanations and schemes of organization by the very limitations imposed upon us by the organizational principles innate in human beings.

It is, of course, absurd to postulate that children learn to speak without linguistic stimulation, and innateness should not be misinterpreted here. Linguistic stimuli provide the raw data upon which the organizing principles can be said to operate. There can be no minimizing of the importance of the environmental influences on the child's learning to speak, for these channel his abilities in certain directions and in many ways exert an influence on the child as great as, if not greater than, the intrinsic structures the child brings to the acquisition situation. Because all languages appear to be constructs with certain general characteristics in common, and because these general characteristics are coded in the child's genetic endowment as a member of the language-using human species, the system of communication he is exposed to will be language, and that language will be of a type already defined for him by his innate endowment. However, without the stimulation of that specific language in that specific language-using community, it would appear that the child will not evolve language. This appears to have happened in the occasional reported cases of feral, or "wolf," children (children supposedly reared by wild animals or in isolation from all or nearly all human contact) and in cases in which severely deprived or maltreated children are brought up in rather eccentric or abnormal human settings entirely lacking linguistic stimulation. For an intriguing contrast between the two situations, compare the linguistic development reported for the eighteenth-century "wild child" Victor, as described by his "mentor," Dr. Itard (1962), and the linguistic development reported for the sequestered twentieth-century adolescent girl Genie, as reported by Curtiss, Fromkin, Krashen, Rigler, and Rigler (1974). Victor had apparently been left in the wilderness as a young child and had somehow managed to survive into his early teens. Genie, on the other hand, was raised in near confinement with minimal human contact until her early teens. Neither of the children could speak or use language when they were first discovered.

Some, like Lenneberg (1967), have speculated that if such children receive no linguistic stimulation until the age of puberty or some such "critical age," their language abilities will be frustrated and possibly never realized. Or perhaps their language abilities will be limited thereafter and realized only partially. However, in past cases of both feral and deprived children, it has been difficult to separate the effects of lack of cultural and linguistic stimulation from natural debilities in intelligence and so forth, especially when the written reports can no longer be independently verified. The inability of the eighteenth-century "wolf-child" Victor to grasp language properly may have been due to other factors besides a lack of appropriate environmental stimulation, but we will never be able to find out. Obviously, such instances are rare, and those that have occurred typically have not been of a kind to provide clear and incontrovertible conclusions, so that such examples prove neither entirely supportive nor unsupportive of this view.

More recently, Curtiss *et al.* (1974) have provided evidence that Genie is making some "steady if modest progress [p. 544]" in acquiring language. This report is significant because Genie first began to learn language when she was about 14 and already pubescent. If there is a "critical age" tied to the completion of the lateralization of cerebral function and if language acquisition by simple exposure to linguistic stimulation is deemed impossible thereafter, Genie's continuing capacity to acquire language would seem to be limited and should end at some time in the future. So far, she has certainly acquired some features of language, though it is premature to predict exactly how much she will develop linguistically or cognitively. We are sure, however, that in normal human beings in normal situations the schedule proceeds apace and there is no stopping it.

Here we should distinguish, as Lenneberg (1964) does, between genetic history and cultural history. Cultural history has about it the ring of purposiveness, a feature by which man implicitly declares to his own kind a rationale for activities, even though those activities may not lend themselves to explanations of rationality at the time of inception. For example, the institution of writing systems can be considered a distinctly cultural development. Other developments can be considered the result of biological development in the evolutionary history of a species. This kind of history, or genetic history, is the result of simple random development and the deciding feature of whether such a development is advantageous to the survival and proliferation of a species or whether it is lethal and thus self-annihilating. Many developments may occur, but only a very small number ever enter into the mainstream of genetic history. An example of such developments may be bipedality and walking in the human species. According to those modern proponents discussed here, language itself is another.

By paraphrasing some of Lenneberg's arguments in taking two clear examples of cultural history and genetic history—writing and bipedal gait, respectively—and comparing them against several criteria, we can form some opinion about whether language belongs to cultural, and thus experiential, development or genetic, and thus innate, development. First, there are no intraspecies variations in the nature of bipedality in normal, healthy human beings, whereas writing differs considerably depending on the system used. Some writing systems attempt to represent entire words, as Chinese does; some portray syllables, as the *kana* writing systems in Japanese do; and some portray single sounds, as the Latin alphabet does. It seems clear that all languages are rather similar in that they are vocal, using the vocal tract from the lips to the vocal cords in the larynx, usually on the exhalation of breath. Each language uses a relatively small number of sound units (phonemes) as its reference points in the language's sound system, and the next level of word building and morpheme building is entirely dependent on the phonological level. That level interlocks with the level of sentence building, where the order of sentences is highly restricted and very much patterned after the small number of rules that govern sentence building. This kind of rule orientation appears to be characteristic of all languages at all times.

Second, whereas there is no recorded history for the feature of bipedal gait, writing is intimately connected with relatively recent developments in our history and is in fact the very vehicle by which recorded history is conveyed. We also do not have a recorded history of language development within the species. Language has constantly changed but has not exhibited a specific evolutionary trend toward development. The structural makeup of speech does not go from primitive to more complicated stages correlated with the cultural and technological development of man. Just as opinions and observations on the cultural and technological development of man may be subjective, so may be any opinion about this aspect of language. Just as in a contemporary sense there is no difference in the basic composition of the languages currently spoken by man, in a historical sense there is no difference that we know of in the languages. We have no evidence other than that all the languages of our acquaintance, past or present, have the same kind of structure. In all, the similarity appears too great to be due to mere chance or even to independent development in different parts of the world. The only viable alternative would appear to be cultural borrowing right across the face of the earth, but this proposition is not entirely feasible, and its viability is further diminished, if not destroyed, by the other facts surrounding language acquisition.

Any child can learn any language with equal ease, and many children learn more than one when placed in a bilingual or multilingual environment. The problem of the child in first encountering language is not entirely unlike that of the scientist faced with a body of data. Both must organize the data into some reasonable system, for it is useless simply to repeat the data. System builders we are, and this quality is exactly what scientist and child alike bring to the problem, except that the child's inductions may be guided along certain innate pathways, while most scientists' inductions are guided by training, experience, and often preference.

Considering the implications of the possible relationships of language, thought, and culture, we should briefly preview the issue of whether language creates thought and is responsible for intelligence or whether thought and intelligence shape language. If proponents of the innate capacity for language acquisition are correct—and their arguments are the most powerful and yet the simplest—neither of those alternatives would seem to be the answer. A third alternative, which would seem to be correct, is that in acquisition language and intelligence are not necessarily related, or at least not in the causality sense that has been examined to this point, and that language is acquired independently of intelligence.

Undoubtedly, however, the two influence each other as they develop, even though there is no causal relationship. This notion of mutual influence can perhaps be extended to the coexistent network of language, thought, and culture. There need not be a causal relationship, but a constant and pervasive one. The innate abilities that the child brings with him are only stimulated by the particular language and culture, and as he grows older, the force of habit may hold him closely in its grasp. But the abilities that he brought to the initial stages of acquiring that language and that culture are intrinsic structures, and he retains them as he proceeds, though the ability to make fullest use of them diminishes as the years pass. Both his having peaked in maturational development and the force of habit may provide the illusion of his being trapped into particular perceptions and patterns.

Developmental Stages in the Acquisition of Language

If the strategies for acquiring language are the same, the sequence of the developmental stages and what is acquired at each stage must somehow correlate highly from child to child and culture to culture.

Before beginning the discussion, we should note that recent research treats child language as structural linguistics might have treated exotic languages. In this approach child language, or rather child languages, for they are viewed as separate stages at separate periods of development, is a separate language, a distinct logical entity. Previous investigations of child language concentrated on assessing the child's deviation from and progress toward adult speech. Such investigations simply assumed that children's language is a very poor reflection of adult speech.

The acquisition of language involves gradual differentiation in all aspects—phonological, syntactical, or semantic. Children start with very general and undifferentiated categories and then constantly expand and change their classifications. Thus, the child begins with a gross category like the concept of sound and proceeds, by a series of differentiations, to establish and re-establish patterns, each successive stage characterized by a system based on oppositions and functional contrast, but still unlike that of the adult speaker. This process of constant redefinition continues until the child's language approximates that of the adult speaker.

The first sounds the baby utters are reflexive. The forced expulsion of air from the baby's lungs initiated or helped along by the slap of a doctor's hand passes air over the vocal cords to create sound and the baby's first cries. The initial cry is a reflex, supplying the fledgling organism with its first breath. During the first month or so, the child proceeds through a period of undifferentiated sound; he is just vocalizing and plainly enjoying it. In the next period the baby realizes the presence of the vocal organs and plays with them just as he might play with other organs and limbs. To adults, conditioned to see meaning and reason in many activities, babies cry for reasons, and to anxious mothers eager to relieve their offspring, such crying appears to signal some discomfort. However, crying does not always signal discomfort; it may be a random, undifferentiated activity done simply for the sake of doing it. The similarity with the child's early activities with his limbs may be the best analogy. They are there, and so is he, vibrant and alive, and he uses them in random and undifferentiated ways.

The sounds of the next period, after the second month or so, are entirely random and bear no resemblance to symbolic language whatsoever except that some of the same vocal mechanisms are used. This period is often called the cooing and chuckling stage, and its most obvious feature is the child's use of vowel-like sounds. He uses his tongue as an articulator in producing the vowel-like cooings and makes sounds unrelated to crying. However, the time of reckoning comes eventually, and the baby gradually becomes aware that certain of these previously random vocalizations have an effect on his environment. The child also seems to respond to human sounds, for he turns his head in the direction of the speaker and may actively look for the speaker–originator of the sounds.

From about the fifth to the sixth month on, the child begins to produce syllable-like combinations, switching from his previous output of vowels to a syllable combination of a vowel plus a consonant. Vowels and consonants thus emerge as distinct entities, and the appearance of the syllable as a unit is contemporaneous. There is some evidence from Moskowitz (1970) and from her reading of Burling (1959) that the syllable may be more than just a unit, that its appearance may in fact be a stage in its own right, though there is evidence of some syllabification from the earliest stages. Syllables are often reduplicated, and parents' joys at overhearing *mama, papa, dada,* and *baba* and their own responses of "goo goo" may be a reflection of this stage. Often called the babbling stage, this period also marks the emergence of intonation as an important feature in the child's vocal behavior. Both the vocalizations exhibited in the babbling stage and those exhibited in the cooing and chuckling stage are probably unlearned and appear to be reflexive. When the child is about 8 months old, the reduplication becomes more frequent, and the intonation patterns become somewhat distinctive.

It is likely that during the latter part of this stage the child discovers the possibilities of combining articulation, the creation of different sounds by obstructing the exhaled stream of breath in various ways, with phonation, the vibrating action of the vocal chords that gives voice to all vowels, nasals, and certain consonantal sounds—/b, d, g, v, z/—and so forth. Shortly after this period the child also discovers the charm of imitating his own sounds, and thus the articulatory and vocal-cord movements he is now experimenting with and mastering become identified with certain auditory stimuli and are equated. That this loop is faulty or lacking in the congenitally deaf may be the major reason they fail to learn language properly.

After identifying his own voice features, the child begins to identify those of others, generally beginning with his mother. It is usually in the latter half of the babbling stage, about the tenth month, that the child shows evidence of understanding gestures, intonations, and sentence structures themselves. In fact, there is some evidence that intonational features (Weir, 1966) are likely the first linguistic features that the child understands and possible the first that he begins to use differentially. Some child-language researchers have even reported that response to intonation may occur as early as the fifth month.

From here on, from the age of about 12 months, the child actually begins to be involved in the fact of communication, and the first suggestions of words appear. The child also shows definite signs of comprehending some words and short, simple commands. Of course, the child's utterances are far from being the kind of language that adults use and comprehend, but they do signal differential use of language abilities. Words begin to appear after this time, at about 18 months, and may constitute an inventory of anywhere from 5 to 50 words, though the words are of course not by any means identical with their adult counterparts. The phonological shapes of the words are often rather opaque, especially to nonparents, and obviously are dependent on the child's stage of development in the realm of phonology. Semantically, the range exhibited by the words is also opaque, and if anything, the range covered by a given term is incredibly broad. As is commonly observed, the term *dog* may refer to everything having four legs, from cows to tables, and perhaps to a few things having more or fewer legs. However, the concept of symbolic reference and abstraction are present, and that is indeed worthy of comment.

Some researchers have interpreted the appearance of single words as also being a stage in syntactic development. They speculate that single words constitute the earliest form of syntactic structure in the development of the child's syntactic and semantic output. Thus, such early single-word utterances are actually syntactic units, albeit somewhat primitive. At this stage single words can be seen to function in communication just as larger units do, conveying a complete semantic proposition. The major difference would be that because of the limited number of words at this early stage, they are pressed into multiple duty and hence convey many, many meanings. The single word *dog* could mean "There is a dog," "I want the doggie toy," "Nice doggie," "See the dog there," or whatever. A grammar of children's syntax at this stage would consist of a single phrase-structure rule, S→W, and a single lexical rule, W→*dog, Daddy,* and so on, signaling that all sentences are single-word utterances and, conversely, that all single words can be and are sentences in their communicative functioning.

So far, the developmental stages in the child's acquisition of language have been presented in a rough chronological order, giving a general overview of the process. Here it may be best to turn our attention to the specific developments in phonology, grammar, and semantics. However, a rough chronology of the developmental stages will be maintained where possible.

Phonological Development

Just as the child begins from gross, undifferentiated categories in his other language skills and constantly enlarges and redefines the categories into smaller, differentiated ones, so does his development of the phonology proceed. The phonology also seems to be built on a set of contrasts, but the set will always be rapidly expanding. Thus, as Jakobson and Halle (1956) have postulated, the first stage may be the simple two-way contrast between the maximal consonant and the maximal vowel. The contrasts continue to be acquired, with the child filling in the blanks with the sound distinctions made in the language of his environment. The important thing is that the distinctions of the adult speech around him enter his developing phonology in a systematic way, again going from gross category to finer distinctions. Moreover, his search for pattern and rule in other areas of language behavior is mirrored in his acquisition of phonological structure. For example, the acquisition of a single distinctive feature like voicing will be extended to all the potential members of the set that are available at that time. Thus, although at an earlier stage the child may have /p–b, t–d, k–g/ as unopposing sounds, using them indiscriminately, once he learns the principle of opposition on the basis of voicing for only one of these sets, say, /p/ and /b/, he will by rule extension generalize to the other pairs, and /t/ and /d/ as well as /k/ and /g/ will become functionally contrasting units.

One of the most detailed discussions of what in principle must go on as the child acquires phonology is that of Jakobson and Halle (1956). Their often quoted work was not based on experimental evidence but was offered as a possible method of explaining phonological development. Their suggestion essentially switches the emphasis from trying to establish the sequence of sounds themselves to trying to establish the sequence of the acquisition of sound categories. The sequence of categories and perhaps even the timing of their acquisition is identical in principle for all languages, according to this theory. Up to this point, we must remember, much research on phonological acquisition was hampered by two serious drawbacks. One was the lack of a comprehensive phonological theory with which to view children's acquisition of various languages. The second drawback was the lack of a comprehensive theory that explained the stages as being independent of adult phonology and counted them as a separate series of phonological models. Thus, as noted previously, the child was to be viewed as a speaker of an exotic language, and his system of oppositions and contrasts was to be assessed at each stage. This was not a common methodological premise of investigations at the time, and Jakobson and Halle's discussion was rather innovative.

Their discussion answered the question of a comprehensive phonological theory with a theory that has since flowered into distinctive-feature phonology's relationship to generative grammar. Briefly, in distinctive-feature analysis sounds can be characterized by a relatively small number of features, which constitute their individuality. Such features are established in pairs of oppositions, which are claimed to be universals of phonology, thus making it possible to discuss or define any sound in any language by simply designating its distinctive feature set from among the universal set. Such an approach also answers some of the most pressing problems in the analysis of children's acquisition of phonology. By proposing distinctive feature oppositions, it is possible to discuss the emerging stages of children's phonology as a series of phonologies, each employing different sets of contrasts, until at last the child's and the adult's phonological systems are identical.

Jakobson and Halle's projected series of contrast splits occurs in somewhat the following way. The first split is that between the optimal vowel and the optimal consonant, /p/ and /a/. Graphically, the opposition looks like the following, with the optimal consonant characterized by maximal obstruction and the optimal vowel by maximal aperture, much like an articulational megaphone at either end, but facing in reverse directions.

$$p \longleftrightarrow a$$

The next stage involves the differentiation of the oral consonant /p/ from its nasal counterpart /m/. Up to this time, all consonants are assumed to be more or less allophonic variants of one overall category called the consonant phonological unit. The next split is that between labial and nonlabial, characterized by Jakobson and Halle as /p/ and /m/ as opposed to /t/ and /n/. What is implied here is that all nonlabial consonantal elements produced are seen as belonging to a single category, the nonlabial.

This last split completes what Jakobson and Halle term the primary triangle of consonantal phonemes /p/ and /t/ and vowel /a/. The contrasts can be graphically represented by the following:

At the same time, the optimal vowel /a/ is being differentiated along the continuum of openness or closeness of the mouth, or in North American linguistic parlance, between the optimally high vowel /i/ and the optimally low vowel /a/. Graphically, the contrast now becomes the following:

The next step is the differentiation of the optimally high vowel into front and back types, and front vowel type, /i/, and the back vowel type, /u/, both still characterized as high. Similarly, there is a split of the velar consonants from the dental, separating /t/ and /k/ as possible phonological entities. Graphically, the basic set can be illustrated as follows:

Up to this point, Jakobson and Halle's theory has attempted to cover the typical kinds and directions of development in languages. If the last stage mentioned is deleted, all languages known to us have at least these contrasts in their phonological inventory, though they may differ in other respects. Even including the last stage results in a framework that is characteristic of most languages, with perhaps Hawaiian, archaic Samoan, and several others being exceptions. Moreover, there is no language having back consonants without also having front consonants. Similarly, one would expect that no language exists that has a close vowel without also having an open one. Such observations have been termed the "law of irreversible solidarity" and refer to the a priori inventory of phonological distinctions in languages. That is, given that such a phonological category appears, it can be assumed that another such category also appears.

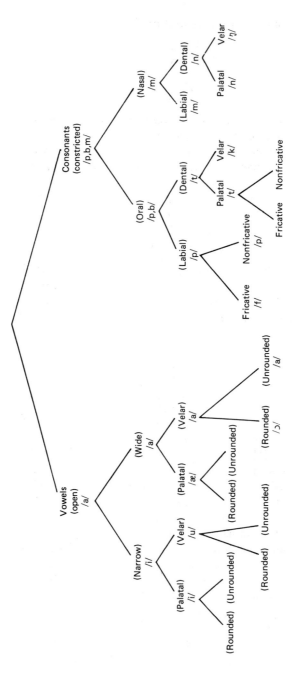

Figure 3.1 A possible order in the sequence of acquisition of speech sound distinctions. [From P. Menyuk, *The Acquisition and Development of Language*, © 1971. Reprinted by permission of Prentice-Hall, Inc., Englewood Cliffs, New Jersey.]

The opposition contrasts acquired after the basic ones are indeed dependent on the specific language to which the child is exposed. Thus, other contrasts, like the oppositions of fricatives to stops for consonants and rounded to unrounded vowels or nasalized to oral vowels, appear later. The specific phonological units that the particular language employs are filled in, from least complex to most complex. The development of the child's phonological system, then, can be considered as simply variations on the basic themes of sonority and tonality. Menyuk (1971) offers the schematization represented in Figure 3.1 of how Jakobson and Halle's formulation might suggest a possible order for the sequence of the acquisition of speech-sound distinctions, with examples from English.

One major criticism of Jakobson and Halle's innovative model has been that the order of contrast splits is too rigid and consequently not entirely representative of the appearance of phonological contrasts in children's phonological development. Older studies, such as those by Leopold (1947, 1961) and Velten (1943), appear to support certain aspects of the theory, though they cannot be considered validations of Jakobson and Halle's position. Basically, such studies support the notion of the acquisition of contrasts in sound categories, but not necessarily the specific sound types in the order of appearance that Jakobson and Halle describe.

There does, however, appear to be some support for their position on the sequencing of phonological acquisition. Irwin (1946, 1947a, 1947b, 1948) reports an early sequence in which low back to low central vowels show a decided increment in their mastery, while there are decrements in front and middle vowel sounds. When consonantal sounds do appear, labials are often first, followed by velars and then dentals. Nasals appear between these stages at the same time that several other distinctions do. Although Irwin's discussion is not a linguistically based one, the initial stages he describes occur in somewhat the same fashion as Jakobson and Halle postulate. Similarly, Ervin-Tripp (1966) presents a consensus of what seems to be the general pattern of sound acquisition, and in its most general form it does not deny the basic framework and the underlying principles of Jakobson and Halle's model. But neither does it clearly support many of their assertions.

Grammatical Development

We now return to the general chronology of the child's development of linguistic skills. At the stage of 18 months, the development of what we can formally call language begins. The earlier stages carried some communicative value, but it is in the later stage that actual language patterning, albeit of a very special kind, occurs. And once this development begins, it is almost impossible to prevent its flowering. From about 18 months on, and certainly after 24 months, then, language is indeed being used as a symbolic activity, and the child's utterances do have some relationship to himself, other speakers, the world around him, and his desires in regard to it. The child shows a marked increase in communicative behavior as such. From now on, his language abilities increase at an astounding rate, until in several years' time he has mastered the basic structure of his language. Then his activity slows to mostly adding new lexical items and new but less frequently occurring grammatical structures, and to learning about language as a social phenomenon. To be sure, this latter activity will be sufficient to occupy his energies and will likely do so for a good deal of his adolescent and adult language-using time. (More on this topic appears in Chapter 5, which deals with language in society.)

From about the age of 18 months, the child clearly has a small vocabulary, and he indeed responds to linguistic stimuli. Around the age of 2 years, the child's vocabulary begins to expand rather rapidly, and his syntactic repertoire now consists of simple two-word sentences. Such sentences do not mean the same to listening adults as their own speech, but syntactic constructions they most certainly are. In adult speech, words are grouped into classes called part-of-speech classes on the basis of whether words can appear in the same places in sentences. If their permissible positions are the same or similar, such words are tagged with names like **noun, verb,** and **adjective** and considered to be members of the same part-of-speech class. This development can be seen in the child's early sentence formulations, though the form classes, or part-of-speech classes, are far different from those found in adult speech. Still, the same organizational principle is there in the child's use of language. At this point, it is too simple to say that children's grammar is a reduced, simplified version of the adult form of speech. It does bear a striking resemblance to adult grammar, but each successive stage in the child's grammatical development can be treated as having a different grammar, with each stage representing a new reorganization of the language data the child is exposed to, dependent on linguistic stimuli as well as his particular stage of maturational development.

The period of the two-word sentence has been studied by a number of researchers (Braine, 1963b; Brown & Fraser, 1964; Miller & Ervin, 1964; McNeill, 1966), and the two form classes have generally been labeled **pivot word** and **open word** classes. The name of the former apparently derives from the fact that such words are fewer in number than open words and serve as pivotal points around which the two-word sentence is organized. Moreover, the pivot class expands rather slowly, while the open class expands much more freely. Then, too, open class words can form one-word sentences by themselves, while most pivot words cannot. In some ways, the distinction is reminiscent of the split between content words (nouns, verbs, adjectives, adverbs) and function words (prepositions, conjunctions, relativizers, demonstratives, articles) that occurs in adult speech. Though the two stages are by no means comparable, it is interesting to note the similarity of their class membership and function.

Table 3.1 gives examples of pivot (P) and open (O) words from three

Table 3.1 Pivot and Open Classes from Three Studies of Child Language[a]

Braine		Brown		Ervin	
P	O	P	O	P	O
allgone	boy	my	Adam	this / that	arm
byebye	sock	that	Becky		baby
big	boat	two	boot		dolly's
more	fan	a	coat		pretty
pretty	milk	the	coffee		yellow
my	plane	big	knee		come
see	shoe	green	man		doed
night-	vitamins	poor	Mommy		.
night	hot	wet	nut		.
hi	Mommy	dirty	sock	the / a	other
	Daddy	fresh	stool		baby
	.	pretty	TinkerToy		dolly's
	.		.		pretty
	.		.		yellow
			.		.
					.
				here / there	arm
					baby
					dolly's
					pretty
					yellow
					.

Table 3.2 Patterning and Semantic Functions of Two-Word Sentences in Child Speech in Several Languages[a]

Function of utterance	Language					
	English	German	Russian	Finnish	Luo	Samoan
Locate, name	there book that car see doggie	buch da (book there) gukuk wauwau (see doggie)	Tosya tam (Tosya there)	tuossa Rina (there Rina) vettä siinä (water there)	en saa (it clock) ma wendo (this visitor)	Keith lea (Keith there)
Demand, desire	more milk give candy want gum	mehr milch (more milk) bitte apfel (please apple)	yeshchë moloko (more milk) day chasy (give watch)	anna Rina (give Rina)	miya tamtam (give-me candy) adway cham (I-want food)	mai pepe (give doll) fia moe (want sleep)
Negate	no wet no wash not hungry allgone milk	nicht blasen (not blow) kaffee nein (coffee no)	vody net (water no) gus' tyu-tyu (goose allgone)	ei susi (not wolf) enää pipi (anymore sore)	beda onge (my-slasher absent)	le 'ai (not eat) uma mea (allgone thing)
Describe event or situation	Bambi go mail come hit ball block fall	puppe kommt (doll comes) tiktak hängt (clock hangs)	mama prua (mama walk) papa bay-bay (papa sleep)	takki pois (cat away) Seppo puttoo (Seppo fall)	chungu biro (European comes) odhi skul (he-went school)	pa'u pepe (fall doll) tapale 'oe (hit you)

	baby highchair	sofa sitzen (sofa sit) messer schneiden (cut knife)	korka upala (crust fell) nashla yaichko (found egg) baba kreslo (grandma armchair)	talli 'bm-bm' (garage 'car')	omoyo oduma (she-dries maize)	tu'u lalo (put down)
Indicate possession	my shoe mama dress	mein ball (my ball) mamas hut (mama's hat)	mami chashka (mama's cup) pup moya (navel my)	tăti auto (aunt car)	kom baba (chair father)	lole a'u (candy my) polo 'oe (ball your) paluni mama (balloon mama)
Modify, qualify	pretty dress big boat	milch heiss (milk hot) armer wauwau (poor doggie)	mama khoroshaya (mama good) papa bol'shoy (papa big)	rikki auto (broken car) torni iso (tower big)	piypiy kech (pepper hot) gwen madichol (chicken black)	fa'ali'i pepe (headstrong baby)
Question	where ball	wo ball (where ball)	gde papa (where papa)	missä pallo (where ball)		fea Punafu (where Punafu)

a From D. I. Slobin, "Universals of Grammatical Development in Children." Reprinted from *Advances in Psycholinguistics* by G. B. F. D'Arcais and W. J. M. Levelt, Eds., by permission of the North-Holland Publishing Co., Amsterdam. Copyright © 1970 by North-Holland Publishing Co.

studies of child language. The dots following the sample inventories of the open class indicate that additional words appear in the complete inventories.

In addition to two-word sentences of pivot plus open word or open plus pivot word, some sentences have a structure of open plus open word. Sentences like *Mommy busy, Mommy bounce, Kathryn sock, umbrella boot, girl dress,* and *bread book* (Bloom, 1970) are not uncommon. They serve to convey a variety of semantic intentions, just as the simpler single-word and pivot–open sentences do. The types of sentences generated up to this point can be encompassed in a single rule that provides for the options thus far apparent in the child's grammar:

$$
S \longrightarrow \begin{Bmatrix} (P) + O \\ O + (P) \\ O + O \end{Bmatrix}
$$

The period of the two-word utterance is relatively brief, which prompts speculation on why it appears at all. Children at this age can respond to fairly complex strings and can certainly string sounds together in utterances longer than two words. Some feel that this period may be the beginning phase in the maturation of the organizational principles of sentence acquisition and production.

The preceding examples are obviously from research done with English-speaking children in North American contexts. But sufficient work has been done in a variety of other languages to enable us to talk about universals of grammatical development in children, regardless of language. Table 3.2 summarizes evidence from German, Russian, Finnish, Luo (Kenya), and Samoan, as well as English, showing that though the patterning is not identical, it is strikingly similar in these languages. The emphasis is on cross-linguistic similarities rather than differences. Note also the type and variety of semantic functions conveyed by two-word sentences in child speech.

There has, however, been some serious criticism of the notion of pivot grammar as a device to account for the child's syntax at this stage. Brown (1973) points out that some recent evidence appears to contradict the distributional claims that constitute the basis of the pivot grammar concept. He also observes that the form of the rules given in pivot-grammar formulations is an inadequate representation of the child's semantic knowledge at this stage.

From the two-word sentence the child's set of syntactic rules expands to include other syntactic classes, such as modifiers, demonstratives, articles, and so forth. The development of the rules proceeds from the undifferentiated syntactic classes to finer and finer subclass distinctions until adult speech is approximated. With the appearance of sentences longer than two words, another important feature of syntax appears: hierarchical structuring. As was pointed out in the discussion on syntax in structural linguistics and phrase-structure rules in generative grammar, a sentence can be analyzed to show the relationships that exist within it. Simply stated, not every item is as closely related to every other item in the sentence; some relationships are at higher structural levels in the sentence's history and others lower. With the onset of utterances longer than just two words, this phase of syntax appears by definition. Thus, in children's sentences like *This a dog* and *That my ball,* the first element in each sentence (*this* and *that*) can be broken off as a constituent part of the sentence whose relationship is to the remaining part of the phrase, *a dog* and *my ball.* Hierarchically, the relationship of *a* and *my* is closer to *dog* and *ball* than to *this* and *that,* respectively. The forms *this* and *that* are tied to the phrases *a dog* and *my ball* on the highest level of sentence derivation.

Children at this stage use order as the guiding principle, make little use of morphological devices like word endings—plurals and possessives for nouns, past tense and progressive forms for verbs, and so forth—and include very few function words like prepositions, articles, and conjunctions. This style of speech, in which only nouns, verbs, and adjectives from adult speech appear, giving the illusion of a style similar to that used by economical adults in writing telegrams, now begins to be replaced by more and more complex sentence structures. The telegraphic nature of this kind of speech does not mean that the child is using an economical version of the complete grammar. Rather, this is the complete grammar the child employs at this stage; the rules are simply far fewer. From this stage onward, the child can do nothing but enhance his command of the language. His vocabulary is the most obvious area for expansion, and the number of words he knows increases tremendously. Sentence structure becomes increasingly complex and more and more like the sentence structure of adult language in the child's environment, though not yet identical. Much of the acquisition process will have taken place between 3 and 4; the phonology and morphology are relatively established, and the syntax progressively approximates adult speech. What will develop more fully from here on is closer experience with and control of the more complex sounds of speech—for example, /l/, /r/, /č/, and /ǰ/—which require subtle control of the articulatory musculature. Also developing at this time is increased familiarity with the morphological rules of the language and their unexplainable, unpredictable, exceptions—*feet* instead of **foots*, *went* instead of **goed*, *better* instead of **gooder*, and so on.

This search for regularity characterizes the child's morphological development as he learns the appropriate phonologically conditioned forms for the plural and possessive endings on the nouns, the third-person-singular present tense, the past tense, the identical past participle ending on verbs, and inflections on other forms. The child comes to possess fairly general—and from the standpoint of adult speech, relatively accurate—rules for generating the appropriate endings on such parts of speech. A discussion of this phenomenon is presented by Berko (1958), who assessed children's inflectional and derivational skills by testing children with nonsense words and the occasional legitimate English form. Berko's study is particularly convincing regarding the existence of children's rule patterning, for the responses of the children in her study can be explained by nothing other than that they were operating according to a set of linguistic rules. After a child saw a picture of what the experimenter called a *wug*, the child responded to a picture of a brace of the same with *wugs*. The words were never experienced before, so the behavior was obviously an extension of the basic pattern learned and used on legitimate nouns.

Curiously, children often learn early the legitimate irregular forms of many words. This is perfectly logical, since the reason such forms have stayed irregular is that they are statistically so frequent in speech. *Feet, went,* and *better* occur relatively frequently, and it is not surprising that children do learn these first. But given a small number of regular forms, such as *dog–dogs, cat–cats, play–played, wash–washed, fat–fatter,* and *small–smaller,* the child apparently seizes on these as the basis for a new rule, and so thorough is his generalization from the rule behavior he has observed in these words that the earlier irregular forms are literally chased out and replaced with regularized forms like **foots, *goed,* and **gooder.* This surge of regularization continues quite far into the child's development, and it is only later that the irregulars are once again re-learned and re-established.

Once their vocabulary skills are unleashed, young children expand their inventory of words very rapidly. The child may increase his vocabulary by 15 times between 18 and 24 months of age. The acquisition of new words in the preceding 6 months proceeded at a much slower pace; the jump from each stage thereafter must be measured in geometric terms. Specifically, by the age of 30 months the child seems to understand most of what is said to him by adults. His vocabulary continues to increase at a phenomenal rate, often several words every few days. By about the age of 3 years, the child's vocabulary consists of perhaps 1000 words, and his language is usually clear enough even to strangers. By the time the child is 4 years old, language is well established, and child and adult language differ more in content than in structure.

It is difficult to pinpoint why such rapid development does take place. One explanation may be that the child grasps the meaning of the concept of words at the same time that he grasps the power attached to their use. He is now in a far more advantageous position to control his environment, and he may simply be taking advantage of his new discovery. Moreover, language is obviously a skill that is used and, in fact, expected of him by the other humans who populate his environment, so he is duly reinforced to use and acquire more and more language.

The child's syntactic development at this age rests on his knowledge of the underlying principles of sentence structure, most of which are now at his command. Familiarity with the more exotic and less frequently occurring structures will come with exposure. But by the age of 5 or 6, children encounter and perhaps master the majority of special cases and complexities. There is, however, some evidence that counters the traditional view that the child has mastered the entire structure of his language by the time he reaches age 6 or so.

C. Chomsky (1969) suggests that some active syntax acquisition continues up to the age of 9 and possibly beyond. She tested the comprehension of 40 children between the ages of 5 and 10 for such complex structures as *John is easy to see, John promised Bill to go, John asked Bill what to do,* and *He knew that John was going to win the race* and found variation in the ages of the children who knew the structures and those who did not. These results suggest a late stage of acquisition for some syntactic structures. However, C. Chomsky proposes that although reliable judgments cannot be made regarding exactly when the child does acquire these structures, reliable judgments can be made on the relative order in which the child acquires the structures.

The child's use of transformational rules begins to appear at a stage after the two-word sentence. Transformations, when they do appear, are necessary from the point of view of efficiency; otherwise, the child is faced with the possibility of saying more and more complicated things but is limited to rather simple phrase structures. Such phrase structures, if assessed from simply an efficiency point of view, are nowhere near the streamlined operations that transformations provide by embedding, conjoining, permuting, and so forth. In addition to that, of course, is the stimulus of adult speech, which uses these operations, but the real stimulus seems to arise from the fact that they are really an integral feature of universal grammar.

The commonly appearing universal transformations, including permutation, deletion, and addition, can be expected to be employed as they are needed for efficient communication as soon as the child is ready for them. It should be noted that it is the type of transformational operation which is a universal, not the structure it may produce in a specific language. For example, English, Cantonese, and Arabic may all use permutation (the changing of the order of items in a string) as a transformational device in their grammatical schemes, but the specific changes effected are likely to be different. Because some of these transformational operations are more complex than others, differential development can be expected. Moreover, when surface structures are generated by a series of transformations, children in the earlier stages should acquire and make use of the transformations one by one instead of all at once.

Semantic Development

Semantic development is far slower than the acquisition of phonology and syntax. One obvious reason is the extreme complexity of the semantic system. Another may be that, even more than syntax, semantics is an ever expanding system, even for adults. We continue to acquire vocabulary items throughout our lives, and because we are obliged to classify, reclassify, cross-classify, and unclassify, the semantic domain is constantly evolving. The development of the semantic system appears to involve two main activities. One is the constant expansion of the vocabulary, and the other is the constant reorganization of the network of relationships between words that constitutes the semantic structure of the language.

Semantic development, like phonological and syntactic development, also involves the progression from gross undifferentiated categories to increasingly finer specifications. Child speech, however, expresses the same underlying semantic notions of case relationships between nouns and verbs—for example, nouns standing in an agent, object or passive, beneficiary, instrumental, or locational relationship to the verb. Children, however, do not yet exhibit much sophistication in dealing with semantically anomalous sentences. McNeill (1970) notes that they are just as likely to accept *Wild Indians shoot running buffalos* as *Wild elevators shoot ticking restaurants*. Some semantic concepts also appear to be different for children at an early age. Several investigations (Donaldson & Balfour, 1968; Donaldson & Wales, 1970; Wales & Campbell, 1970) report on the development of semantic comparison and relational terms for children and how they differ from adult conceptualization and use. One finding is that the distinction between the terms *less* and *more* does not seem to be apparent to the majority of children at the age of 3½; indeed, children of this age seem to regard the two terms as synonymous. The same appears to be true for other terms of relation or antonymic opposition, but not always as dramatically as for the distinction between *less* and *more*. Donaldson and Balfour's results with *more* and *less* seem to indicate that the unmarked form *more* has been overextended by the child to cover *less* as well, a feature that Clark (1973) finds to be common to such oppositions at this stage of semantic development. At the age of 4, there is less uncertainty over the two meanings, and later the distinction crystalizes. It would appear that the child proceeds through stages of undifferentiation of sets of related terms to eventual complete differentiation of the meanings of the terms.

Similarly, Donaldson and Wales report that *same* and *different* are treated as synonyms at this stage. Clark (1972) also found that for children at the age of 4 the word *big* is even overextended to cover many of its fellow unmarked adjectives, like *long, high, tall,* and *wide,* while *small* or *little* is similarly overextended to cover the marked adjectives, like *short, thin, low, young,* and *shallow.* The marked–unmarked distinction, incidentally, relates to the fact that only one of a pair like *tall–short* can appear in sentences that name a dimension and give the physical extent of that dimension. Thus, one says *He is 6 feet* **tall,** *The Terminal Tower is 32 stories* **high,** *A yardstick is 3 feet* **long,** *He is 32 years* **old,** and *The river is sometimes 20 feet* **deep** *in winter,* but not **He is 6 feet* **short,** **The Terminal Tower is 32 stories* **low,** **A yardstick is 3 feet* **short,** **He is 32 years* **young,** and **The river is sometimes 20 feet* **shallow** *in winter.* One cannot use the marked adjective in such sentences unless, of course, they are intended to be cute, metaphorical, or punning.

Clark (1973) has formulated a semantic-feature hypothesis that articulates what the child must be learning about the meaning of words as he acquires his language. Clearly, the child often does not know the full meaning of words even though he may use them (or their reasonable facsimiles) at early stages. To Clark, this implies that the child has only partial semantic descriptions of such words, such that the semantic-feature configuration characterizing these lexical items for adults is only partially present in the child's mental lexicon. The child's progress in the acquisition of semantic structure, then, is to be

Table 3.3 Some Overextensions Related to Shape[a]

Source	Lexical item	First referent	Extensions and overextensions in order of occurrence
English	*mooi*	moon	> (cakes) > (round marks on window) > (writing on window and in books) > (round shapes in books) > (tooling on leather book covers) > (round postmarks) > (letter O)
French	*wawa*	dog	> (small white sheep)
French	*nénin* (breast)	breast, food	> (button on garment) > (point of bare elbow) > (eye in portrait) > (face of person in photograph)
German	*bow-bow*	dog	> (fur piece with glass eyes) > (father's cuff links) > (pearl buttons on dress) > (bath thermometer)
Georgian	*buti* [<*burti*] (ball)	ball	> (toy) > (radish) > (stone spheres at park entrance)
English	*tick-tock*	watch	> (clocks) > (all clocks and watches) > (gas-meter) > (fire hose wound on spool) > (bath scale with round dial)
English	*kotibaiz*	bars of cot	> (large toy abacus) > (toast rack with parallel bars) > (picture of building with columns)
English	*tee* [<*Timmy*]	cat	> (dogs) > (cows and sheep) > (horse)
Serbian	*wau-wau*	picture of hunting dog	> (small black dog) > (all dogs) > (cat) > (woolen toy dog)
Serbian	*deda*	grandfather	> (picture of Vuk Karadzić in postcard) > (photos of grandfather and King Peter of Serbia)
Serbian	*kutija* (box)	cardboard box	> (match box) > (drawer) > (bedside table)
Serbian	*gumene* [<*dugme*] (button)	coat button	> (collar-stud) > (door-handle) > (light-switch) > (anything small and round)
French	*bébé*	reflection of child (self) in mirror	> (photograph of self) > (all photographs) > (all pictures) > (all books with pictures) > (all books)
Serbian	*vata* [<*vrata*] (door)	door	> (shutters in window)
Danish	*vov-vov*	dog	> (kitten) > (hens) > (all animals at zoo) > (picture of pigs dancing)
English	*ball*	rubber ball	> (apples)

[a] Adapted from E. Clark, "What's in a Word? On the Child's Acquisition of Semantics in His First Language." In T. E. Moore, Ed., *Cognitive Development and the Acquisition of Language*, 1973. Reprinted by permission of the author and Academic Press, Inc., New York.

seen as the addition of more and more features of meaning until the semantic-feature configuration of lexical items is identical for child and adult.

This approach is an exact parallel to the view that the acquisition of language proceeds from gross categories to finer and finer distinctions until the distinctions made are identical with the linguistic features exhibited by the adult members of the linguistic community. Thus, the child may learn the word *dog*, but the criteria for the category will be somewhat primitive in comparison to those for the adult configuration for that category. The child may simply use the feature of *four-leggedness* and overextend the word *dog* to include an amazing variety of four-legged objects—perhaps dogs, horses, cows, lions, a stuffed panda, and a jade elephant on the coffee table. Clark reports that the results of a detailed survey of very young children's use of words as reported in the numerous diary studies during the past two centuries show such overextension to be common. She speculates that overextension is probably language-independent, occurring in all languages, and thus universal in language acquisition. Table 3.3 lists examples of overextensions related to shape from several languages. Table 3.4

Table 3.4 The Restructuring of a Semantic Domain[a]

	Word(s)	Semantic domain
Stage I	*bébé*	reflection of self in mirror; photo of self; all photos; all pictures; books with pictures; all books
Stage II	(a) *bébé*	reflection to self in mirror; photo of self; all pictures; books with pictures
	(b) *deda* (grandfather)	all photos
Stage III	(a) *bébé*	reflection of self in mirror; photo of self; books with pictures; all books
	(b) *deda*	all photos
	(c) *ka'ta* (karta = card)	all pictures of landscapes, views
Stage IV	(a) *bébé*	reflection of self in mirror; photo of self
	(b) *deda*	all photos
	(c) *ka'ta*	all pictures (not of people)
	(d) *kiga* (book)	all books
Stage V	(a) *bébé*	self; small children in pictures
	(b) *deda*	photos
	(c) *ka'ta*	pictures
	(d) *kiga*	books
	(e) *slika* (reflection)	reflections in mirror
	(f) *duda* (Douchau, own name)	photo of self

[a] From E. Clark, "What's in a Word? On the Child's Acquisition of Semantics in His First Language." In T. E. Moore, Ed., *Cognitive Development and the Acquisition of Language*, 1973. Reprinted by permission of the author and Academic Press, Inc., New York.

presents data from an early description of the acquisition of French and Serbian. The child goes through at least five stages until the various semantic domains of self (*bébé*), photos (*deda*), pictures (*ka'ta*), books (*kiga*), reflections in the mirror (*slika*), and photos of self (*duda*) are differentiated by specific words. Note that at the first stage all these are undifferentiated and represented by a single lexical item, *bébé*.

Clark also notes that the primary features used as criteria attributes at this stage are derived from the perceptual input of the child. Thus, it is not surprising that the primary features used at this stage often fall into categories like movement, shape, size, sound, taste, texture, and so forth. Interestingly, color does not appear as a criterial attribute here.

With the development of word classes, or part-of-speech classes, children also begin to form notions about the semanticity of such classes. As Brown (1957) has pointed out, for children most of the items they do encounter as count nouns, mass nouns, and verbs fit the traditional textbook definitions given them. For children most nouns are indeed concrete, tangible objects; verbs, on the other hand, are concrete, physical actions. Children also seem to have fitted a notion of mass noun together, and these three, count nouns, mass nouns, and verbs, are easily recognized by their structural signals as belonging to this or that form class. Given nonsense words fitted into appropriate slots—for example, *This is a niss, Have you ever seen any niss?*, and *The man is nissing*—children invariably recognize them as belonging to a particular form class (count noun, mass noun, and verb in these example sentences) and, furthermore, recognize certain semantic attributes as characterizing each of the members of the different classes.

One interesting observation comes from several earlier studies by Brown and Berko (1960) and Ervin (1961), who assessed possible word-association differences between children and adults. Apparently, children under the age of 8 differ from adults in the associations provided to stimulus words. To use Brown and Berko's terms, associations that are paradigmatically the same, or belonging to the same part-of-speech class, can be termed homogeneous responses. Associations that are not and that seem to arise from the stimulus and response words having been linked together in syntagmatic relationships, as partners in sentence construction, can be termed heterogeneous responses. Pairs like *table–chair, boy–girl, to send–to mail,* and *fat–heavy* are thus homogeneous by part-of-speech associations, while pairs like *chair–sit, boy–run, to send–letter,* and *fat–girl* are heterogeneous. It appears that young children make a significantly high proportion of responses on the basis of syntagmatic association and that the change to homogeneous responses takes place at about the age of 6 to 8.

The Role of Stimulation, Imitation, and Reinforcement

In conclusion, some comment must be made on the influence of environment and imitation on the learning of language. The notion of language capacities as an innate factor in human development does not by any means deny the importance of the child's stimulation by his environment and the language within that environment. As has so often been pointed out, children reared in institutional settings often are rather different from children reared in normal settings. However, children do not appear to learn on the basis of direct tuition. No one teaches children the rules of language. No adult has the time (and few adults have the energy) to teach a child all there is to know about language. Besides, parents are usually no more aware of the rules of phonology, syntax, and semantics than is the child. The imitation is of a kind dependent on the child's environment; he learns to behave in the manner in which those in his environment behave. Thus, the child learns to speak as those in his environment do. But imitation is not the source of the behavior itself, and there is a very deep philosophical difference between an interpretation which sees linguistic experiences as the ultimate source and an interpretation which simply views it as necessary input. A simple behavioristic approach tends to view imitation and reinforcement as the source of the behavior, while the former approach regards it as only the data that are correlated with the innate capacities for generating that particular kind of behavior. The result is the specific kind of linguistic behavior we do see.

The search for ruled and patterned linguistic behavior seems to contradict the role of imitation and actual practice. One example is the child's abandoning of earlier learned irregular verbs in favor of regular and patterned inflections that are then extended to the irregular forms as well, despite their prior appearance. Another example is response approval by parents. Often the child asks a question or makes a response that, from the point of view of the adult grammar, is clearly wrong or inadequate, but the child is praised for it, or at least not corrected. In fact, parents are generally too busy to correct their children's speech, and are usually delighted at any gem they utter. They seem to reinforce children on the basis of the correctness or appropriateness of the general idea, not on the basis of the actual linguistic form of the utterance itself. It would appear that behavioristic learning theory cannot account for what takes place in the first example. As for the second example, if reinforcement were the ultimate source of linguistic viability measures, the clearly incorrect forms being reinforced by parental action would be the ones to be ingrained. The influence of environmental stimulation on the child's developing abilities, both cultural and linguistic, is undoubtedly strong. If, however, one claims that learning itself—and specifically language learning—derives only from conditioning, reinforcement, extinction, and so forth, the behavioristic approach becomes philosophically as well as practically overextended.

Simply put, children learn specific languages, like English, Bulgarian, and Hindi. It is true that the innate capacity is there, but it must be stimulated by a child's particular linguistic environment, and the patterns that will emerge as his linguistic competence will be founded on the linguistic data fed to him in his surroundings. Without that specific linguistic experience, no grammar of any kind is likely to emerge, and no language is likely to be spoken in any fashion. The child thus grows up speaking a specific language in a specific language community.

Language,
Culture, Thought,
and Universality

The Question of Linguistic Relativity

Perhaps one of the most intriguing of all language-related topics is the relationship of language to thought and culture. Is it possible that thought is responsible for and causes language? Or is it possible that language is responsible for and causes thought? Or do language and thought perhaps influence each other, such that the language one speaks does influence thought but thought initiates certain verbal processes?

Anyone who has had any experience with another language finds that certain things cannot be directly translated from one language into the other. Some languages seem to express certain things in certain ways, and such feelings or experiences can be expressed only by long-winded circumlocutions in the other language. If we take such a casual observation to its logical extreme, we come up against what the linguistic relativity controversy essentially has been about. Put in another form, our question becomes something like the following: Is it possible that the way in which the structure and vocabulary of our language are organized in any way organizes the way we view the world and deal with it? Our inability even to translate simple feelings or experiences from one language into another to our complete satisfaction may be only symptomatic of some underlying philosophical issue. Perhaps the issue really revolves around whether languages are compatible after all and whether the structure of one's native language structures his thought process along particular lines, affecting his world view.

Probably the best known of the proponents of this linguistic relativity hypothesis has been B. L. Whorf (1956), although the notion has been a popular topic of discussion for the past several decades. If we accept this hypothesis, we could speculate further that our dealings with the exterior world would be in some way different if we had grown up speaking another language. If we agree with Whorf that thinking is more or less a reflection of the pervasive cultural phenomenon we call a language—so that thought and culture are inextricably linked—we must at least consider the possibility that much of what we think or perceive or expect is heavily culturally oriented. The common analogy between mathematical systems and language is well taken, for both are efficient, self-contained systems, brooking little interference from competing systems. Whatever the final conclusions one draws about the ultimate influence of languages on thought patterns, they do at least have the hypnotic, spell-binding capabilities of habits. Thus, it becomes difficult, though not impossible, to break their hold, and all new activities are filtered through previous experience.

Whorf's contention was that English, like all other languages, forces upon us an *a priori* categorization of reality and, without our even knowing it, preclassifies our experiences. Interestingly, theorists in many fields have found it necessary to invent a **metalanguage,** a language using natural language but with meanings over and above it and highly restricted for technical use, in order to talk about some of the things that interest them. Physics and philosophy are certainly two of these fields. Some have nevertheless maintained that the static, quantitative aspect of modern sciences came about because the discoverers in such sciences have spoken Indo-European languages, which have certain structural features. Put thus, the question is an intriguing one: Are philosophers and physicists and others really discovering the immutable laws that govern the universe, or are they somehow simply superimposing their own cultural and linguistic modes of thought upon the vast array of data known as reality? To take a specific example, in the popular conception of physics, the world is populated with physical objects. Such physical objects can be considered as fixed and as exhibiting certain properties, such as size, shape, color, weight, and so forth. The laws of the universe as described by physics, then, are laws that describe the changes in these stable objects. But the dichotomy between objects and activities or changes remains as a fixed popular conception, and to one convinced of the linguistic relativity approach, that dichotomy is strikingly similar to the Indo-European linguistic separation of nouns and verbs, with nouns representing objects and verbs representing the activities that affect them. Indeed, our concept of time, the most observable changing factor in our lives, views time as a stable constant, such that one can save time, keep time, and put away an hour, a day, a week, as though they were negotiable commodities. Still, all we can say about time as we popularly know it is that it is constantly moving onward. What we have done is to take the changing continuum we inhabit and put some kind of order into it, calling it time. Of course, some modern theories of physics on the nature of time are rather different; they view the world as flux or constant change and time as not necessarily moving forward and at a consistent pace. One must be careful not to consider the results of observation as immutable laws of the universe instead of simply convenient summarizations of and predictive constructs for the events that seem to structure our environment.

If we take language in its simplest sense to be a collection of vocabulary words, which makes up the lexical content of the language, and a collection of rules of arrangement, which makes up the grammatical structure of the language, we must wonder about the effect of such habits on the way we interact with the real world. For example, if we are told that such-and-such is a table and that so-and-so is really a friendly fellow, we may tend to behave toward that something or someone in certain ways. Perhaps we would act in measurably different ways if we were told that the chairlike item is really a conversation piece and that the person in question is extremely hostile and invariably difficult to get on with. Similarly, grammatical habits in a language, like the obligatory expression of plurality, past or progressive tense, experience as opposed to hearsay information, and so forth, may also lead us to behave in certain ways. For example, does the plural category in English, by which we designate nouns as being either singular, like *dog, cat, boy, rose,* and *aardvark,* or plural, like *dogs, cats, boys, roses,* and *aardvarks,* predispose us in any way to order numerically the items in the universe? Or does the fact that Slavic verbs express masculine or feminine gender by overt endings in their past-tense forms lead speakers of such languages to pay more attention to such external-world features? The question is whether language is some kind of cognitive organizer of an obligatory type.

Indeed, when speaking of the social, political, and intellectual relationships that groups speaking different languages find themselves in, we cannot help but speculate on the quality of the interaction and how much may be distorted by virtue of their differing expectations about certain concepts. The Russian and English words for peace, translated across the board as English *peace* = Russian *mir,* as if they were perfectly equatable in all senses, may lead to discussions in which the one's expectations are rather different from the other's. The Haida of the Queen Charlotte Islands off British Columbia's coast may have the word *x̣a* for *dog,* but the generic term *x̣a* for the furry, four-footed creature may not have the same range of inclusiveness as our English term *dog.* After all, before the incursions of the white man, *x̣a* likely referred to a single, rather uniform species, quite different from the range of dachshunds, St. Bernards, Newfoundlands, and cocker spaniels included in our term *dog.* And, of course, the expectations may be entirely different, especially in the parts of Southeast Asia where dogs are occasionally on the bill of fare.

Looking back over our own intellectual history in western Europe, we also cannot help but wonder how much of past and present traditions resulted from the reevaluation of important ideas and documents through the filtering device of our own culture and language. What did documents like the Old and New Testaments say in the original tongues in which they were written? What were the meaning expectations of the people speaking one of those languages at that time? What was the significance of such a writing style or literary genre at that period in history for that particular culture? There can be little doubt that ideas have been altered quite unconsciously over time to fit the expectations of individual personalities as well as cultural outlooks, and that some of what we know, we know only vicariously and incompletely.

Whorf's position can be taken quite literally, or it can be modified to a more habit-oriented position. The stronger version that all higher levels of thinking are entirely dependent on language is perhaps the claim that has been seized on by the majority of his critics. And perhaps rightly so, for this makes for some uncomfortable reasoning when one must account for the nature of bilingual activity on the part of many speakers. The notion of linguistic universals becomes impossible, and one is left with the distinct impression that any pedagogical study in which language and language-oriented activities are involved would prove impossible. It is hard to believe that Whorf would have intended this interpretation, and one cannot help feeling that the extreme viewpoints attributed to him would have been modified had he lived on to continue the debate. The idea was not Whorf's own to begin with; it had been around for some time. In fact, Whorf's contentious position seems to be the logical extreme of an opinion voiced by Sapir (1931), who likened language to a mathematical system that "records experience, in the true sense of the word, only in its crudest beginnings but as time goes on, becomes elaborated into a self-contained conceptual system which previsages all possible experience in accordance with certain accepted formal limitations [p. 578]." Whorf was a sometime student of Sapir, and it was Whorf's writings and lectures that turned attention back to this notion and created an extreme popular as well as scholarly interest in it again.

This tradition can also be seen in the nineteenth-century German philosophical speculations on whether traditional Aristotelian logic would have developed in the same fashion had Aristotle been an Aztec or something other than a western European. Humboldt, that amazingly inquisitive investigator of the past century, entertained the idea in a slightly different fashion. Others, such as the communist Marr in this century, tied language development to the intellectual and cultural development of man, thus implying that there are stages of evolutionary development in language. However, prestige or power associated with some modern languages is due entirely to chance. French at one time was used in many of the courts of Europe and for diplomatic contact, but not because the language is "inherently beautiful" or "extremely logical." English is probably now used for trade and commercial purposes by more people than any other language, but that is not a reflection of its "sturdy scientific basis" or its "Yankee horse-trader" qualities. It is simply the fortuitous result of certain social and historical events that have placed the groups speaking these languages in the positions of relative importance they now occupy.

Some speculation on the notion of cultural evolutionary development has again appeared. This resurgence of interest seems to be implicit in certain current anthropological investigations of cultural universals, and particularly evident in the ethnolinguistic treatment of color-terminology comparisons presented by Berlin and Kay (1969), as well as descriptions of the possible evolutionary semantic status of ethnobotanical and ethnozoological terminology. The notion of linguistic relativity itself does continue to intrigue a number of scholars in other fields, and it has enjoyed a varying degree of notoriety in the writings of modern popular philosophers like Alan Watts. Such philosophers, who insist on examining and experiencing Eastern modes of thought and behavior, would obviously find linguistic relativity considerations attractive.

This desire for theoretical constructs congruent with particular philosophical or methodological concerns is not unknown in the history of social science, either. For example, consider the status of anthropology and linguistics at the turn of the century and immediately afterward. The intellectual atmosphere soon became highly receptive to the notion of linguistic and cultural relativity. The basic theme of universality of reason and thought was prevalent, and the methods of language analysis were highly restricted in terms of the languages of Europe, most of which belonged to the same Indo-European family of languages. But with the efforts of Boas, Sapir, and others to describe Amerindian languages, awareness increased that such languages must be described in their own terms, and not according to the modes of the classical tradition handed down from previous Latin and Greek descriptions. Some have said that this was only the second time in Western intellectual history that such an event occurred, the first being Panini's grammar of Sanskrit, a development that was also unhampered by contact with classical grammatical tradition.

The aftermath can only be interpreted as a consistent subtle interplay between field research and theoretical development. Researchers began to analyze and describe communities and their languages, and a new procedural paradigm grew up around the beliefs that would underlie the methodological organization of the actual research itself as well as its final formulation. Each culture and each language was to be considered as an entity unto itself and described in exactly those terms without any unneccessary outside reference; and each was considered as being the ideal language or culture for that particular environment and world view. The term **culture** here, of course, refers to how a human group organizes its activities—physical, mental, and spiritual—on a day-to-day basis to cope with the exigencies of life. Such designs can be explicit or implicit, and whether members of a given group can articulate their existence is irrelevant to their presence and pervasive influence. Moreover, one does not easily call such life patterns rational or irrational, for they are often nonrational and are simply potential guides for behavior.

Anthropology and linguistics at this stage had a great deal in common. In fact, in North America they were most often either under the same roof or only recently separated, whereas in Europe classical philology and linguistics often maintained close ties. One need only look in the anthropological literature of earlier decades at the full-blown debates over whether ethnographies could be properly written without a full understanding of the language to see the underlying similarities between linguistic and anthropological methods and concerns. The Whorfian hypothesis fits into this era perfectly, for what better correlative to a methodology that treats each culture and each language as an entity unto itself is there than a belief that each language makes for a world view that is radically different from all others? Thus, one would have as many different descriptions of the universe as there are languages and, of course, cultures speaking them, and the task of the social scientist would be to describe for posterity just that language and culture.

One cannot help but make the comparison between this stage in the history of linguistics and the current one of Chomskyan generative transformational analysis. The nature of the former made the development of a theory of language difficult, if not impossible, though very informative classification systems and a rigorous methodology envied by many in other social sciences were developed. Similarly, discussion of such things as linguistic universals was not readily forthcoming, since this notion ran counter to the theory. On the other hand, the modern viewpoint postulates a theory of language and encompasses keen discussions of universals in language. Whorf might have enjoyed noting the degree to which specific methodological and theoretical concerns that are formalized in scholarly theoretical languages influence their users.

A literal reading of Whorf's position is undoubtedly rather exaggerated. He probably depended far too heavily on the literal use of words and grammatical structure, as the outsider often does. Language is indeed a habit and, as such, is comfortable, like favorite old shoes; one does not pay a great deal of attention to the deep-down properties of each and every word. For example, to most of us a sentence like *The Russians have found an element lighter than hydrogen* is a sentence like any other, to be quickly passed over with its meaning only half-digested. Unless we have a specific purpose, we do not make any more of it than that if it is true, our understanding of the chemistry of the universe will have to be reordered. But even this possibility does not seem too earth-shaking, and perhaps we have already begun to think in new directions to accommodate this new world view. It has not changed much in our world; it only necessitates a reordering of the data presented to us. Fortunately, man is able to adapt to this constant need to reorganize and reperceive the shifting of the cosmos around him, though of late we have been presented with evidence that there are future-shock limits to the amount of reorganization that can take place over given periods of time.

Applying Whorf's notions to the English language, one could come to the unfounded conclusion that we are an extremely religious people by all our *good-by's* (*God be with you*) and *God bless you*'s or, similarly, that we are particularly animistic in our beliefs about the power of nature and whatever controls the elements. After all, in common phrases like *It is going to rain, It is cloudy, It is windy,* and *It is sunny,* what is the *it* but perhaps the unseen all-powerful forces of nature? Obviously, that is not so, and such turns of phrase are mere linguistic habits.

Several other arguments diminish the power of any extreme linguistic relativity point of view. First, if each language is so distinct from any other that it cannot possibly enter the world of another, how was Whorf able to convey the sense of the argument to us by way of example at all? Why are we able to argue alternative metaphysical systems if they are in effect unavailable to us because of the cognitive limitations imposed a priori by our language experiences? Conversely, how can certain philosophical positions, like Henri Bergson's *élan vital* lifestream of thoughts, processes, and events, have been conceived of in an Indo-European language and conveyed to the rest of us? Bergson's philosophical position seems very much like the Hopi metaphysics that Whorf was so fond of using as an example.

Second, if Whorf was right, it would appear that a good many of us are wasting our time teaching and learning foreign languages or that we will have to content ourselves with always having an imperfect knowledge of the other languages, rather like looking through opaque glass; the light filters through, but nothing is really visible. Moreover, if he was right, we can question whether any intercultural and interlinguistic exchange is an exchange at all. According to a strong version of the linguistic relativity position, the communication must always be somewhat distorted no matter what efforts are made to safeguard the good intentions. Although one can easily agree with the possibility that some distortion may occur, it is hard to negate the millenia-old practice of inter-linguistic exchange. True or not, it would appear to be somewhat unsatisfying as an objective truth, and besides, what other alternative have we but to continue as best we can to attempt to understand one another?

The only objective method of evaluating the stronger version of the linguistic relativity hypothesis was proposed relatively early by Lenneberg and Roberts (1956). They suggest that there is really only one area in which the hypothesis can be tested. This area they call the language of experience, those linguistic devices that express the elementary forms of experience, such as the sensations of light, color, temperature, and so forth. Man superficially orders these different stimuli perceived by his senses in systematic ways, and the ordering systems used in various cultures can provide frames for description with corresponding linguistic ethnosystems. The data to be used in such cross-cultural investigations must be universally occurring, must exhibit variation, and are hopefully characterized by simplicity in that the fewer parameters of measurement the better. Apparently, only under such conditions can the investigation of linguistic data and their relationship to the language and culture hypothesis contribute to our understanding of whether there is a relationship between language and perception. It is one thing to claim that there are superficial differences in the ordering of experiential domains in languages and another to claim that there are categorical differences in human perception as a result. The two are obviously entirely different phenomena.

The extreme view of linguistic relativity is that just so many molds called language exist into which thought is poured. The weak, or conservative, view holds more promise for those willing to concede a level of language that includes performance and not just theoretical capabilities. The weaker view would accept the idea that the structure of a language only predisposes its speakers to pay more attention to some kinds of perceptions than to others and to group these perceptions in one or another category more consistently. Thus, in general perceptual capabilities one human being is not unlike any other human being, but in specific task-oriented behaviors he may use certain capacities much more often. This notion therefore distinguishes between habitual and potential behavior, or as Herskovits (1948) has called it, **cultural focus.** The focal area of a given culture will involve elaboration in the lexicon and possibly certain grammatical categories. But we must be careful in discussing lexical and grammatical categories and habitual behavior. Many of the grammatical features of a language are purely superficial aspects of linguistic structure. One might well ask whether it means anything that French has two gender classes, masculine and feminine, while English nouns no longer have such a designation. Or that English has a third-person-singular morpheme for verbs like *He eat–s* and a progressive-verb ending *–ing.* These are grammatical features, yet they may not have any meaning other than that they are structurally present in the particular language. Even seemingly compulsory categories can be paraphrased in most languages. For example, one might insist that English requires its speakers to choose between singularity and plurality for nouns except those in the mass-noun subclass. However, sentences like *Dog owners are obliged to buy licences before March 1* and *Too many cooks spoil the soup* can be paraphrased as *Everyone who owns a dog is obliged to buy a licence before the first of March* and *More than one cook can ruin the soup by getting in* *one another's way.* The latter sentence shows that often sentences, phrases, and words are really saying something that the lexical meaning of the individual units does not convey. More on this phenomenon appears in Chapters 6 and 7, which deal with nonverbal communication and semantics.

Linguistic Names, Linguistic Categories, and Perception

To approach this topic, visualize a stack of perceptions in which the most common ones are those at the top of the stack; the others are either habitually or potentially available but are closer to the bottom of the stack, so that they are less readily at hand. The people in a particular culture are differentiated into many subgroups, and we can expect different individuals with different concerns to use different specialized vocabularies, with consequent differences in their perceptual expectations. The generic term is left to the majority, who neither need nor use finer shades of distinction for a given topic, while the specific term is always there for those who use it regularly as well as those who may wish to use it. Having names for different kinds of stimuli certainly must facilitate responding to and remembering them. However, having names for things does not really affect the ability to discriminate among items that bear similarities along a single continuum, like color, shape, and so on. Individuals who regularly engage in such activities as discriminating between certain kinds of stimuli and who consequently learn lots of names for those stimuli may not have any better objective discriminatory powers than average citizens selected at random, unless, of course, the former were preselected specifically for sensory abilities related to particular tasks.

On the other hand, having such highly codable terminology for certain kinds of stimuli does seem to aid greatly in their recall and use in memory tasks. In other words, it is handy to have a name for a thing. Brown and Lenneberg (1954) have suggested that codability in English is directly related to the frequency of use of a given term, which in turn may be a reflection of how often a given type of judgment is made. In the first part of their research, they established that a series of colors differs in what was termed their codability, or the fact that such colors are named easily and promptly and with a high degree of agreement. In the second part of the experiment, Brown and Lenneberg demonstrated that the codability of such colors is closely related to their recognition on memory tests calling for such abilities. In fact, some subjects even reported that they actually named the colors to

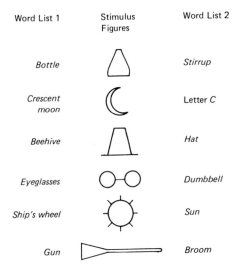

Word List 1	Stimulus Figures	Word List 2
Bottle		Stirrup
Crescent moon		Letter C
Beehive		Hat
Eyeglasses		Dumbbell
Ship's wheel		Sun
Gun		Broom

Figure 4.1 An example of the influence of specific names on the reproduction of objects. [From L. Carmichael, H. P. Hogan, and A. A. Walter, "An Experimental Study of the Effect of Language on the Reproduction of Visually Perceived Forms," *Journal of Experimental Psychology* 15 (1932): 73–86. Copyright 1932 by the American Psychological Association. Reprinted by permission.]

themselves while the colors were exposed the first time and later used the names as an aid in recalling the colors when asked to find them on the color chart. A similar experiment was repeated with Zuñi, an Amerindian language of the southwestern United States, and similar results were obtained (Lenneberg & Roberts, 1956). Although the actual codability of the colors was different in Zuñi, the principle that those colors easily named in the language are most accurately remembered was the same. Conversely, color ranges that were not well coded in Zuñi by specific linguistic forms resulted in more difficulty in recognizing and remembering colors.

A similar finding was reported much earlier from a classical experiment by Carmichael, Hogan, and Walter (1932). In this study, individuals were presented with ambiguous figures that could be linked with either of two linguistic labels. The figures and the labels are shown in Figure 4.1. Reproduction of the pictured figure was found to be affected by the original stimulus word naming the ambiguous figure at the first exposure. For example, if the figure was called *eyeglasses,* it was likely to be reproduced as

On the other hand, if the same figure was called *dumbbell,* it was likely to be reproduced as

    Clearly, the implication is that having a highly codable name for something makes it easier to remember it and to discuss it. By extension, one would surmise that some topics are more easily handled in memory and discussion activities for certain groups because the languages they speak or the technical jargon they use makes these exercises easier. Consider, for example, a thing or an experience for which we have no name. A discussion of such a topic could be difficult and somewhat distorted until we make up a label for it.

    From the results of other language–perception and language–memory experiments, it appears that part of the human strategy of coping with such tasks is to use language as a helpful device. Internalized verbal cues are an important factor in solving certain artificial problems presented in experimental contexts; the same is obviously true for daily activities. Here language can be seen as acting as a verbal cue in the storage of certain kinds of information or is itself the information to be stored. Language is thus one extremely important feature in the discussion of memory, but by no means the only one.

    Indeed, when one considers how sematic structure is stabilized for most children, the way in which a word is named and the manner in which it is learned reflect in a very definite way the same kinds of judgments and perceptions made by adult members of the speech community. The popular belief that ideas and things in the immediate environment have a single name is, even when matched against common-sense evaluations of the question, just not true. There are many names for the same thing, depending upon one's use for, appreciation of, and learned attitudes toward the item in question. However, by the same token, the terms or names given to children are remarkably uniform in given speech communities, and to this degree we can speculate on the notion of linguistic and cultural relativity and on frequency observations, but without believing that these tendencies have direct consequences for intelligence and perception in a contemporary sense or overtones of evolutionary history in a developmental sense.

As Brown (1958) has pointed out, Zipf's law, according to which the length of a word is inversely related to its frequency in a language, does not really answer the question of why the degree of uniformity in the naming terms given to children in their acquisition of the vocabulary structure of their native language is so surprising. Frequency no doubt plays a role in language use and is ever present in the development of language patterns, but it does not answer the question of why specific names turn up for items in the development of language by children. Why, for example, do they use the word *dime* instead of all the other available names? Why the particular four-letter word *dime* for the metallic object that used to buy so much and now obtains so little? The reason may be, according to Brown, that the word *dime* gives a clue to the level of usual utility for a term—that is, immediately carrying with it connotations of what the item does, what it means in the handling of it, and how we can and do perceive it. In other words, our nonlinguistic practices are embodied in our linguistic practices, and as a result, the way in which an item is named is a direct reflection of what it in fact means to us. Thus, the child's naming practices quickly approximate those of the adults surrounding him, and he grows up with the same kinds of terminology. In this way, one generation passes on to the next its ethnolinguistic systems. A term or a name denotes the level of usual utility of the thing as seen by the members of that culture and constitutes its identity as opposed to all other things in those people's surroundings.

The weaker form of the linguistic relativity hypothesis is most appealing; all we are admitting—and without necessarily conforming to Whorf's views of language or to the linguistic relativity hypothesis itself—is that language in certain of its aspects can serve as a medium of information storage and information retrieval. To the degree that language is successful in this role, it can lead those who use it to be predisposed to act and perceive in certain ways rather than in others. Language can become just as powerful in this role as any other habit—or just as weak. It by no means determines perceptions, memory tasks, or actions of other kinds, but it does by its very convenience, availability, and habitual use tend to become rather permanently fixed as an influencing factor.

As Fishman (1960) has so aptly summarized, the linguistic relativity hypothesis can be interpreted as making statements about the lexical organization of a language or the grammatical organization of the language. It can also be interpreted as making statements about the sense-perception abilities or the culturally determined cognitive sets of speakers. To summarize, we must conclude that sensory perception is the same for all normal human beings the world over, regardless of language and its syntactic and lexical organi̇zation. However, we can distinguish between this aspect of perceptual behavior and the aspect of behavior called culture and agree that language continues to some degree to be the codification of the culture. It is not surprising that distinctions made in the culture will likely, though not necessarily, find their way into the language as distinctions on the lexical, but not grammatical, level. The vocabulary of a language is much like a telephone directory for a city; it gives a handy set of clues to the population inventory. But just as there is no causal relationship between telephone directories and cities, it is difficult to admit of a causal relationship between language and culture. The relationship is more of a codificational one, and between grammatical structure and culture there is no such relationship.

The assumption that grammatical structure influences sensory perceptions is obviously less tenable, for one cannot readily point out instances in which the language of experience is perfectly commensurate with the grammatical structure of language. A classic investigation of this problem was done by Carroll and Casagrande (1958), who examined sorting tasks performed by English-speaking and Navaho-speaking Navaho children. The Navaho children were either Navaho-dominant or English-dominant in speaking ability and they were asked to carry out sorting tasks in which it was possible to use either the shape or the color of the object. Navaho, being an Athapaskan language, has grammatical endings on certain verbs that signify the noun-subclass membership of the co-occurring noun in the sentence. Such subclasses are established primarily around the feature of shape. In the experiment, Navaho-dominant children sorted things by shape rather than color about twice as frequently as their English-dominant counterparts did. However, when a group of monolingual English-speaking children in New England was given the task, they performed the sorting task more on the basis of shape than even the Navaho-dominant children did.

Perhaps some see a relationship between grammatical structure and general culturally oriented behavioral patterns. This conclusion also appears to be untrue. It would mean that French is suited to diplomacy because of its logic, English to commerce because of its mercenary qualities, Italian to romance because of its amorous qualities, and so on. Such a conclusion is reminiscent of the old aphorism about using Italian for making love, German for giving orders, Spanish for praying, and so on. But there is no proving it, and as Lenneberg and Roberts (1956) have pointed out, the argument is tautological and entirely dependent on terms for which there is no objective agreement. To use their example of language conditions and national character traits, the "harsh sounds" in Japanese cannot be purported to correspond to "harsh discipline"; the "complicated sentence structure" in German cannot be purported to correspond to "complicated philosophical thoughts"; and the "preponderance of monosyllabic words" in English cannot be purported to correspond to "conciseness and thriftiness." Such assertions about the relationship between language and national character should be questioned on the basis of exactly what the terms at both ends of the proposition are supposed to mean and what objective measure they refer to. Statements like these seem to be only reflections of our myths and beliefs about a certain culture. Language, which is one of the most overt signs of a given people and their culture and accomplishments, is simply a handy place to hang an evaluative hat.

Yet we must admit the obvious, that human culture as we know it does not exist without language. The fairest conclusion is to admit the fact of an interdependent relationship between language and culture, but not the deep-seated causal tie that some have suggested. The matter of the relationship between language and thought is less clear, and a final statement on this topic may not be in order until after a brief look at Piaget's and Vygotsky's notions on cognitive development in the child. However, we must conclude that languages do not really differ so much in what it is possible to say, but rather in what is relatively highly coded in them and easier to discuss as a result. This conclusion leads directly to the matter of universality, which more and more disciplines are examining. Anthropologists are becoming more interested in the underlying similarities of cultures, linguists in the universality of language, and psychologists in cross-cultural studies. This interest can only be appropriate at a time when man's numbers have swelled to such immense proportions and the ease with which we trade, communicate, and war with one another has put each of us into the other's lap.

The Notion of Universals

Trends toward the investigation of cultural universals and an evolutionary approach to the study of culture have been in evidence in anthropological inquiries. Ethnographic and ethnolinguistic studies have been numerous during the past two decades and were motivated by the attempt to describe societies from the viewpoint that some aspects of culture are equivalent to rules for appropriate behavior in well-defined situations. Some examples are those by Frake (1962, 1964a,b), Goodenough (1964a,b), Conklin (1962, 1964a,b), and Louns-bury (1964). Such studies have often focused on a single subset area of the total culture and have set out to specify exactly what one should know, do, reflect, or categorize in an approved and appropriate fashion. This shift toward the problem of both **formal** and **substantive** universals in theoretical linguistics is paralleled in ethnography, although that development is not surprising, considering the number of ethnographic descriptions. Still, much work in identifying universals has been largely dependent on a viewpoint in which universals are taken as empirically identifiable phenomena in languages and cultures.

Interestingly, the search for universals in ethnographic descriptions has not been limited to the investigation of **synchronic** universals; increased attention has also been given to possible **diachronic,** or developmental, universals. Research on particular lexical domains points to the possibility of semantic stages of evolution for certain areas, such as ethnobotany, ethnozoology, folk medicine, and folk diagnosis of disease and illness. For example, in the area of color categories, Berlin and Kay (1969) found that there is a universal set of basic color categories from which all other color terms are drawn. Thus, although languages encode different numbers of basic color categories in their lexicons, the color terms in any given language are ultimately derived from a total universal inventory of 11 color categories. These categories—black, white, red, green, yellow, blue, brown, pink, purple, orange, and grey—also appear to be sequentially ordered in the semantic history of various languages. The order of appearance of these categories seems to be so predictable that if one knows the actual number of colors in a given language, he may be able to predict exactly which terms they will be. Berlin (1970) has pointed out the following distributional restraints on the appearance of color terms[1]:

1. All languages have color terms for black and white.
2. If a language has three terms, the terms will be black, white, and red.
3. If a language has four terms, the terms will be black, white, red, and yellow or black, white, red, and green.
4. If a language has five terms, it will have terms for black, white, red, green, and yellow.
5. If a language has six terms, it will have terms for black, white, red, green, yellow, and blue.

[1] From B. Berlin, "A Universalist–Evolutionary Approach to Ethnographic Semantics." Reproduced by permission of the American Anthropological Association from *Current Directions in Anthropology,* Bulletin of the American Anthropological Association, Vol. 3, No. 3, Pt. 2, p. 8, 1970.

6. If a language has seven terms, it will have terms for black, white, red, green, yellow, blue, and brown.
7. If a language has eight or more terms, they will include the foregoing, and in addition, gray, pink, orange, and purple.

Interestingly, the distribution is such that of a possible 2048 combinations of the basic 11, only 22 color-term combinations, or a mere 1%, actually occur. Moreover, Berlin and Kay (1969) suggest that the chronological order may also be interpreted as a sequence of evolutionary stages, such that the categories are encoded in the history of a given language in a somewhat fixed order, indicated in the following ordered rule[2]:

$$
\begin{bmatrix} \text{white} \\ \text{black} \end{bmatrix} \longrightarrow [\text{red}] \begin{matrix} \nearrow \\ \searrow \end{matrix} \begin{bmatrix} \text{green} \\ \text{yellow} \end{bmatrix} \begin{matrix} \longrightarrow \\ \longrightarrow \end{matrix} \begin{bmatrix} \text{yellow} \\ \text{green} \end{bmatrix} \begin{matrix} \searrow \\ \nearrow \end{matrix} [\text{blue}] \longrightarrow [\text{brown}] \longrightarrow \begin{bmatrix} \text{purple} \\ \text{pink} \\ \text{orange} \\ \text{grey} \end{bmatrix}
$$

Just what one can make of such semantic development in relationship to the possible evolution of cultural stages of development is still open to discussion. However, the interesting point is that there appear to be universals, albeit semantic universals in this case, from an empirical point of view as well as possibly from a theoretically based point of view.

Linguistic Universals

The question of linguistic universals raises the question of what a universal is and how it is to be determined. The notion of linguistic universals is treated differently within different theoretical frameworks, depending on whether they aim at a structural comparison of different languages or attempt to account for the nature of language. With the first type of framework, one proceeds on a purely empirical taxonomic basis and tabulates elements that appear in all languages, or at least in all those for which we have documentation. This position assumes that a given feature can be considered a universal by virtue of its actual appearance in all the languages examined and is akin to Hockett's reminder (1966) that for an item to be truly universal it must be a feature or property shared by all languages. According to this view, universals are to be discovered, not postulated, and one cannot afford to be anything but inductive in one's approach. Universals in

[2] From B. Berlin and P. Kay, *Basic Color Terms: Their Universality and Evolution.* Copyright © 1969 by The Regents of the University of California; reprinted by permission of the University of California Press.

this sense become a list of properties, either item tabulation or item-arrangement tabulation, arrived at by survey, observation, and extrapolation from language investigations.

Such universals can also be of the type termed **implicational** by Greenberg (1968), by being stated in terms of prior conditions under which two or more features can be seen to occur. Such conditions can be stated as follows: If such-and-such is present, then such-and-such must also be present, and in specific directions. For example, if there is a dual-number category in the language, as there remains from proto-Indo-European in Slovene and Lusatian (two of the smaller Slavic languages), there must also be a plural-number category in such languages. As you will recall, according to Jakobson and Halle's suggestion (1956) of a law of irreversible solidarity, a language will not exhibit back consonants without also having front consonants. However, the reverse is not necessarily true; languages can exhibit a plural-number category without also having a dual-number category and front consonants without back consonants. One has been said to imply the existence of the other. Whether this is necessarily reflected in the acquisition and development of language by the young child may be a different matter, though one would expect to find developmental parallels to make such speculation plausible.

The description of those features that occur in nearly all languages presents valuable information, just as does the description of what the upper limits are to the appearance of certain kinds of features. For example, the number of phonemes, upper limits as well as lower limits, gives us some idea of what the range of phenomena in language actually is, and in a way that a priori categories can never provide. Thus, Greenberg (1966) has provided evidence from some 30 widely scattered languages, differentiated by geographical, genetic, or typological considerations, and has listed 45 universals of word order, such as the observation that the dominant order of subject, object, and verbal element in declarative sentences is almost always one in which the subject precedes the object, provided both subject and object slots are filled by nominals.

Moreover, Greenberg (1968) reasons that a considerable number of important observations can be made about such features as the structure and inventory of phonemic systems, permissible sound sequences, morphological categories, syntactical order in surface structures, and semantic systems. There seems to be as much justification for investigating what actually does occur in language as for postulating the processes by which it occurs. A satisfying discussion of universals, if it is to be representative of language as a universal phenomenon, must include some survey of the various surface manifestations in the syntactic, semantic, and phonological components of the forms of communication we call English, Cantonese, and Indonesian.

However, although those universals that are empirical generalizations holding true for all languages are handy for our understanding of language, they may not be particularly useful for our understanding of language behavior. Thus, other universals can be expected to answer important questions about the nature of the organizational processes that underlie language behavior. Such universals may be features that are included in a specific theory of language like generative grammar. These universals may not be readily observable in the sense that those listed in taxonomic fashion are, but they are still universals, since obviously certain kinds of knowledge and certain kinds of abilities need not be immediately observable to exist.

Generative grammatical theory proposes that each grammar has a base component that characterizes the underlying syntactic structure of sentences in the language (deep structure) and a set of transformational rules that modifies the base component by a series of operations into the natural form of the language (surface structure). The hypothesis of a base structure and transformational rules across languages is a statement of the general form of language and is considered by N. Chomsky to delineate the essential properties of language. These properties make explicit the manner in which all languages are reflective of the same general linguistic mold. This concept is distinct from Greenberg's categorizing synchronic universal in that Greenberg is generalizing at the level of the surface structure.

Such linguistic universals can be classed into two types, formal universals and substantive universals. **Formal universals** provide the general formal structure of the kinds of rules to be found in each of these components of the language. **Substantive universals** provide the theoretical symbol vocabulary upon which such rules operate. Thus, substantive universals are those elements that actually appear as elements in the grammar. As such, substantive universals are specific statements about language properties, and such category symbols as sentence (S), noun phrase (NP), complex symbol, phrase marker, and noun (N) are examples of substantive universals across language. The same can be said for the concepts of distinctive features and semantic features in the phonological and semantic components of the grammar, while such commonly occurring transformations as permutation, deletion, and addition are seen as universal process operations. Thus, this notion of universals hinges on a theoretical formulation that outlines the general boundaries of the form human language can take.

Chomsky and others have extended this theory of language to account for the phenomenon of rapid language learning by young children. They suggest that for such a theory of language to be a complete explanation it must also account for the child's acquisition of language. Chomsky (1965), McNeill (1970), and others have commented on the likelihood of a "language acquisition device" as part of every human being's innate linguistic capabilities. This device would consist of the set of assumptions about the form of the grammar on the basis of such formal and substantive universals. It would also likely contain a set of procedures with which it processes adult language and produces natural language patterns by a series of successive approximations. Because the acquisition device is so equipped, it need only focus on the unique features of the language in question as being outside the scope of the innate assumptions it brings to bear.

Piaget and Vygotsky

One who has within the last decade become increasingly familiar to students of cognitive development has been Piaget (1952, 1955, 1970a,b; Piaget & Inhelder, 1958). Although a good portion of Piaget's work dates back several decades, his ideas about cognitive development have only fairly recently become a more familiar feature in the North American psycholinguistic landscape. It may have been that Piaget's notions were all the more inaccessible in the original French to an era uninterested in questions of innateness, let along the postulation of innate schedules of cognitive development. Be that as it may, there have been a surprising number of recent translations of Piaget's work from the French as well as English summarizations of his ideas. Piaget is more at home in the current psycholinguistic scene with his beliefs that man's capacity for logical thought is embedded rather than learned. Perhaps some of his current popularity also stems from the fact that his ideas, although he has been until recently abstemious with respect to promulgating their implications for pedagogy, have far-reaching ramifications for education if correct. Correct or not, many of his notions have found supporters and practitioners among proponents of educational settings in which children are encouraged to observe, invent, and manipulate personally in order to discover knowledge.

Piaget has most recently found his way into developmental psycholinguistics, and much attention has been paid to the application of Piaget's thoughts on sensorimotor development to the structure of child language. As Nelson (1974) summarizes, the parallel between his description of the basic categories of thought and their progression from birth to 18 months of age and the basic semantic relations found in the child's primitive sentences is striking. This has led some researchers in child language to see some of Piaget's notions as crucial to developmental studies of language, and this particular parallelism is seen by some as a cornerstone for an understanding of the relation between language and thought. In addition, these researchers have thought of Piaget's stages as in some general way explaining the sequence involved in the actual development of language.

As a young man, Piaget worked under the direction of the famous Binet of the Stanford-Binet Intelligence Test. His stay at Binet's laboratory facilities in Paris provided him not so much with an interest in IQ testing and results as a fascination with the large proportions of wrong answers at different chronological stages for children. Piaget was interested in how children come to know what they know and what it is they know at different stages. Intelligence tests that measure the adult knowledge in a society, when applied to children, seek to determine the different norms of knowledge for different age levels. Piaget was intrigued by what seemed to be uniformities in the cognitive beliefs of children preceding these stages (as shown by the wrong answers children **regularly** gave on the tests) and was led to inquire into the nature of the developmental stages, not the end results of what children know. We know what adults know, or at least we think we do. What Piaget was interested in is what stages of imperfect knowledge children pass through on their way to the totality of adult knowledge and conceptualization. One cannot help drawing an analogy, as some have done, between the anthropological aims in ethnoscientific investigations discussed earlier and the types of child ethnoscience Piaget has carried out. Piaget has in a sense treated the developmental stages of the child as an anthropologist might treat other cultures.

Piaget's concern with language is more of a secondary one; research on the the development of thought has been his primary concern. To Piaget, language is important in the child's later development primarily as a reflection of his intellectual growth as a result of verbal interaction with others. Piaget's main interest in language appears to be in the functions of language and the needs it serves for the child. Piaget sees two stages in this aspect of the child's development and labels them **egocentric speech** and **socialized speech.** Egocentric speech may appear when the child is alone or when he is in the presence of others; the important characteristic is that it lacks any communicative intent on the part of the child. Thus, as the child progresses from one stage to the next, he essentially moves through a phase in which he speaks solely for himself, without any conscious effort to involve or satisfy other parties. In moving to socialized speech, the child becomes conscious of the point of view of other speakers. When his utterances reflect some communicative intent, he has entered the world of socialized speech.

For Piaget, cognitive growth has a developmental sequence all its own, and though language may in some cases touch upon the same areas involved in cognitive development, the two processes are separate and distinct. Cognitive growth seems to be more impressive and more important in the child's development. The child develops by direct contact with objects, by formulating and reformulating ideas to explain his environment, and cognitive development proceeds apace. One cannot help agreeing with Piaget in certain respects, if only from personal experience. Certain kinds of activities are best explained and best remembered simply by doing, not by verbalizing. A case in point experienced by most of us as children and later as adults and parents is the tying of shoelaces. This experience is learned through direct action, stored as an activity involving certain complex motor-skill sequences, and recalled as such. Language plays a small part in shoelace tying, except when the child or the teacher–adult voices exasperation.

Vygotsky (1962) is another whose speculations about the relationship of language and cognition have attracted increased interest among North American psychologists. Until recently, knowledge about Vygotsky's work was limited because of similar translational problems from the original Russian, but his work is now available in English and is becoming more widely read. Vygotsky was to some degree influenced by Piaget, though for reasons of translatability and availability it is only recently that Piaget has been conscious of his Russian counterpart's work.

Vygotsky also believes that linguistic and cognitive development are independent processes, though they share a very close association in the child's earliest stages of development. Vygotsky plainly believes that the structure of thought is not at all identical with the structure of language, and as a result, there is no easy and immediate equation between the units of the two systems. However, for Vygotsky, language and thought are separate and distinct at least until about the age of 2, when they merge and serve to initiate a new form of behavior. The child discovers the symbolic function of words and their value. This may correlate with the rapid increase in the child's vocabulary after this point and with a lengthy questioning period in which the child actively seeks out the names for objects and classes.

Vygotsky also envisions language as the means by which thought is conveyed from one person to the next. Thus, some aspect of the child's intellectual growth is tied to his learning of the social means of thought—or language. Language is in this sense the overt means through which certain thought sequences come into observable existence. However, whereas language in its observable forms consists of discrete elements, units strung together by the various rules that constitute the system part of language, thought is a single simultaneous panorama, much like a fine tapestry. Language by its nature must take the tapestry apart and present it thread by thread and stitch by stitch in an attempt to portray all that is embodied in the holophrastic and all-at-onceness nature of thought processes.

Vygotsky's conceptualization of language also pays attention to the importance of its social functions, and he firmly believes that an important part of the child's general development does include the expressive use of language in order to communicate with those around him. Unlike Piaget, he would find less difference in the primary function of language between adults and children. Both use it for communication, and the essential difference between the two is the ability to achieve this goal. Still, for Vygotsky, thought and speech have separate and distinct roots, and in the child's development there is a stage of vocalization and verbalization that does not involve thought at all. Similarly, in the child's cognitive development there is a stage that does not involve speech at all. The two thus emerge and develop quite independently until they meet at a particular point in the child's maturational development. At this time, thought takes on some verbal characteristics, and speech becomes rational as the expressive outlet for thought.

If the motivation for language is important, we can also question the origin of motivation for thinking. If we change the question of "Why language?" to "Why thinking?" we get a different perspective on the relationship between the two. Thought is to a large degree the child's response to situations in which discriminations, recognition, and concept formation and retention are vital to his understanding of and participation in his environment. Part of this environment includes others, nonselves, and with these must the child interact. Piaget's and Vygotsky's notions of the child's development as a panorama of changing and maturing abilities, with language being only one of these, is most attractive and most realistic. For Piaget and Vygotsky, the motivation for language may lie within the realm of the child's developing repertoire of discriminations, recognition, and concept formulations; it is but a subset of the total repertoire and though a most important one indeed, still a part, not the whole.

Language and Society

Language as a Social Phenomenon

The place of language in society is an important one, for without language society as we know it would likely not exist. Just as people carry about their cultural expectations in unfamiliar as well as familiar situations, so do they carry their societal expectations with them. As the child acquires language, he is also being assimilated into a particular society, and he learns that language is used for social purposes. He will now embark on another path of acquisition, one that will be more subtle and will continue much, much longer: that of the place of language in the society of which he is a member. His language abilities do not stop at simply acquiring certain phonological and grammatical abilities but will now begin to include learning what to say under which circumstances.

Learning to speak is thus more than just learning which words refer to which objects, for there appear to be many similar words or forms in a language. The choice among such terms is not dependent on their semantic and grammatical reference alone, but rather on the way in

105

which language is intended to manage the social interactions between those who are speaking. Thus, language is connected not only to the real world in its ability to symbolize but also to the social world of speakers. The choice of a specific item from the linguistic repertoire may express the attitudes and beliefs of a speaker or a group of speakers, of the person or persons being spoken to, and, perhaps, where there are intragroup differences, the entire social context. The situations one encounters are infinitely varied, but as in the case of grammatical competence, one learns and employs a limited, finite set of rules to cope with those situations. Typically, certain basic rules underlie all social situations in a given culture, just as a certain simple number of phrase-structure rules outline the general nature of syntax.

In fact, we are fairly constrained as speakers of real languages, for interaction by speech is a far more ritualistic activity than we may imagine. With each passing phase in the interaction, moreover, we are more restricted in our number of choices. This is, of course, countered by the popular injunction to achieve completely free, unrestricted, and spontaneous speech. However, being completely free and random in one's speech may lead to misunderstanding, hostility, or downright rejection, which are likely to be the outcome when one intentionally contravenes the norms of sociolinguistic interaction. Since we are inhabitants of human societies, the primary means of satisfying those immediate needs that we cannot personally fulfill is by interacting with our fellow members of society. This interaction is commonly carried out by speech, and to make the flow of speech seem even easier, different combinations of interactions are carried out on the basis of type similarities. We all occupy a range of roles, and roles differ according to the other individual and what he is doing at the moment of interaction. The speech repertoire that can accompany these role settings and serve as a medium of communication between individuals as role representatives is also relatively fixed as some part of the total language repertoire.

People are prone to classify others on the basis of their speech characteristics until they have had a chance to get to know the other person and confirm or deny their original impression. As a result, many cultivate, consciously or unconsciously, certain styles of speech in order to be identified with and receive the same treatment as certain groups. Or one may cultivate a particular style that he feels is appropriate to a particular role, such as that of distracted professor, eager young executive, bronzed lady killer, local tough guy who considers himself the razor's edge, and so forth. The roles are many, and there are appropriate styles to accommodate virtually everyone.

Depending on the particular language, such exchanges are provided for in larger or smaller part by certain mechanisms in the language. Occasionally, some of these exchanges are so fixed that they become almost static, unchanging styles, and only a departure from these styles becomes an original communication of any kind. Excellent examples of these fixed styles are found in short book reviews, letters of recommendation, and cocktail conversation among strangers. If you have difficulty in comprehending that there could be anything in the slightest degree patterned about the nature of conversation, do not say anything in the middle of the next conversation you are involved in when it is your turn to speak; just continue eye contact by continuing to look into your interlocutor's eyes. Fillers like *uh* and *hmm* are not allowed. You will quickly find that both you and the other party are embarrassed by the silence and the failure of the conversation to regenerate itself, and end by feeling somehow inadequate or that something is not quite right. The feeling is much enhanced for the other party if you stop abruptly in mid-sentence and continue eye contact. The implication is that there are rules of the road for conversational exchange that govern respectable periods between utterances, when to speak, how to break in, and so forth. Like hand signals in driving, certain verbal signals indicate that the rules are being observed. For example, an injected *uh* signals that the pause is legitimate and that the listener should be prepared to wait momentarily and politely until one recaptures one's train of thought and continues the sentence.

Such patterns can be called **norms.** These social norms simply constitute an expectancy that certain regularities in interpersonal behavior will consistently appear. They provide a picture of what is normally appropriate for a set of situations and, by implication, what is not. Sometimes the norms are explicit enough that what is inappropriate is actually spelled out, but more often than not, it is the appropriate—or the plus side of the ledger—that is anticipated. These norms are simply guides to behavior that specify what can be said by whom to whom and in what situations. Moreover, because of the stratification found in most societies, such norms often express the social stratification in a given group, for what can be said by whom to whom is usually dependent on variables that correlate highly with such factors. The part that deals with situations can imply settings, or it can signify persons with whom one interacts. Each person is positioned somewhere along the parameters that the society measures itself by, and the scale is always a sliding one. The reason that the scale is constantly being adjusted is that the relationship between any given pair of persons is not dependent on any specific objective characteristics of the individuals concerned. The adjustment is dependent upon what the society considers important and how the two individuals relate to each other in that light. A given person may have one kind of relationtionship with a person in one situation and another kind of relationship in another situation. We are parents one minute, children the next; acquaintances one time, lovers the next; students one day, teachers the next. The kaleidoscopic range of our activities is constantly changing. For example, a student enrolled in a graduate program may react one way to his advisor at the university and react another way in his capacity as a part-time instructor at a local community college with colleagues who are in the same field. One may react differently with co-workers on the basis of age, sex, familiarity, and occupational status. The scenario changes as soon as another person enters it, for we all find ourselves in different positions related to others.

Dialects and Evaluative Judgments

In general, certain groups speaking different types of dialects may find themselves in particularly advantageous or disadvantageous positions by virtue of the social connotations attached to their particular form of speech. Not only is the form of speech important but also the manner of speech. Up to this point in our brief discussion, we have assumed that all members of our hypothetical society speak in exactly the same fashion and that all a discussion of language and society need concern itself with is an assessment of just what the uses of language in a uniform range of social settings might be. However, societies are rarely composed of uniform individuals (uniform parts of the community and all speaking the same variety of the same language). Most societies are composed of a number of groups, some larger, some smaller, some in the majority, some in the minority. Taking North America as an example, we would find that although almost all the inhabitants speak English, there are dialect variations dependent on geographical variation as well as social variation. The wrap and woof of the fabric of sociolinguistic patterning is based on variation corresponding to social differences and variation corresponding to geographical differences. Sometimes geographical variation comes to be identified with social variation through the move from one area to another by a substantial number of speakers of the same dialect. This has happened several times in the history of American urban development. For example, during the prewar and wartime era, large numbers of South Midland speakers and Southeastern speakers moved to Northern urban industrial cities to find work. The same thing happened when large numbers of Southern blacks migrated to urban centers throughout the United States. In such cases, what originated as a geographically defined dialect comes to be a social dialect identified with a specific group and their mode of living, aspirations, socioeconomic status, and so forth.

Some speech varieties come to be considered as having prestigious qualities, while others do not; some are considered as being definitely unprestigious and suffer from unwarranted negative connotations. But like interpersonal reactions on the individual scale, such evaluations are purely subjective within the society and also vary according to the individuals involved. Thus, for example, although some consider urban black English as unprestigious, it has increasingly become the pattern on which certain segments of the population, both black and white, have modeled their speech.

Where the question of prestige and the concept of a standard dialect are concerned in North America, the notion is purely a social one. From a technical point of view, dialect differentiation can be examined with a keen but objective eye, just as the taxonomic botanist might be drawn to the compelling varieties of butterflies. There is no official standard for English in North America as there are standard varieties of languages in other countries, like France, Italy, and Germany, where the process of natural language change has been working for much longer and the varieties are very different—in fact, so different that two inhabitants of the same country may not be able to understand each other. In such countries one variety has been promulgated as the officially sanctioned medium of communication for all. The amount of differentiation in North America is nowhere near that great yet. Still, some insist on maintaining that one variety be considered more prestigious than others, but this judgment usually originates in an evaluation of which group is advantaged and which is not. Thus, for English in North America the connotation of terms like **substandard, nonstandard, unstandard, unprestigious,** and so forth is that the form of speech in question simply does not conform to the variety spoken by the people considered to be in some advantageous position. There may be more than one group of such people, and the groups may differ in their preferences for emulation.

Dialect variety may also contribute to the ethnic solidarity of a community if there are other racial, social, or historical characteristics to support the crystalization of a particular speech form as a locally admired standard. Such communities may maintain their original dialect with tenacity as the outward symbol of their unity and the badge of their difference from the outside world. An excellent example is the case of so-called pidgin English in Hawaii. Pidgin English is no longer a true pidgin, but it is certainly very different from other dialects of English. As such, it serves as a quick indicator of whether one is a native of the Islands or a *haole* mainlander. Attempts by the educational system to stamp out the Hawaiian variety of English are not very likely to succeed as long as the speech form is so intimately tied to considerations of ethnic and social solidarity.

Certain groups have even attempted historically to create an idiom to serve as a mark of differentiation from the rest of society. Some groups have simply stuck by a reverse prestige motive; they consider their variety of language as the prestigious one and ostracize anyone deviating from it. With situations like these, attempts to make education attuned to such feelings of language consciousness seem well advised. One is first socialized by means of a specific form of language, and that form of language will likely continue to be the one through which one's keenest emotional ties are felt. "He speaks like us; therefore, he is one of us" seems to be the feeling engendered by such attitudes. One who learns his ideals through this form of speech comes to admire and attempt to emulate those who measure up to the same ideals. Surely, with relatively few exceptions, one will not happily trade in one firmly fixed set of attitudes for another, especially not on the basis of fear and guilt inculcated because of the negative attitudes of other segments of society. Those whom one admires would then give the linguistic lie to one's own verbal behavior, and to talk the way they do is to be like them. One uses his speech in many more ways than just to ask whether lunch is ready or to obtain a match or to inquire about the time. One's speech is the embodiment of his societal expectations and beliefs and, in many cases, the reflection of what other parts of that society believe as well.

Dialect variation is still very controversial when people come to speak of educational practices. Take black English, for example. Here is a dialect of American English that is used by a large number of people, is geographically undefinable, and is considered prestigious by some and unprestigious by others. Some educators say that children must be afforded the opportunity to be educated in their own dialect forms, while other educators insist that children should be educated in a form that is either standard or prestigious in its social position. The former argue from the standpoint of the child's immediate benefit, the latter from the standpoint of longer-range benefits.

This topic is perhaps even more controversial in an age in which educational funding is being increasingly cut. Some opinion leans in the direction of providing the maximum opportunities for the child to be educated in his own native tongue, and legislation emphasizing bilingualism has been passed in the United States and Canada. The same sort of thinking has been applied in practice in situations in which dialect variation is of sufficient magnitude. Many sociolinguistically oriented educators appear to advocate this approach and, if given the proper arrangements and resources, would implement it. An interesting discussion of the wedding of such sociolinguistic and educational functions of language in the classroom is provided by Cazden, John, and Hymes (1972).

Specifically, the topic can be narrowed to an example of the range of task-oriented decisions facing educators in situations involving dialect differences. Learning to read is difficult enough for children, given the confusing degree of fit between the orthography of English and its actual sound system. Our writing system is in many respects better representative of Chaucer's Middle English than of our twentieth-century speech. The reason is a fairly simple one: While the language was changing, as all languages do endlessly and irrevocably, the writing system, being fixed in two-dimensional black and white, was not changing but becoming a permanent fixture. Add to this the difficulty encountered by children speaking a variety of English other than the one the orthography is normally taken to indicate by some schools, and the teacher has to lead the child not only through the trauma of a confusing spelling system but also through the inexplicable logic of a writing system that does not appear to represent his phonological values at all. The result can only be frustration and perhaps bitterness on the part of the child.

Then what are the alternatives? One can teach the child to read in the standard dialect, and that has been the traditional approach simply because the teacher in the past was perhaps unaware of the possible far-reaching differences between the variety of dialect certain children had been brought up with and the standard dialect. In fact, some teachers may have been in general unaware of or uninterested in dialect differences except that for them such differences were associated with intelligence and capability differences. The consequences were often two-fold: Either the differences were not tolerated and attempts were made to eradicate them as logical defects, or children who persisted in their use were relegated to the back of the class, to sink, ever deeper into unproductive behavior. There are few things more devastating than a rejection of one's speech; one can hide or disguise other forms of behavior, but not speech if only one variety is available each time one opens his mouth. And how many varieties are available if they are not taught? There is, nevertheless, the one obvious advantage to this method that children do learn to read the standard dialect one way or the other.

A recent alternative to this traditional exercise has been to treat dialect varieties as though they were foreign languages by using the methods of applied linguistics developed in the structural linguistic period. Using techniques like contrastive analysis, in which one would make a detailed summary of the differences between the structures of the two speech forms, a teacher can produce pedagogical materials stressing practice on the differences between the two systems while capitalizing on the similarities. Drills are developed in which the learner produces and reproduces the patterns of speech until they become second nature, just as language is. The problem with treating dialect varieties as though they were foreign languages is that they are not foreign languages. Moreover, the standard may suffer the same fate as foreign language instruction in certain programs; because only a limited period of time is devoted to foreign language instruction, and because much of the conversation carried out in the language is limited to rather stilted exchanges that could only happen in schoolrooms, the language does not proceed beyond the classroom and is forever considered an artificial, perhaps esoteric, activity.

Some interesting progress has been made, however, in various bilingual programs advised and surveyed by Lambert and others (Lambert, 1969; Lambert, Tucker, & d'Anglejean, 1972) in Montreal with French and English. In such programs bilingual teachers use only the target language for instruction in all subjects, as though no other language existed. Following the children's development in school has shown that these programs have been surprisingly effective. Admittedly, however, Canada is constitutionally a bilingual country, and the children of many middle-class and upper-middle-class English-speaking families living in a large French-Canadian urban center like Montreal have a sufficiently high degree of motivation to learn French. The situation is not unlike that of the millions of immigrants to North America whose children went to schools in which there was no other language but English; they mastered it and the curriculum taught in it. The motivation was exceptionally high, and there was no other choice. More on such bilingual educational programs appears in Chapter 10.

Another problem involved in this manner of teaching the standard form of a language is that social judgments are placed on the other dialects in one's linguistic environment. The child learns these as well as his native speech, so that regardless of the techniques used to teach him the standard form, he may have acquired or been exposed to attitudes that cripple his motivation to learning it. Thus, although the administration and the individual teacher may try to provide him with a variety that for larger social reasons may serve to enlarge his future prospects, he may scorn the speech form as the marker of a larger society he has little use for and does not care to join. In this way, teacher and official can think that an ability to use a standard form is a useful thing to have while the student thinks of it only as a damnable assault on his identity.

The other alternative is, of course, to educate each child in his own dialect, with or without a later switch to the standard form. This alternative is encountered in the use of other languages in primary instruction for such groups as American Indians and Hispano-Americans and such immigrant groups as Slavs, Italians, Scandinavians, and Germans. Recent legislation has allowed for the language needs of the first two groups in educational settings; the latter have traditionally formed their own associations, often centered around religious, social, or insurance-benefit organizations, and schools and ethnic newspapers have done much to keep the mother tongue alive. The former groups are increasingly demanding that some education at the primary level can and will be carried out in their native languages wherever possible.

Again, the question of social judgments enters. Should we reinforce the dialect variety at the expense of the standard form, which carries, for better or worse, certain favorable connotations? What we gain in bolstering the child's pride in himself and his origins may be lost, some would say, by his later failure to participate in the larger society because of his speech. Although academicians and educators may be increasingly in favor of bidialectalism and bilingualism, the determining factor is what the larger society wants or believes it wants. The academic community may have some ability to influence the larger society, but success or failure will ultimately depend on what that larger society deems desirable or appropriate.

Sociolinguistic Rules and Verbal Interaction

The relationship between language and society is in part a matter of individual differences and in larger part a matter of group differences. On the level of individual differences, investigation centers on those linguistic features that can be varied in response to societal norms and on the choices made in regard to their total communicative value. Features of language that are always the same are of no interest. Members of society can readily recognize instances of such rule-governed choices, though they may not be able to verbalize the reasons for their choices. Just as grammatical competence consists of a rule-governed grammatical behavior that speakers cannot explain or verbalize about, communicative competence, or the rules that actually govern social-performance uses of language, lies beneath the surface of immediate awareness.

The linguistic code itself can be considered as a variable in communication, just as any single feature in individual exchanges can be. In these cases the entire code is a signaling feature of the person's conception of himself, the co-locutor, and the situation. In some cases it may be signaled by a shift from one variety of a language to another, with the difference between the varieties more or less extreme. In other cases it may be signaled by a shift from one language to another. The remainder of this chapter provides examples of both individual and group differences in the use of language as well as their relationship to code switching.

One of the most important facets of individual exchanges involves the exchange of address forms. How to address the other person is a crucial matter in many cultures, and it is not surprising that in many languages this area of sociolinguistic activities is a highly elaborated one. Obviously, where forms of address are elaborated, one exhibits both one's own position relative to one's co-locutor by the forms of address chosen and one's attitudes about the situation and the way society codes that situation.

An excellent example of a highly patterned situation in the exchange of address has traditionally been offered by Japanese. Martin (1964) points out that Japanese has a substantial number of polite formulas designed to smooth over most social situations. The exchange of address in Japanese forces upon the speaker an obligatory choice of forms, for the address component is expressed in inflectional affixes for verb and adjectival predicates. Unless one avoids such part-of-speech categories altogether, one must inevitably choose one form of address or another. Even nouns and pronouns in Japanese may be restrictive. For example, a number of noun affixes, as well as noun choices, are socially informative, and so are all of the pronoun forms. Thus, one is left with only prepositions, and one obviously must make a choice in speaking unless one is adept at carrying on conversations limited to function words like prepositions. Such far-reaching and unavoidable constraints can be termed **obligatory categories,** for in employing the language one is perforce obligated to make some choice regarding the manner of speech.

In Japanese the obligatory choice is between **plain** or **polite** speech levels, and it is indicated by appropriate suffixes on the verb forms. The plain style is used for addresses judged to be alike or inferior on the social scale according to factors of ingroupness versus out-groupness and status by position, age, or sex differences, and in that order of importance. For example, one would use plain-style verb endings on the verbs *nomu* and *taberu, to drink* and *to eat,* respectively. On the other hand, one would use the polite style for those judged to be superior on the scale according to the factors mentioned. The verb forms in this case are *nomimasu* and *tabemasu.* Plain style thus takes an affix $-(r)u$ on the end of verbs and polite style an affix $-(i)masu$, depending on whether the verb stem is a member of the vowel class or the consonantal class.

Japanese, incidentally, also has an **axis of reference** (Martin, 1964), in which speakers must indicate their attitudes and social positions on the scale relative to the person they are speaking about. This axis of reference calls into play the same factors of age, sex, social position, and outgroupness differences, but in this relative order instead of the one given earlier. In Japanese, then, one must be careful to employ an appropriate style both when speaking to someone and when speaking about someone. The levels of style on the axis of reference are the **humble,** including oneself, one's kin, and close ones; the **neutral,** those on a social par with oneself; and the **exalted,** those judged to be in a position above oneself. The differences in reference might be exemplified by the different verbal forms employed in speaking about one's younger brother, one's friend, and one's professor—using the humble, the neutral, and the exalted referential styles, respectively.

One can imagine some amount of constraint on Japanese interaction, with a careful sorting of variables guiding such speech-level selection. Much of this situation seems to have been changing since the postwar era in the direction of a leveling off of some of the more stringent rules governing such interaction. Younger generations are less prone to continue some of the distinctions, and it seems likely that in the not-too-distant future an entirely different configuration of sociolinguistic patterns in Japanese will emerge, highly reminiscent of the previous system, but not at all a carbon copy of it.

A similar example of a highly stylized form of sociolinguistic repertoire has also been traditionally offered by Javanese. As Geertz (1960) has pointed out, the three identifiable social groups of peasants, townsmen, and aristocrats have their own social spheres of activity and yet must at the same time interact with one another in the larger scope of Javanese society. This is accomplished by what Geertz (1960) has characterized as a situation in which "the patterns of linguistic etiquette modulate, regularize, and smoothe the processes of social interaction into . . . an unvarying flow of quiet, emotionally tranquilizing propriety [pp. 254–255]." Such clear social divisions have been traditionally the case in Javanese society but are showing indications of change under the influence of a leveling social process. Nevertheless, it is still not difficult to separate the three groups by their economic, religious, and social practices. All speak Javanese, and their respective varieties are mutually intelligible, but the variety also provides overt cues to their social affiliations and their expected attitudes toward their interlocutors.

Javanese speakers must choose between three different speech levels, but unlike the sociolinguistic affix system employed by Japanese, Javanese **stylemes,** or speech levels, are dependent on lexical choices. Each styleme is characterized by lexical sets, so that the speaker must choose one vocabulary set over the other two, and the formality or deference of the relationship is conveyed by these stylistic vocabulary choices. At the moment of the first vocabulary choice in sentence construction, the speaker more or less commits himself to a style that will then be consistent in the selection of vocabulary items thereafter. Beside the three basic sets, it is also possible to raise the lowest level and the highest level by an additional set of honorific terms. Thus, it is possible to raise the lowest-level styleme somewhat by a set of low honorifics or to raise it even more with a set of high honorifics. It is still thought of as the lowest level and does not contradict or overlap so much into the middle level as to obliterate the distinction. Similarly, it is also possible to raise the highest level somewhat with a set of high honorifics.

Thus, Javanese exhibits at least six separate and somewhat distinct levels, all based on vocabulary markers. However, the same range of levels is not employed by all Javanese speakers, and their uses are dependent on their social affiliations. Although the lowest level of unadorned speech is learned first by most children, it is thereafter usually observed in mutual adult speech by members of the peasant group in their interactions with one another and the townsmen group. However, because it is the basic core of the language around which the other styles are built, it is also used by intimate adult members of other groups in mutual exchange when there is no disparity of status, age, and so forth. It is also used when addressing someone who is one's social inferior, either within the same group or a lower group.

The middle level is used between townsmen who share no intimacy of relationship and by peasants addressing superiors or members of the next group up, the townsmen. The highest level is used between aristocrats who share no intimacy of relationship and by townsmen addressing superiors or members of the next highest group, the aristocrats. Thus, depending on the degree of familiarity and social superiority or inferiority, the first level in its plain or elaborated fashion will be used, while the middle level will be used more commonly by townsmen in their dealings with one another. The highest level is more characteristic of the aristocratic group, although townsmen will also use it, given the appropriate occasion.

If the possibilities for interaction between members of the three groups are assessed, the reason for the separation becomes obvious. Not all members of the three groups have the same opportunities for interaction, and the general rule seems to follow the assignment of the three levels to each of the three groups between themselves in formalized settings. On addressing the next highest group, there is the added possibility of speech embellishment by the honorifics or simply a move up to the next level where possible. The question of familiarity or intimacy also enters the picture, and, dependent on this variable, speakers will move down a stylistic rung on the six-possibility sociolinguistic speech ladder. In addressing inferiors within the same group or members of the next group down—for example, aristocrats to townsmen or townsmen to peasants—the customary choice is a level or more lower. Moreover, just as setting plays an important role in stylistic choice in all languages, in Javanese the setting provides for a choice on embellishment of one of the basic three levels or possibly a move to the next level.

As with Japanese, it may be that some of the niceties underlying the choices are being worn down under the pressures of social change. For example, in modern Java politicians addressing potential or real constituents in mixed settings face the problem of possibly offending and thereby losing rapport and vote alike. Bahasa Indonesia, the officially recognized national language, has come to fill the void by virtue of its freedom from restrictions in such matters and its status as a foreign language to most Javanese. Although it may not please all concerned, it certainly does nothing to offend anyone, so it is the perfect medium for the ambitious politician.

Lest such examples seem somewhat exotic, we have only to turn to members of our own Indo-European language family for examples of similar highly structured forms of exchange. Such categories in Japanese and Javanese can be called obligatory categories, for at some very immediate point in the conversational flow, the speaker is constrained to choose and thereafter employ that form of speech deemed to be appropriate for the addressee and the situation. Many Indo-European languages afford a choice of the form of pronominal usage employed and, in those languages that have maintained the Indo-European inflectional system, verb forms as well. These can be termed **semiobligatory categories,** since they do not figure as heavily in the total configuration of the language forms, though they do require choices at some strategic points in the structure.

Such languages may maintain a distinction between the second-person-singular pronoun and the second-person-plural pronoun that has to do with the dimensions of social superiority and social familiarity. Plurality obviously has to do with addressing more than one person, and this is, of course, the original purpose of the pronominal distinction. For example, the French distinction between the forms *tu,* second-person-singular *you* or *thou,* and *vous,* second-person-plural *you,* is only one of plurality when the distinction to be drawn is obviously one of plurality. French speakers may also use both of these pronouns when speaking to a single person, and the meaning of their use in this respect is to be found in their sociolinguistic functions. Similar uses are found in many languages of Europe that deploy their pronominal forms of address to convey sociolinguistic information. The *tu–Usted* distinction in Spanish, the *du–Sie* distinction in German, the *ty–vy* distinction in Russian, the *ti–vi* distinction in Slovene, and many more are examples of the same sociolinguistic fashion that swept through European courts in imitation of prestigious behavior, and have remained ever since.

As Brown and Gilman (1960) have pointed out, such languages use the pronominal forms of address to express two dimensions embodied in most social interaction, the dimension of power and the dimension of solidarity. The power dimension is dependent on factors like age, social position, and occupation, while solidarity can be considered the degree of intimacy or at least like-mindedness between individuals. The use of the address forms will vary according to the relationship of the speaker and listener along the dimensions of their equality or inequality along the power continuum and their degree of familiarity along the solidarity continuum. A choice may have to be made even if the pronouns are missing, for in those languages that have verbal inflectional endings tied to person markers, the verb ending will signal whether the choice has been the familiar singular pronoun or the unfamiliar plural pronoun. For example, a phrase like the French *Dites quelque chose,* or *Say something,* signals the second-person-plural pronoun even though the pronoun itself is not there. The signal is the verb ending *–es,* which tells French speakers the same thing as the pronoun.

If the speaker judges the addressee to be familiar on the solidarity continuum, the usage will involve a mutual exchange of second-person-singular pronouns, or to use the French pronominal forms as an example, a mutual exchange of *tu.* If the addressee is judged to be unfamiliar, the exchange is likely to be a mutual exchange of *vous,* the second-person-plural pronoun form. Once familiarity is established, the direction of change will be toward the mutual exchange of the familiar form *tu.* Many languages have names for the initiation of such familiar exchanges, and sometimes even a tiny celebration accompanies the establishment of the intimate exchange. In German the transition from the form *Sie* to the intimate *du* is of sufficient importance to be expressed by a lexical item, *Bruderschaft,* and traditionally involves a ritual toast to each other's health and well-being and the continuation of friendship. In French and Spanish, the terms *tutoyer* and *tutear,* respectively, can be translated as *to exchange the familiar form of address,* as implied by the syllable *tu–.* Slovene, a Slavic language of Yugoslavia, has the contrasting forms *tikati* and *vikati* for the familiar and unfamiliar exchanges of address (implied by the syllables *ti–* and *vi–,* respectively). All of the foregoing indicates that the sociolinguistic behaviors are not only implicit in the workings of societal interchange but also consciously formalized for some speech communities.

If a speaker judges the addressee to be equal along the continuum of power, the form *tu* will be used. If he is judged to be superior, the form will be *vous;* if he is judged to be inferior, the form will be *tu.* The two dimensions interact such that the choice of variables will be dependent on the overlap between the two axes of power and solidarity. For example, in addressing a child who is unfamiliar, the power factor is clearly the first point of reference, and the form of address will be *tu,* while in the case of a visiting dignitary both unfamiliarity and social inequality will demand a *vous.* In the case of an employer or a boss at work, the first mode of address will likely be *vous,* with the inequality of occupational status often over-riding the possible familiar aspects of the similar work setting. The new employer or work superior, on the other hand, may use the *vous* form because of the nonsolidarity factor or the *tu* on the basis of occupational status differences. If the address exchange is to change in the direction of mutual exchange of *tu,* the change is usually initiated by the person with the greater status, age, or position. The change is not likely to be initiated by the lower-status person for possible fear of inappropriate linguistic behavior and of giving offense. On the other hand, the mutual exchange of *vous* on the basis of absence of solidarity between equals is a process initiated by either or both, since no status variables are contravened in this case.

Certain of the rules are in conflict because of the contradictory status of the power and solidarity variables, in which case the choice of form of address is neither entirely straightforward nor simply determined. Speakers may in this case choose the more formal and gradually move toward the less formal. Less is risked with initiation of formal exchanges, and change can typically proceed toward the more familiar exchange; if, on the other hand, familiar exchanges are initiated but are deemed inappropriate by the other party, there is nowhere to go but back to the formal exchange, and this involves the risk of social embarrassment and possible rejection, particularly for the initiator.

In the social upheavals and restructuring of certain orders of society over the past several centuries, certain aspects of the system have changed, with the order of change generally involving a reinterpretation of power factors as solidarity factors. As Brown and Gilman (1960) point out, the nonreciprocal aspect of the power factor is more obviously associated with stable and relatively static societies in which status is given, not attained, and in which power is maintained and not disturbed. This, of course, has not been true of European societies over the past several centuries, and the changes that have occurred are mirrored in the changes that have taken place in the exchange of address forms. In general, more reinterpretation along the solidarity continuum has taken place as a direct reflection of the emphasis on egalitarian principles in Western society.

As has been pointed out by Brown and Ford (1961), English address, though not tied to pronominal choices of address indicating social familiarity and status differences, does use the exchange of **first name** or **title plus last name** to achieve the same ends. Both first names—*Joseph, John, Joe, Jack, Bill,* and so on—and title-plus-last-name sequences—*Mr. Smith, Dr. Jones, Father Pawley, Dean Peters,* and so on—are forms of address. As in the case of choosing the forms of pronominal address, the selection of address form depends on the relationship between the speaker and the addressee. One simply does not call another person by any name chosen from personal fancy—first name, nickname, title plus last name, or whatever. Neither is the form used predictable from the individual alone unless, of course, he has some absolute status; but even then his immediate relationship with the speaker may be one of an extremely familiar and intimate nature.

Following Brown and Ford, we can abbreviate the forms of address as FN for first name and TLN for title plus last name. Only three options are possible in North American English: mutual exchange of FN, mutual exchange of TLN, and nonreciprocal exchange of FN and TLN. The mutual exchange of TLN is usually used by adults meeting for the first time. After a period of time, they may move to an FN exchange on the basis of familiarity, shared values, frequent contact, and so on. The younger the pair, the sooner the change may occur; in fact, the young often use the FN form as their first medium of exchange. The same is true for members of the same sex, where mutual FN exchange is faster than between members of the opposite sex.

The exchange of FN implies familiarity on the part of adult speakers in similar occupational or status positions or both. The nonreciprocal exchange of FN and TLN may imply a difference in age between the parties, perhaps about 15 years, though the line is relatively hazy. It may also signal the fixed relationship between the two parties, such as that between adult and child. Even in family settings the fixed terms for parents or relatives can be taken as titles, and the first name of the child, no matter how young or old, can be taken as a first name. Nonreciprocal exchange may also signal differences in occupational status, either temporary, as with a store clerk or deliveryman, or more permanent, as with a doctor, priest, section chief, or employer. In those instances in which the two may conflict, as, for example, in the casual, after-hours, in-office meeting of a young executive and the middle-aged janitor, it is likely that nonreciprocal exchange will still result, with the status ethic dominating the age ethic. Our society may place more importance on status than age, especially in cases of achieved status. There may, however, be a mutual exchange of FN if the younger executive has been acculturated to pay deference to age or simply if he is embarrassed by being addressed by TLN by an older man. The situation may also result in a mutual exchange of TLN, thus preserving the equilibrium of the situation, with the young executive's status being paid deference to by the TLN and the janitor's age by the TLN. In other situations setting dictates the form of the exchange. For example, there is little question in military settings about who receives the appropriate address, regardless of age or extramilitary status differences.

In cases of nonreciprocal FN–TLN exchange, the recipient of the TLN normally holds the key to rearranging the form of address to a mutual FN. Take, for example, the case of an older employer who says to an employee one day after a long exchange of FN–TLN that it is indeed unnecessary to address him as *Mr. Hodgkins,* that *Bill* would be just fine. However, even in cases in which the two individuals have worked together for a long time and the change in address has been invited by the elder superior, as in the *Mr. Hodgkins*-to-*Bill* transition, the FN recipient may still find it difficult or impossible to acquiesce. Fortunately, English offers an alternative with *you,* since there is no distinct form for *you* singular or *you* plural. One can always avoid potentially embarrassing or difficult address situations by simply using *you* in an oblique fashion.

There are other forms of address in English; the FN and TLN variations are simply suggestive of the factors that govern exchanges. The use of last names alone, titles without last name, multiple first names, nicknames, and so forth are all indicative of the personal and socially conditioned forms of expressing relationships that form the basis for interaction in our society. One of the best examples of other forms of English address is the use of multiple first names or nicknames. Multiple use would appear to indicate greater familiarity, as any casual glance at the large inventory of terms used to address a loved one or close friend will show. There is a compelling similarity in the cultural relativity suggestion that the more important an area of experience is in the lives of a people, the more elaborated it will be in the vocabulary stock of that language. Just as one accepts the rationale of countless words for snow in Eskimo, one can easily accept the rationale for countless terms of endearment for loved ones on the individual level of language use.

From the data examined and reported on in a fairly large number of languages, it would appear that a possible sociolinguistic universal in the manner of address is reflected in such descriptions. Where such obligatory or semiobligatory categories exist in language, their usage is surprisingly similar in principle, which has prompted some (Slobin, Miller, & Porter, 1968) to suggest that their patterning is perhaps a sociolinguistic universal. For example, our sample languages each code the two social factors of familiarity or solidarity and status or position. There are obviously cultural differences in what constitutes solidarity and status in the various languages, but each codes that aspect that is important to it, and the two concepts find a place in the total sociolinguistic system.

Moreover, it would appear from the investigations so far that another possible sociolinguistic universal is at work here. The familiar form of mutual address, whether it be first name, pronominal usage, or whatever, is also the form used for going downward in address patterns from superior to inferior. Thus, the familiar form is either signaling intimacy between equals or social gaps between nonequals; the formal form either signals nonfamiliarity between likely equals or deference on the part of the one using it to someone he does not know. Slobin and his colleagues also comment on the commonality of certain kinds of sociolinguistic variables, such that the address term exchanged between intimates (the familiar pronoun, first name, and so on) is the same term used in addressing social inferiors, and the term exchanged between nonintimates (the "polite pronoun," title plus last name, and so on) is employed to address social superiors. There is obviously no logical reason for this being so; it just happens to be a characteristic of the languages surveyed, and one would surmise that it may be present in many, many more.

So far, most of the discussion has involved the exchange-of-address situation from the point of view of the speaker. The addressee is also affected in that he is likely to be treated as he is addressed. Occasionally over the phone one may commit himself to a formal nonreciprocal exchange of address without the aid of visual cues. On actually meeting the person, who is perhaps not only younger but in a similar or lower occupational status, one nevertheless almost feels obliged to continue the form of exchange until it is resolved. Most of us can probably recall the discomfort of not fitting into the right slot as the result of our own actions, and the situation can be difficult for all concerned. This situation is not unlike the experience of having been described to others as a socialist or a hippie or a fool and then at least partially reacting on the basis of the immediate expectations already provided to the persons with whom one is speaking.

Linguistic Variables and Sociocultural Differences

Another fruitful area of investigation in the relationship of language to society has been analysis of ingroup and outgroup attitudes toward linguistic diversity. Individual differences in linguistic style can give some information about the individual using them; group differences provide another kind. Moreover, the individual's use of features correlated with different groups is another very informative component in social interaction, for it expresses group membership and the values of that group and its attitudes toward itself and other groups within the total context of society. Numerous studies of what can be termed communicative competence have begun to appear, and they complement what work has been carried out on the level of theoretical linguistics. The full measure of a language is the part it plays in actual use among members of a linguistic community. Moreover, a full description of a speaker–hearer's ability will include a description of his language behavior in different social contexts.

Labov's much quoted study (1964) of social stratification and speech patterns on the Lower East Side of New York City is an excellent example of such sociolinguistic studies. Labov found that the use of linguistic variants was not haphazard and that the stylistic choices were closely patterned on social norms. He was fortunate in having a sociological sample already constructed and was able to approach directly the investigation of linguistic factors that might conceivably correlate with these given social differences. He employed several phonological variables that he considered to be potentially diagnostic of social affiliations and tested the presence of these phonological features in several different speaking situations. Such phonological variables as the presence of postvocalic /r/ (*cah* for *car*, *pahk* for *park*, and *yahd* for *yard*), the substitution of /t/ and /d/ for /θ/ and /ð/ (*ting* and *dat* for *thing* and *that*), and the vowel qualities found in word sets like *dog*, *walk*, *talk*, and *all* and *bad*, *Ann*, *dance*, and *cash* are examples of the variables Labov was looking for. The speaking styles were differentiated into a careful interview-type style, a casual, normal speech style, a text-reading style, and a style employed in reading isolated words in list form. When deviations from the prestige forms were tabulated, the number of deviations reflected the socioeconomic divisions already outlined in the sociological information.

Before prestige forms are discussed further, some commentary should be again offered on the meaning of the term. Traditionally, the dialect of American English spoken in New York City has had certain characteristic features, just as any other American or Canadian English dialect has its own characteristic features. One tends to think of the next fellow's speech form as dialectal, substandard, and perhaps even deficient, while one's own is not. Each individual speech form is ultimately a variety of the language and can be characterized by those features that distinguish it from the next variety. In New York speech some of those features are the ones mentioned earlier—the postvocalic absence of /r/ that characterizes most of the Atlantic seaboard from Newfoundland through New England and down through the Southern states, the /t/ and /d/ replacement for the fricatives /θ/ and /ð/, and the particular New York vowel qualities in words like *walk*, *dog*, *can*, and *Ann*. Recently, other forms of North American English not sharing these characteristics have acquired an aura of prestige through their consistent use on radio and television broadcasts, in movies and plays, and so forth, and New York speakers have occasionally attempted to model their speech on these patterns rather than continue with their own traditional dialect features. **Prestige** in this sense, then, refers to

Table 5.1 An Example of Sociolinguistic Differences[a]

Category	Casual	Careful	Reading	List
(a)	105	75	35	25
(b)	35	20	5	0
(c)	19	15	0	0

[a] From W. Labov, *The Social Stratification of English in New York City*, 1966. Reprinted by permission of the Center for Applied Linguistics, Washington, D.C.

the coming and going of certain features in a dialect that speakers attempt, but never altogether successfuly, to pattern after another dialect they consider more elegant, more important, more advantageous, or whatever. Labov was thus measuring the deviations from what would be a perfect correspondence between this dialect and the usages of speakers who were attempting to pattern their speech after the prestige variety.

For example, typical usage of the fricative /θ/ in the categories illustrated by (a) a workman of Italian ethnic origin, (b) a white-collar worker, and (c) a college-educated professional might be as shown in Table 5.1. Labov's method was to count deviations from 0 (that is, no deviations from the standard /θ/) to 200 (that is, no instances of the standard /θ/, for all are replaced by /t/).

Labov found that in general the higher a man's socioeconomic class, the more likely it would be that the percentage of his usage of the prestige forms would be higher. This does not mean that his usage would be perfectly identical with prestige usage but that his usage would more closely approximate that form of speech. Thus, the upper-middle, upper-working, lower-working, lower, and lowest classes approximated the prestige forms in that order, with the upper-middle class showing the closest approximation and the lowest class the lowest percentage of approximation. The only apparent exception to this rule was the lower-middle class, which approximated the prestige forms even more closely than the upper-middle class. One inference that can be drawn from this exception is that the striving for upward mobility by the lower-middle class is exhibited in their language behavior, while the upper-middle class, being relatively confident of their social and economic status, have no need to prove themselves, and this fact is mirrored in their language behavior.

Figure 5.1, for example, shows Labov's relationship between class stratification and the use of the final and preconsonantal /r/. Higher scores reflect more use of the prestigious /r/, and the scores correlate with class stratification. The other interesting point, of course, is the

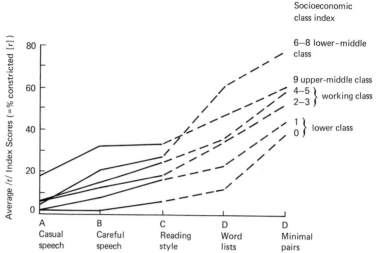

Figure 5.1 Class stratification and the use of the final and preconsonantal /r/. [From W. Labov, *The Social Stratification of English in New York City,* 1966. Reprinted by permission of the Center for Applied Linguistics, Washington, D. C.]

general slope of the style shifting. Compare the slopes of the lines in Figures 5.1 and 5.2. As Labov (1972) observes, the highest and lowest groups have the shallowest slopes. The other groups have steeper slopes, particularly the second-highest group, the lower-middle class. It would seem that upward aspirations characterize the middle groups more than the highest and lowest groups.

However, all speakers on all levels appear to be more restricted in their usages as they move from the least careful to the most careful style of speech. Most of the deviations from the prestige form occur in the casual style, the next most in the careful style, the next in the

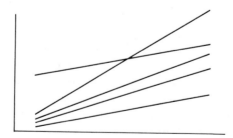

Figure 5.2 Generalized slopes for sociolinguistic indicators according to the social class. [From W. Labov, *Sociolinguistic Patterns,* 1972. Reprinted by permission of the University of Pennsylvania Press, Philadelphia, Pennsylvania.]

reading style, and the fewest of all in the isolated words in list form. Even higher correlations are found in the reading of supposed minimal pairs. Conversely, such phonological changes are in effect made greater by highly charged, emotional topics. The actual number of deviations may vary from group to group, but the ratio is proportionally the same for all in terms of most to least number of deviations from the prestige forms. Labov terms such variables **markers,** and points out that they are indicative of both role and style switching according to the self-monitoring activity of the speaker.

It is also useful to survey the functions of code switching in societies in which well-defined codes for style, dialect, or even separate languages are available. In these societies the codes employed by individuals will differ according to setting and co-locutor. In such cases the two different forms of the same language are distinct enough to form two completely different systems recognizable as such by all members of the speech community. One example found in most literate societies is the difference between the forms of language used in written and spoken styles. In English, for example, specific styles are set apart for certain kinds of writing, prose or technical, and other styles are set apart for speaking occasions. Other languages have more classical connotations attached to the form calcified in writing, as is the case with classical forms of the language, like the past use of Latin in the Catholic liturgy, Arabic in Islamic practices, Hebrew in Jewish religious functions, and until recently, Old Church Slavonic in Russian and Ukrainian Orthodox religious services.

This situation may also be reflected in differences in the various modern spoken renditions of the same language. Certain spoken styles may be considered appropriate for certain speaking situations and other spoken styles for other situations. In such cases one can talk of the formal and colloquial varieties of the language, with the formal being typically reserved for those social situations judged to be of a formal nature and the colloquial reserved for more ordinary conversational exchanges between familiars, equals, or superiors to inferiors. Two formally distinguishable dialects of the same language may also be used differentially by a certain segment of a society or by the entire society. The dialects are likely to be a standard variety of the language, or perhaps simply a prestigious form of the language, and a local or regional variety of the language. In such instances the standard form is the one used for the formal settings, and the regional variety is the one used for colloquial, intimate settings. An excellent example of this phenomenon is the relationship between the use of Standard German and regional Swiss German dialects in Switzerland, though the same kinds of principles of code switching can be seen in such diverse languages as Arabic, Modern Greek, Haitian Creole, and countless others. Ferguson (1964) has introduced the term **diglossia** for this kind of standardization situation in which two varieties of the same language coexist within the same community, with each having a definite role to play.

It is also possible for the choice between two entirely different languages to have diglossic connotations, with one of the languages being reserved for more formal, commercial, or nonintimate exchanges and the other reserved for colloquial, friendly, or personal exchanges. The relationship between Spanish and Guarani in Paraguay (see Rubin, 1968) is apparently of this type. In Canada the use of English and French by French-Canadian bilinguals exhibits certain of these connotations. In these two cases, Spanish (in Paraguay) and English (in Canada) are taken to be formal, prestigious, and nonintimate forms of speech. Obviously, in such situations bilingualism is more than just fluency in the two languages, and some account of the basis of code switching is in order in any description of such bilingual activity.

In the use of two or more languages or varieties of the same language in the same community, one variety is usually the higher and more formal style and the other the lower and less formal style. The lower form is usually learned first and the higher form much later. Moreover, since the latter is often learned in a formal setting for use in formal situations concerning formal topics, it rarely is used for intimate affairs in the speakers' lives. These situations are usually reserved for the lower style, in which certain personal exchanges are most readily transmitted. In some societies the formal may well be a foreign language for many who never come to feel completely at home in it and are only too aware of its more artificial situational status. Other societies may not consider it as dramatically distinct as this but are still aware of its status as the medium of exchange for certain topics or in certain settings. For example, Blom and Gumperz (1964) discuss such switching between the local dialect and Standard Norwegian, in which the use of the dialect or the formal language reinforces or at least parallels the content of the message. Thus, a pair of Norwegian students who had been close friends in a small Norwegian village may, upon their return home from college in two different urban centers, employ the local dialect when discussing local matters and switch to Standard Norwegian when discussing matters more directly related to their more formal pan-Norwegian lives as students, urban dwellers, and so forth.

Diglossic and bilingual variation also imply attitudinal beliefs.

Speech differences set off a chain reaction of responses from listeners who take the verbal cues as denoting that the speaker is to be taken as friend, colleague, and social equal or as the opposite. This is an integral part of the plot of George Bernard Shaw's play *Pygmalion* and its modern spinoff, *My Fair Lady*. For Henry Higgins, removing Eliza Doolittle's original speech patterns and establishing the right verbal cues to elicit the right responses were the keys to passing her off as a lady.

Labov (1966) found some interesting correlations between his New York data and the ability of listeners to predict correctly the social status of the speaker. Ongoing studies by Lambert and others (Lambert, 1969; Lambert, Frankel, & Tucker, 1966; Lambert, Hodgson, Gardner, & Fillenbaum, 1960) have taken the interesting tack of having native bilinguals produce passages in both Canadian French and Canadian English. In evaluating the speakers on a number of personality and physical characteristics just on the basis of the spoken passage, both English and French speakers rated the English speakers higher than the French speakers on all but one scale, that of height. That the speakers of both the French and the English passages were the same was, of course, unknown to the listener–evaluators, and their evaluations of the speakers say a great deal. What is obviously indicated in such evaluative reactions to speech differences is not the evaluation of the speech form itself but the evaluation of the group that uses that speech form, the most overt marker at the moment being the language sample.

To speaker and listener, then, the manner in which linguistic information is carried through the channel of linguistic variety is an all-important one, for the information conveyed by the variety may be of far greater significance to the listener. Moreover, the style does not have to be entirely drawn from a single variety to convey the impression of a specific style. In fact, listeners are notoriously prone to stereotyping speakers on the basis of incomplete information or even a small percentage of deviation. Labov (1966) found that although members of some of his lower-class samples might have used certain phonological variables only 40% to 50% of the time, they were often judged as doing it all the time.

Such sociolinguistic notions have powerful implications in the area of language and nationalism. Contrary to popular belief, most nations have more than one language, and more often than not, many languages coexist within the same political boundaries. The problem would appear to be a twofold one. First, countries attempt to ensure that their own national identity is sufficiently established to distinguish themselves from neighboring countries whose inhabitants speak the same or related languages. This is the case in newly emerging countries and has been traditionally the case in Europe, where nationalistic movements have often been identified with language. Even in areas in which one would least expect it, linguistic nationalism arises. In English-speaking Canada, for example, with a rich and powerful neighbor to the south speaking the same language and many inhabitants living close to the long border even speaking the same or a similar dialect, one may feel nationalistic pressures to establish a more distinctive form of speech to rally around.

Second, countries in which large segments of the population speak varying languages, whether similar and related or dissimilar and unrelated, are faced with sociolinguistic problems of maintaining equilibrium among the languages concerned. Czechoslovakia and Yugoslavia, for example, have a number of closely related languages within their borders. Even so, local nationalistic movements inevitably spring up, with a particular language as a rallying point. The recent rift between Serbian and Croatian in Yugoslavia and the Croats' apparent preference for recognition of Croatian as distinct from Serbian and the official terminology of Serbo-Croatian is a perfect example of such tendencies.

India, Malaysia, New Guinea, and other countries with vast land areas and diverse populations present the other side of this aspect of the problem in attempting to maintain equilibrium between numerous languages that are often not even related but that, for obvious social and political reasons, must interact with one another. An added problem is establishing a standard language for official uses that is acceptable to all—a far from simple question. India presents an example of what can happen in the attempt to establish a language as the official form of communication. India has a large number of languages and a population in the hundreds of millions. Until its disassociation from Britain in the late 1940s, the use of English very efficiently solved the problem of which language would best serve as the official medium of communication; the British authorities simply proclaimed that English was the official language. However, upon receiving independence, the Indians began to give serious thought to replacing English, with its colonial overtones, with a language native to the area. Thus, the Indian constitution of 1950 provides for an official regional language for each of the 16 states; the country as a whole, the Union of India, would continue to use English until 1965, when it would be replaced by an Inidan tongue. Hindi was a likely prospect and was promoted by some, but when it came time actually to implement the native-language stipulation, India erupted into grim riots at the suggestion of Hindi's being the one. The result was that English continues as the semiofficial language for as long as is deemed necessary, which appears to be a long time indeed. Though it is a language Indians associate with a colonial period in their history that they do not want to be reminded of, they have no choice but to maintain it as a medium of communication. The alternative is to select a native language, which would have serious overtones of race, caste, religion, geography, and so forth, and it is better to shake one's fist at an absent and unassailable opponent than to kill one's easily accessible neighbor. The situation in India is repeated less dramatically in countries like the Philippines, Malaysia, New Guinea, and so forth, where colonial languages have been kept for social, political, educational, and other purposes because of their apparent social neutrality now that those who introduced the languages have gone.

Language and Nonverbal Communication

Nonverbal Channels of Communication

To anyone who is a speaker of one of the world's several thousand natural languages, it comes as no surprise to learn that there are a number of communicative systems that parallel language in their ability to communicate information between human beings. Our senses are constantly bombarded with information that is being communicated by means other than spoken language as such. Even when we are not immediately aware of it, we are unconsciously paying heed to a number of nonverbal features present in the behavior of others. Though we may not be able to verbalize the exact rules of behavior that are being realized in any given interaction, we are certainly well enough aware of such features for our reactions to reflect our interpretations of what is happening. These nonverbal channels are constantly being employed to convey subtle but powerful information.

Some of this information comes from the voice set and vocal qualities that accompany the actual verbalization of words phrases, and sentences as indicated by the common remark, "It wasn't what he said so much as the way he said it." This manner of transmission can modify, amplify, or even negate the basic verbal message. There are many ways of saying "yes," and not a few of those ways include presentations that in fact negate the verbal content of the message. Such nonverbal messages are essential to our understanding of human communication; indeed, the way in which something is said **is** often the message, and the verbal exchange is simply chatter. In such cases, it would perhaps be more proper to say that the verbal communication is accompanying the nonverbal communication.

Other systems that communicate information may not be characterized by vocalization at all. One of these is body motion. Overt gestures and body movements in general—for example, facial expressions, eye movements, and posture—all convey information that can also affect the basic verbal message by amplification, modification, or negation. Or, in the absence of a verbal message, they convey their own message concerning the speaker's attitudes about a given situation or his general disposition at the moment. Similar to but not necessarily the same as body movement and gesture is our use of socially recognized personal space and our perception of that space as personal territory. Dependent upon cultural considerations, man projects an area of personal space that is his; crossing the boundaries of that space, except for socially and culturally approved kinds of interaction, constitutes a violation and is a communicative act in itself. According to this notion, there are culturally sanctioned distances for various kinds of activities, and adherence or nonadherence to these distances is a kind of communication. Moreover, when language does enter the picture, kinds of verbal output, as well as the vocal qualities surrounding it, correlate highly with variables on the scale of social and personal distance.

This viewpoint, of course, implies a partial shift in interest from the communicator to his behavior in communicating. Since this form of communication is multichanneled, we will concentrate on specific channels of the overall nonverbal-communication system, and consider which other channels of social interaction provide a matrix for verbal communication and exactly how they do so. Just as there are various types of verbal communication, there are different types of nonverbal communication, which differ in both form (the **how** of how things are communicated) and content (the **what** of what things are communicated).

The three modes of nonverbal communication are **paralanguage** (vocal qualifiers and nonverbal vocalizations), **kinesics** (body movements and gestures), and **proxemics** (social and personal space). It is noteworthy that only recently has research been directed at detailing the confines of each of these areas with any degree of success. It may seem strange that topics so known to us all in our communicative interaction with one another should have waited so long for detailed examination, but we need only recall that it is only in the past century or so that our knowledge of the details of language itself has grown to proportions sufficient to boast of.

Paralinguistics and Intonational Phenomena

Trager's early discussions (1958, 1961) set the stage for the examination of the nonverbal vocal behavior he has termed paralanguage. Trager envisions three kinds of events that employ the speech apparatus. The first of these is language itself. The second and third types, which differ from the structural features and content of true language in significant ways, Trager has termed **vocalizations** and **voice qualities,** respectively. Vocalizations are those noises that do not have the structure of language but are nevertheless audible and potentially communicative. Vocalizations are in fact easily identifiable as specific vocal noises or aspects of vocal noises. Trager here includes such diverse types of vocalizations as laughing, crying, yelling, belching, whispering, yawning, whining, coughing, clearing the throat, sighing, and so forth, as well as such vocal segregates as the *uh–uh*, *uh–huh*, *uh*, and *tsk–tsk* in English for negation, affirmation, pause, and sympathy or sarcasm, respectively. Such vocal segregates can be expected to differ according to language. For example, the items listed are characteristic of English, while a long breath (*sssss*), usually drawn in over the teeth (used much like *uh* in English pausing) is a vocalization characteristic of Japanese.

Vocalizations may also be of a third type, vocal qualifiers, which provide modificational characteristics, such as the intensity (loud–soft continuum), the pitch height (high-pitch–low-pitch continuum), and the extent (the drawled-speech–clipped-speech continuum), of the articulation. Vocal qualifiers, of course, have been of particular interest to psychologists and psychiatrists insofar as they can be construed as indicative of an individual's mood or affect. An obvious prior consideration is noting which particular pattern of vocal qualifiers is characteristic of a given dialect, class, or ethnic heritage. For example, common notions are that a slow drawl is characteristic of some American Southern dialects and that the intensity "soft" is typical of much normal middle-class North American speech.

Voice qualities, on the other hand, are modificational aspects of language itself as well as modificational aspects of the kinds of vocalizations already mentioned. Such qualities can, according to Trager, be sorted out from what is said and what is actually heard. They might include such qualities as pitch range, vocal lip control, glottis control, pitch control, articulation control, rhythm control, resonance, and tempo.

It should be pointed out that paralanguage in this respect is not to be confused with the functionally operating units that comprise intonational phenomena in natural languages. Linguists have already paid some detailed attention to the problems of pitch, stress, and juncture in language, and paralanguage studies explicate related areas only when they are not coextensive with linguistic areas or when they modify them in a secondary sense. For example, English uses pitch, stress, and juncture in fashions that are analogous to phonemes in their uses for distinguishing between meaningful elements in the language.

Linguists taking a structural view are generally agreed that English uses four distinctive levels of pitch in intonational contours. In a normally uttered declarative sentence like *John went home,* we will hear a level mid pitch at the beginning of the phrase. It then shifts upward to a higher pitch on *home.* After reaching the higher pitch on the sentence-stressed word *home,* the pitch comes back down through the level pitch heard at the beginning of the sentence and goes even lower, finally trailing off into silence. We can thus distinguish so far among at least three pitch levels, low, mid, and high. If the sentence is turned into a question, *John went home?,* *home* is again the point at which the pitch goes to a level higher than the mid starting point, but this time it remains there. We can characterize the two sentences as having differing pitch patterns up to this point and mark the differences with the numbers $/1/$, $/2/$, and $/3/$, corresponding to the three levels of low, mid, and high, respectively. Pitch levels are normally marked at the beginning of sentences and phrases, at the points at which they change, and at the end. In short sentences like this, the most heavily stressed word in the sentence normally also receives the highest pitch. Thus, *John went home* as a statement would be [2]*John went* [3]*home*[1]; as a question, the sentence would be [2]*John went* [3]*home?*[3] Add to this set another sentence in which *John went home* is said to indicate surprise, and the speaker will likely go up another pitch level, to extra high, and stay there. Thus, the sentence of surprise can be transcribed as [2]*John went* [4]*home!?*[4]

There are not only different pitch levels but also extra rises or falls in intonation toward the next level of intonation up or down, but not quite reaching those levels. For example, in both the question and surprise versions of *John went home,* we notice a slight rise in the voice above and beyond that reached in levels /3/ and /4/, respectively. This can be considered a rising terminal, as distinctive a unit in the phonological system as the consonant /p/ or the pitch level /3/. Similarly, in the statement, *John went home,* we note that there is a falling in pitch and trailing off into silence at the very end of the sentence. This can be considered a falling terminal. Finally, in a sequence like *John went home, he said,* the transition between *home* and the quotative segment, *he said,* is usually neither rising nor falling but a sustained pitch from the phrase quoted to the segment *he said.* This pitch variable can be considered a sustained terminal, making the terminal total three. These are variously marked with arrows, ↗ for rising, ↘ for falling, and → for sustained, or with a single bar /|/, double bar /‖/, and double cross /#/, respectively. The differences are only in symbols and terminology, for they represent the same linguistic phenomenon.

Our three sentences (declarative, question, and surprise) can now be partially transcribed as the following:

²*John went* ³*home*¹ ↘   ²*John went* ³*home?*³↗   ²*John went* ⁴*home!?*⁴↗

We can look at the question of stress in a similar fashion. In English, stress is the relative prominence of articulation given one syllable as opposed to others. In monosyllabic words there is no question of stress, since words of one syllable can offer no differences in stress between different syllables. However, when we expand our horizons to two-syllable words, we find pairs like *permit* and *permit* that are identical in all phonological respects save one—they differ in stress placement. The verb *permit* has a strong stress on the second syllable, *–mít,* with a weaker stress on the first syllable, *pĕr–.* The noun *permit* has the opposite pattern, with the strong stress on *pér–* and the weak one on *–mĭt.* We thus have at least two degrees of stress, strong and weak, which for convenience we can mark as /´/ and /˘/, respectively.

Next, in polysyllabic words like *dictionary* and *animation,* we find a third degree of stress, intermediate between the strong and the weak one. The word *dictionary* appears to have an extremely strong stress on the first syllable, *díc–,* but another stress not quite as strong on the third syllable, *–nà–.* The symbol /`/ is used to indicate this tertiary stress. The remaining two syllables, *–tĭon* and *–rў,* appear to have very weak stresses, not at all as strong as the preceding two. We can thus transcribe the stress placement in *dictionary* as *díctĭonàrў.* On the other hand, the polysyllabic word *animation* appears to have its strongest stress on the third syllable, *–má–*, and a less forceful stress on the first syllable, *à–*. The other two syllables, *–nĭ–* and *–tĭon*, appear to carry weak stresses. We can thus represent the stress placement in *animation* as *ànĭmátĭon*.

If words occurred only in isolation, only three degrees of stress—primary, tertiary, and weak—would suffice to make all stress patterning. And, as a result, most dictionaries of the English language mark only three degrees of stress, for by and large what they obviously set out to do is to present words in list form in isolation. For larger constructions, some argue that another degree of stress may occur intermediate between the primary and the tertiary. This stress, the secondary stress (marked /ˆ/), occurs in longer constructions. In the adjective-plus-noun combinations, the noun head of the phrase still receives a stress, but the modifying form takes the primary and strongest stress. For example, say the following phrases and notice the stress placement: *a green house, a white house, a high chair,* and *a blue fish.* On the other hand, look-alike compound nouns may or may not have vowel differences, but they will definitely have stress differences in both kind and placement. Compound nouns in English usually have a primary stress on the first word and a tertiary on the second. For example, say the following phrases and again note the stress placement: *greenhouse, White House, highchair,* and *bluefish.* The stress differences can be illustrated as follows: *gréen hoûse* versus *gréenhoùse, whíte hoûse* versus *Whíte Hoùse, hígh châir* versus *híghchàir,* and *blúe fîsh* versus *blúefìsh.*

In adjective-plus-noun combinations, there is always a short but noticeable pause between the first word and the second. This pause is called by structural linguists the open juncture [or plus juncture, from the symbol (/+/) used to transcribe it] and is taken to be one of the distinctive units in the phonological structure of English. However, unlike the other kinds of phonological units, it is an open-ended abstraction that accounts for linguistic pauses and the phonetic variations that occur on either side of the pauses. The classic example used to illustrate the pause and the concomitant changes in the surrounding phonological environment is the words *night rate* and *nitrate*. First, notice that *nitrate* seems to flow on without the kind of interruption, or juncture, being discussed here, while *night rate* seems to exhibit such a pause. Moreover, the articulation of the /t/ before the /r/ in *nitrate* appears to be slightly rounded because of influence from the rounding of the following /r/. There is also fricativization, or turbulence of the airstream, a feature that normally accompanies /t/ before /r/ in English. On the other hand, the first /t/ in *night rate* exhibits none of these qualities and in general acts just as /t/ might in a final position. Rather than account for the allophonic variation in the two manifestations of the same phoneme /t/ by detailed explanations, structural linguists found it easier simply to establish a pause phoneme, the open juncture, and to note such changes as normally occurring phonetic variations on either side of the juncture. Thus, a full transcription of *night rate* and *nitrate* would have to include the juncture symbol and would look like *night + ràte* and *nítràte*.

We have up to this point discovered that besides the normally observable consonant and vowel phonemes that we have as a matter of course taken to constitute the phonology of the language, there are subtle but nonetheless describable phonological phenomena connected with systematic variation of the features of pitch, stress, and pause. We have counted no less than 12 such units, 4 of stress, 4 of juncture, either terminal or open, and 4 of pitch. A complete presentation of the phonological system of the language would just as dutifully include the pitch levels /1,2,3,4/, the stresses /´ ˆ ` ˜ /, and the junctures / ⟋ ⟍ → +/ as it would be the consonants /p,t,k,b,d,g,f,θ,s,š, h,v,ð,z,ž,č,ǰ,m,n,ŋ,l,r,w,y/ and the vowels /i,e,u,o,a,ɪ,ɛ,u,æ,ɔ,ə/ of the system.

The point to be made here is that such systems as the ones presented from English are known to occur in language, and they either have been or can be described for language structures. The variables of pitch, stress, and pause illustrated are part of the verbal behavior side of language and may differ from language to language, but they are nonetheless part of language. In talking of paralanguage, we are aiming at vocalizations that modify speech over and above these elements. In talking of pitch range, for example, Trager and other paralanguage investigators are talking about the variations in pitch range over and above the ways in which pitch is already used in distinctive and functionally contrasting ways. For example, in English this would mean over and above the specific uses of pitch already pressed into service by the language structure. Similarly, intensity would deal with the force and prominence of articulation over and above that implied in stress differentiation in words in English. Thus, the use of particular features in language structure must not be confused with their use as paralinguistic features.

And, incidentally, just as one can expect to find differences in the superficial aspects of phonology from language to language, one can expect to find differences in a paralinguistic sense. The intonational system of Russian differs in its use of pitch, stress, and juncture in a linguistic structural sense, and it is likely that paralinguistic features differ as well. Unfortunately, it may be premature to speculate about the nature of universals in paralanguage or, for that matter, in most other areas of interest in the study of nonverbal behavior. Most studies have concentrated on cultural differences in such nonverbal behaviors rather than seeking universal principles.

Some features are, of course, outside a speaker's conscious control. They are the result of certain physical characteristics that are either permanent or temporary, depending on the chronological stage of development. Certain physiological features, like the size of the resonating cavities, oral, nasal, and pharyngeal, as well as the length of the vocal tract, the bone structure of the head, and the presence or absence and condition of dental structure, all contribute to the voice set that particular speakers have. Linguists struggling to capture the nature of quickly disappearing languages have often had to rely on informants with damaged or missing dental structures for their analysis of phonological samples, and such oral characteristics obviously have an effect on the general nature of the speech set as well as production of certain segmental phonemes.

Other qualities are the result of differential development associated with chronological maturation. The voice of the child is indeed different from those of adult males and females, whose voices also differ. The child's voice will change in a way that is similar to other physical changes taking place as he matures. Such differences—for example, pitch levels—are present for man, woman, and child but are not equivalent in the physical sense. The pitch levels operate in a relative sense from speaker to speaker, such that a high (/3/) pitch level for a male is not the objective physical equivalent for a child or woman. But in relation to the other pitch levels within the child's system of pitch ranges, it is considered high, just as a high pitch level for the adult male or female is defined by reference to the other pitch levels in their relative systems of pitch usage. When we consider, for example, the differences in voice quality that such physiological disparity is responsible for, the communicative differences in voice set are immediately obvious. Some differences can be reproduced within the boundaries permitted by manipulation of the physiological apparatus to attain the desired effects. But such attempts take effort and practice and are not always possible, nor are they generalizable across a population.

Different voice sets characterize different language groups and even subgroups within our own English-speaking continuum. The quality that characterizes English in the West Indies or English on the Indian subcontinent is a learned behavior, much like the kind of vocal set that characterizes our North American voice set, and serves as a kind of signature behavior, as much a characteristic of membership in a specific cultural grouping as is body-motion behavior. It is not always easy to distinguish between the learned and unlearned aspects of such voice modifications, for most speakers are capable of modifying their basic voice-set qualities somewhat. Some professional entertainers are exceptionally adept at this kind of artifice and make an excellent living by masking their own voice characteristics to give surprisingly accurate imitations of other speakers in the community. It is difficult to assess just what degree of success is derived from imitation of voice set and other paralinguistic features and what degree is derived from both lexical content and other nonverbal behaviors coupled with **our own** expectations. Still, the mere presence of such people is sufficient to convince us of the existence of such markers as paralinguistic features.

Kinesics

The study of body movements, or kinesics, the term coined by Birdwhistell (1952), has received a great deal of attention in the past two or three decades. The popular eye has also recently focused on it under the guise of "body language." Kinesics as developed and elaborated by Birdwhistell (1952, 1966, 1968, 1970) seems an excellent point to begin discussion of the place of body movement in communication. Anyone who has learned how to behave in public is implicitly aware of the communicative quality of body behavior. To Birdwhistell and others, the kind of behavior exhibited in body motion, facial expression, and posture is expressive of an underlying system of behavior that is culturally conditioned and learned. It is comparable to language in the superficial structure that characterizes it as a coded system and in being different according to cultural settings and learned as a culture-specific kind of behavior.

There are other kinds of body movement that can be mentioned in passing but that are not the kind of body-motion activity focused on in such kinesic studies. For example, such stylized movements as the art of pantomime, the sign language employed by the deaf, and the sign language reputed to have been used by certain of the Western Amerindian trading tribes fit into the former category. So do stylized gestures used by trained public speakers and the individual gestures like the simple hand wave for *good-by* and the beckoning finger for *Come here!* Needless to say, such gestural movements are part and parcel of systematic behavioral codes and are worthy of study as such, but not in the sense intended here. Moreover, we must assume that such body-motion activities as blinking in reaction to dust particles, wild punches, and glare from the sun are also movements of a different order. The latter are truly instinctive and communicate less about the individual organism than they do about us as members of a species with specific abilities and ranges thereof.

Birdwhistell has devised a system of notation for all possible aspects of body movement. His system of notation is very similar to the levels of analysis in structural linguistics, with units like allokines and kinemes looking very much like allophones and phonemes. The ascending levels in structural linguistics are paralleled in kinesic explications of body behavior. Thus, a simple movement like the lift of an eyebrow and its return to its normal place can be a meaningful movement, signifying perhaps slight doubt, questioning, or uncertainty. Moreover, such kinemes may occur with features of language, thus modifying the meaning. The upward eyebrow movement might well occur with the terminal contour of a raised pitch at the end of a sentence, usually expressing a question or a request to repeat part or all of the message.

Although the facial musculature can produce possibly 20,000 expression variations, only a small number seems to be used in each language group. Birdwhistell claims to have so far isolated some 32 kinemes for middle-class North Americans in the face and head area alone. Such differentiated body movements include head nod, head tilt, brow variations, like lifted brow, lowered brow, and knit brow, eyelid variations, like overopen eyelids and squeezed eyelids, nose variations, like wrinkled nose and flared nostrils, and mouth variations, like protruded lips or overopen mouth, as signaling units in the communication system of body behavior. Meanings of such kinemes in isolation are difficult to establish, but, for example, overopen eyes might indicate surprise and astonishment, while an overopen mouth might indicate vacuous innocence as the "Oh, not me—I was just minding my own business" kind of look.

Usually, however, as with the features of language, it is not always possible to tell exactly what each given feature in the system means without reference to co-occurring features in the immediate behavior. The meaning of a specific gestural movement will be one of its possible signaling repertoire, dependent on the surrounding contextual features. This is highly reminiscent of the question of the meaning of words and disambiguation. Although more than one reading is possible for many lexical items, the co-occurring items in the sentence provide clues to exactly which of several possible semantic readings is actually intended.

Body motion and congruent body behaviors, like eye and facial expression, head disposition, body disposition and posture, and so forth, can be media of communication independent of verbal communication itself. However, Birdwhistell has found that such body-movement behavior comprises a system very much like that of spoken language in both the units that comprise it and the manner of their arrangement into longer, ordered sequences. Birdwhistell (1966) has also found that some features of this system of body behavior can be highly correlated with certain aspects of spoken language. For example, head, eye, and hand movements can be used to accompany pitch changes in the intonational contour that accompanies the syntactic unit.

Thus, the audible patterns of change in the intonational modification of language will also find parallels in the visible changes exhibited by such body parts as the head, the eyes, the eyelids, or the hands. In general, there appear to be three kinds of such markers. Speakers may drop both pitch level and body part at the end of declarative informational sentences, or they may raise pitch and body part with question sentences. Or, in the production of a series of words, phrases, or short sentences, speakers may hold both pitch and pertinent signaling body part level until completion of the entire unit. As a more specific example, our previous example of the raised eyebrow accompanying a final rise in pitch can be expanded to include the lowering of eyelids at the completion of sentence units to signal completion of the intonation contour and, consequently, the phrase or sentence. Or the eyelids may remain half open to signal points of continuation, just as a steady-pitch terminal juncture, without change by lowering or raising pitch, was seen to do the same.

Birdwhistell (1966) has also noted other kinesic markers closely associated with other linguistic features of discourse. For example, in referring to persons or things other than himself, the speaker may accompany his use of the appropriate pronoun by a distal movement of the head, hand, or finger. Conversely, in employing pronouns referring to himself or his people, proximate or metaphorical, the speaker may use a proximal movement. Similarly, differentiated movements may be associated with the pronouns *on, over, under, by,* and so forth.

Some, like Scheflen (1973), see the entire body orientation as being a metacommunicative commentary on the communication situation as well. Thus, a particular position is taken and maintained while some activity like explaining, passive protesting, listening, and questioning is engaged in. This position is held until the activity is completed or until it is interrupted by others. Because upon cessation or intention of cessation of this unit of behavioral activity the speaker will invariably shift his entire body placement or body orientation, it is a meta-communicative act. Obviously, such movements as head or eye movement or a shift in body posture are important facets of the feedback situation in communication interaction and play an important part in informing speakers whether listeners are agreeing, disagreeing, or even paying attention. Such movements also convey a fair amount of information to listeners about the relationship of the speaker to the message. For example, students can invariably deduce their teachers' interest in their subject, in teaching the subject, in entertaining questions in discussion or in private, and so on.

Such learned features on the part of a segment of the population are reminiscent of variety in language arising from social and regional differences. Such markers can accurately pinpoint membership in certain regional and socioeconomic groups. In this respect, the study of certain kinds of kinesic activities can be viewed as similar to dialectology; in fact, Birdwhistell has proposed kinesic dialectology as a viable area of investigation. These features contribute to what can be called signature behavior in that they contribute to identifying characteristics in the close-knit groups of family, community, and region.

We have been examining cultural norms for kinesic behavior. However, individuals may develop their own personal and idiosyncratic variations on these gestural themes. The result is that a given person or family, or even perhaps all the males in a family, have a particular variation of the expected kinesic behavior in a form uniquely theirs. This can be seen in a shake of the head, an averting of the eyes at certain points, or a deferential moving of the hand across the face. Some, like LaBarre (1964), find nothing untoward about the possibility of idiolects in such activities as walking, and we can only surmise that just as signature behavior marks us as belonging to one or another relatively well-defined group, some characteristics set the confines of our own personal and idiosyncratic signature behavior in that larger scene.

Posture is also an important feature, and as Hewes (1957) has pointed out, the body is capable of assuming about 1000 static postures that can be maintained in comfort for a reasonable period. Besides the physiological considerations that limit posture choice, there appear to be cultural preferences in usage. Although the variety in basic postures is not as startling as that of more observable superficial characteristics, it does prompt one to speculate on the effect of such differences in man's cultural evolution in different areas of the world. Since such postural differences are often linked with such amenities of everyday life as clothing, tools, furniture, and so forth, some of these articles of material culture may have been influenced by postural behavior in various groups as well as by the more obvious factor of the environment (heat , damp, mud). For example, in Japan one traditionally finds low furniture, the cushion-like *zabuton,* and sleeping *futon* for use on *tatami* mats woven of rice straw. These can be contrasted with high furniture, chairs, desks, and beds as solid immovable fixtures in North America. It may be that, as Hewes implies, the origin of such differences lies in the different postural behaviors traditionally found in these two parts of the world. One cannot pursue this topic too far, but the speculative glimmer it provides may be well worth considering at least momentarily.

Proxemics

The area of personal and social distance has been recently studied by Hall (1963, 1966, 1968, 1972) and others. Hall has labeled this inquiry the study of proxemics, and the choice of name at least suggests parallels between proxetics and proxemics and other kinds of etic–emic investigative enterprises in linguistics and anthropology. Hall has also provided a detailed notational system for proxemic behaviors along a number of dimensions, such as postural–sex identifiers, voice loudness, and factors like closeness and the potential for actual body contact.

That spatial separation and appropriate distancing serve an expressive, communicative function can be tested simply enough by moving into another's personal and intimate space. The other person will react by either retreating or acquiescing to the approach by subtly changing his behavior to make it more congruent with the kinds of behavior deemed appropriate for such distances. Such distance zones apparently vary with the degree of familiarity and intimacy and, if language is actually involved, in the kind of content to be discussed. The distances vary from culture to culture and are correlated with other kinds of behaviors, like eye contact, voice volume, and so forth. For example, in North American culture eye contact apparently invites some kind of interaction, and if intimacy already exists or if it is desired by one or both of the individuals, it will be present or will be actively sought. On the other hand, to ensure personal privacy in walking down the street, for example, one's eyes may be averted from those of others, thus discouraging any kind of interaction. Or people on buses or in waiting rooms in depots and airports may seek appropriately spaced seating arrangements to ensure their own personal space. If such seating is unavailable because of a large crowd, they will at least avert their eyes so as to avoid contact and thus discourage interaction.

Hall has described four main spatial-distance relations that North Americans normally use in their interactions. These four zones, intimate, personal, social, and public, correlate highly with vocal qualities, especially the volume of articulation. For Hall, then, these are spatial zones appropriate to various types of interactions. If one crosses the boundary of a particular zone, the other person is likely either to move back or to change his behavior to comply with the pattern of interaction deemed appropriate to that particular distance. For example, intimate distances are reserved for our most personal and private activities, and clearly for those alone who are intimate enough to enter this zone without discomfort. At such a distance as the intimate zone, individuals are obviously fairly closely involved with each other, and their awareness of each other is heightened by the coordination of the other senses, since at this distance olfaction, touch, body heat, and breath sensations all combine to signal the presence of another being. One can immediately see why violation of this particular zonal boundary, with its special connotations, can be either insulting or threatening when it is unexpected and uncalled for. Individuals immediately become wary when this and other boundaries are overstepped unexpectedly, and they react appropriately. Members of cultures that use spatiality in ways different from those of general North American white culture are thus easily misinterpreted when they read a specific distance with their usual cultural values. The same can also be true of individuals within the same culture, as, for example, when an upper-middle-class Anglo-Saxon descendant marries someone of second-generation or third-generation eastern European immigrant background; the differences are there and may lead to misunderstanding.

The next zone, personal distance, is the spatial zone that is commonly employed in conversations with familiars or casual acquaintances without undue intimacy or formality. Personal distance, or "keeping someone at arm's length" in Hall's figurative term, is a distance at which one is close enough to observe details of his colocutor's features. The inside area of the zone brings the individuals close enough for further physical interaction, such as touching or shaking hands. Social distance, from 4 to 12 feet, is commonly employed for a range of activities from impersonal exchanges to conversation at social gatherings. Impersonal exchanges of a business-like nature, such as transactions with clerks, milkmen, handymen, bank tellers, and so forth, also take place at this distance. The inside area of this zone appears to be used by people who work together. The public zone is the one used by speakers in a public or formal capacity, such as teachers, lecturers, politicians, and chairmen of meetings. Each of these spatial zones—intimate, personal, social, and public—has closer and farther areas, and greater involvement is implied by use of the closer area in a particular zone.

In attempting to show possible correlations between voice volume, verbal content, and the spatial zones of interaction, Hall (1959) earlier postulated eight spatial zones of interaction somewhat like the following. The very close zone, from 3 to 6 inches, is characterized by a type of interaction best described as top secret or intimate, and the voice volume appears as a whisper; the close zone, from 8 to 12 inches, as very confidential, and as an audible whisper; the near zone, from 12 to 20 inches, as confidential, and as a soft voice; the neutral zone, from 20 to 36 inches, as personal subject matter, and as a soft voice at low volume; the neutral zone, from $4\frac{1}{2}$ to 5 feet, as impersonal information, and as a full voice; the public zone, from $5\frac{1}{2}$ to 8 feet, as information available for others to hear and as a slightly overloud voice; the across-room zone, from 8 to 20 feet, as a loud voice directed to a group; and the hailing-distance zone, from 20 to 24 feet indoors and up to 100 feet outdoors, used in departures and calling utterances in a loud or shouting voice.

The Question of Universals

Other approaches to the study of nonverbal communication have been seen in those studies directed less toward explaining the nature of nonverbal behavior than toward relating aspects of nonverbal behavior to emotive content, personality characteristics of the communicants, their reactions to the communication situation, and other variables. For example, work done by Ekman and his colleagues (Ekman & Friesen, 1967, 1968; Ekman, Friesen, & Tomkins, 1971) has attempted to fill in such gaps by investigating what kinds of information can be carried by nonverbal behavior of the body-motion kind. In general, they have found that such nonverbal behaviors as body movement, body and head postures, and facial expressions do in fact transmit valuable information about the emotional state of the one emitting the nonverbal signals. Moreover, such features also provide substantial clues to the intensity of the emotional state of the individual. The information conveyed by such features appears to be regularly and reliably agreed upon by others and, as such, would appear to be an important index of attitude and emotional state.

Ekman and his colleagues have also found that posed facial behavior is judged as depicting the same emotions across a number of cultures, both preliterate and literate. Contrary to the previously discussed view that posed (or rather unposed) facial behavior is a set of culturally bound and culturally learned conventions, Ekman's investigation of such posed facial behavior across a dozen cultures has challenged the view that such behavior has no relationship to spontaneous facial behavior. By extension, one can argue that it is highly unlikely that a number of divergent cultures would have independently developed the same facial poses for the portrayal of such emotions. What may be reflected, suggest Ekman and his colleagues, is that we may be tapping some universal element in the use of facial behavior in the expression of emotions, or at least in the expression of particular emotions. The implication is clearly that there appears to be a universal association, regardless of culture or country, between particular facial poses and particular emotions. This does not necessarily mean that all aspects of facial poses are universal. Although the musculature involved appears to remain constant, the stimuli that give rise to a particular facial pose may differ from culture to culture, as well as the manner in which the pose is displayed and the consequences of it. According to Ekman and his colleagues, these do vary greatly from culture to culture in their more superficial culturally conditioned aspects. Such investigations, of course, carry the vestiges of the universals-versus-specifics argument seen in previous discussions. Many, especially those anthropologists like Birdwhistell and Hall working in this area, would see much nonverbal behavior as entirely culture-specific and culturally relative. On the other hand, according to the results of an increasing number of investigations, like those of Ekman and his colleagues, certain nonverbal activities appear to be species-specific and, as such, are universal in their use and their meaningfulness.

Ekman and others' work can best be discussed in the light of the argument over what is specific and what is universal. It may be that certain kinds of nonverbal communication, like the gestures and kinesic activity that accompany language and the general kinesic activity and spatial sets that are systems in themselves, are culture-specific. On the other hand, certain activities may be similar, identical, or even universal across culture lines. Some of these may include those activities related to dominance and superiority, courtship and mating, expression of emotions, and so forth. The problem at this point, of course, is that we are not entirely sure of where to draw the line between the end of universals and the beginning of specifics though both types of studies inevitably flesh out our knowledge of this highly challenging field of human activity.

Hesitation Phenomena

A fair amount of work has also been done on what have been termed speech disturbances and hesitation phenomena in speech and what these may tell about the speaker. Such disturbances in the speech flow as stuttering, pausing, repeating, sequencing, and so forth have been suggested as possibly being indicative of emotional states of speakers. However, most such investigations have been related to interview situations in psychotherapy and similar settings, as examination of the literature exemplified by Mahl (1956), Pittenger, Hockett, and Danehy (1960), Gottschalk (1961), Matarazzo, Wiens, and Saslow (1965), Matarazzo, Wiens, Matarazzo, and Saslow (1968), and McQuown (1971) serves to indicate. Because such investigations concentrate on the interactive and possible predictive and/or behavior modification aspects of such characteristics for interview purposes, they are not pursued any further here.

However, some studies of hesitation phenomena have provided valuable information about the nature of the structure of speech itself. Goldman-Eisler (1964, 1965) has provided evidence for hesitation pauses preceding the least redundant items in speech processing. Thus, there appear to be relative difficulties at the various choice points as the stream of spoken speech progresses, and hesitation phenomena become much more likely and much more frequent at those points where greater lexical choice or greater syntactic planning is involved. Her work also suggests that the structuring of sentences is to some extent a matter of linguistic skill rather than of planning, a consideration that overlaps with experimental psycholinguistic concerns.

Goldman-Eisler (1964, 1968) also reports that the length of the pause correlates significantly with the content to be expressed by the rather ingenious device of asking individuals to state the point of captionless cartoons. Prior to this task, individuals were required to describe captionless cartoons. Obviously, it is more difficult to state the point of a cartoon than simply to describe it, and this was taken as a measure of difficulty of content. Not surprisingly, the length of the pauses in the former exercise was twice as great as in the latter exercise, and obviously not at all related to syntactic complexity.

Maclay and Osgood (1959) earlier also showed that a pause is more likely to precede lexical, or content, words than function words. Such function words—determiners, prepositions, and so forth—may in fact be repeated together with a recorrected lexical word, almost as if they were an integral and automatic part of the phrase. Goldman-Eisler (1968) has more recently summarized her work on spontaneous speech and what it shows of the processes in speech production. To Goldman-Eisler, pauses, in both their location and their distribution, are vital clues to the underlying cognitive processing involved in the production of language, with pausing often accompanying decisions of a content kind as well as of the grammatical kind. However, this is not to say that pausing as such is not an integral part of language use; on the contrary, Goldman-Eisler observes that the actual percentage of pausing time, though obviously subject to individual variation, is sufficient to consider pausing as much a part of speech as actual vocal utterance. For example, spontaneous speech, even at its most fluent, can be shown to be highly fragmented, with as much as two-thirds of the spoken language coming in chunks of less than six words.

Nonverbal Communication and Education

In concluding, we must admire the contributions that have systematized areas that were often by-passed because of their seeming inaccessibility. The systems developed by such researchers have been highly detailed ones and suggestive of other areas of inquiry as well as providing the methodological tools for application in these other areas. Some of the earlier major contributions, however, were directed at the analysis of the structural aspects of what constitutes such nonverbal communicative systems of behavior, not at what such nonverbal behavior communicates about the personality structures of the individuals using them. Some recent popular magazines publicizing body-language approaches by providing reference glosses to what various movements and postures may mean, and how to understand and perhaps take advantage of them, have been somewhat misleading on the state of our knowledge. Still, some service has been done by again calling our attention to this facet of interaction and suggesting that closer attention be given to such matters in pedagogical and social practice. For example, in pedagogical practice many of us spend at least a decade, and possibly two, learning various aspects of spoken language in the form of reading, writing, public speaking, literature, and so forth, but not very much attention is given to the process of nonverbal communication. It would appear that our pedagogical interpretation of interaction is one very much like caricature figures, immobile cutouts on a plain field of white interacting with one another through the medium of word-carrying balloons issuing from our lips. However, as evidenced by what we do about it, and not what we say about it, such nonverbal cues as body movement and posture say a great deal about us and how we view ourselves and about the situation we find ourselves in at the moment, so this process may yet find a place in our educational approaches to socialization.

As Byers and Byers (1972) so aptly point out, our traditional educational concept of communication has been one of information, parcels of knowledge in the form of facts, concepts, and beliefs easily packaged and easily transferable from individual to individual. A good deal of pedagogical practice is directed at enlarging the possibilities for storage capacity or filling that capacity with valuable information to meet whatever social contingencies may arise in the individual's progression through his intellectual and social life. In fact, a good deal of social evaluation, according to this point of view, is assumed to be based on just how much knowledge can be stored and just how accessible it is in terms of recall and reproduction under the appropriate circumstances. Language is, of course, the carrier for such attitudes and is the means by which such practices are effected.

Although such attitudes are perhaps the ones that are used in actual accomplishments in the fields of science and technology, they may not be conducive to other desirable attributes in interpersonal communication, other than the learning and transmitting of content. If we instead look at the situation as a process, it becomes obvious that some concern with the range and interpenetration of verbal and nonverbal communication is required. Since it is clear from the preceding discussions that there is a great deal more to the act of communication than simple verbal transmission of factual content by words, it seems only reasonable that this fact be reflected in our other pedagogical practices as well. Indeed, if verbal competence merits so much of our energies in a descriptive, analytical, and pedagogical sense, it should follow that a similar treatment of the code of nonverbal competence is also in order.

7

Language and Meaning

The Meaning of *Meaning*

All would agree that verbal labels are of significance in the realm of abstract ideas. Without the ability to make abstractions on the one hand and the possibility of symbolic behavior on the other, our linguistic powers would be of small use. An analysis of the relationship between language and meaning attempts to examine just this relationship between abstraction and symbolic representation. Needless to say, there have been many approaches to the study of meaning, each concentrating on some aspect of what the relationship might be.

Probably more than any other area of language behavior, the argument over the meaning of *meaning* serves to recall the importance of agreement on the exact boundaries of the object of one's investigation or theoretical constructs. The best approach for us is to survey some of the avenues to meaning that have been used over the past several decades and to review what information these have provided about the nature of meaning in language or language-related behaviors. From the outset, it may be wise to acknowledge that there are different subsets of the concept of meaning in such investigations, so that we

153

are really talking about meaning$_1$, meaning$_2$, meaning$_3$, and so on. Simply because they have all been pursued under the same label of *meaning* does not mean that they are all compatible in a single theoretical view of language or that they fulfill the same functions in language behavior. This is simply a function of the procedural fact that one must methodologically overlook all other aspects of the phenomenon to concentrate on one's own, but doing so does not invalidate or deny the existence of the others.

Scholars have usually attempted to break down the larger question of "What is meaning?" into smaller, more modest questions. Obviously, the answer to each of such questions is in some way a part of the answer to the total question. The point is that answering such subparts of the total meaning question gives us grounds for establishing what fits into the realm of semantics to be explored and correspondingly answered by the specific theory of meaning we are interested in pursuing. Each of these and other questions on the nature of semantic properties will have to be answered before a theory of meaning can be forthcoming. Another major problem is how to frame the theory that will express these semantic properties and semantic relations. Again, the solution will lie in what is considered to be part of the semantic domain and what is not. It will also very directly relate to the format of the theory and will obviously provide its own input for work in experimental psycholinguistics thereafter.

In a structuralist vein, meaning was taken as representing an area of human experience too diverse to account for adequately without resorting to man's knowledge of the universe. Bloomfield (1933) and those with similar methodological beliefs saw language as being composed of two aspects, one physical and the other psychological. The former was the expression side of language, its actual manifestations in sound patterns, discernible by other speakers–hearers of the language. The latter was the content side of language, the meanings intended to be conveyed by these discernible sound patterns. The problem of how to describe meaning was often by-passed in favor of more accessible areas of language, but certain units were labeled as the possible carriers of meaning. Phonemes were viewed as only those signaling units that could potentially differentiate meaning-bearing units, as for example, in *pit* and *bit*. The morpheme was seen as the possible carrier of meaning, be it lexical or structural.

The dichotomy between lexical and structural meaning was recognized as necessary to account for the qualitative differences in information conveyed by linguistic elements. In a sentence like *Nero gave the boy the slave*, whatever one knows that is not a direct result of the lexical meanings of *Nero, gave, boy, slave,* and perhaps *the,* can be attributed to structural meaning. Dictionary-like definitions of the listed words do not give anywhere near the total semantic configuration of the sentence; a great deal of information is yet to be accounted for. For example, if the sentence read *Nero gave the slave the boy* or *The slave gave Nero the boy,* the semantic reading of the sentence would be different even though the elements composing the sentence remained the same. Such information, of course, was considered the stuff grammars were to be made of.

Relational Ties between Words

Words never played a very large part in such investigations of language because precise definitions were emphasized, and words do not readily lend themselves to precise definition. Hockett (1958) once suggested that any sentence segment bounded by points at which pausing is possible constitutes a possible definition of the word. This seems a tautological definition at best, but it represents the best effort to define a concept like word in terms of structural requirements alone, without reference to what the word does in carrying meaning.

There is little doubt of the speaker's awareness of words as some kind of unit in language, as Sapir's findings (see Mandelbaum, 1949) regarding teaching Indian informants how to write down their own languages imply. Perhaps speakers of languages that have writing systems have had less success in defining the nature of words because of conditioning by years of experience with the idiosyncratic nature of word representation in black and white. The notion of word has had a kinder history in psychological usage and has figured heavily in a number of such investigations, such as word-association studies.

Structuralist activity thus turned from what was felt to be linguistically irrelevant to the linguistically relevant and from the unattainable to the attainable. Investigations in this genre had to avoid any reference to psychological factors that might imply related mental processes. There could be no other meaning than the situations in which speakers might use linguistic utterances and the responses those utterances might bring from those who heard them. It is little wonder that Bloomfield himself felt that the study of semantics would not progress very far until our knowledge was greatly expanded, for in his view, a knowledge of semantics could be equated with man's knowledge of himself and the world he inhabits.

At least we can agree with the view that there is more to the question of meaning than immediately meets the academic eye. Meaning has many faces, and claiming that any one approach has extracted the true essence of meaning would be to overlook the other meanings of *meaning*. Even if one entertains the simpler notion of the dualism of sound and sense as being the essence of meaning, the situation is not as straightforward as one might wish it to be. If language were other than human and thus not predictably imperfect, every referent in the real world might have only one name in each language. Assessing meaning would then be simply a matter of inventorying each word and its single referent. Moving from one language to another would just involve the translation of lists of words and the things they stand for. But, as Ullmann (1962) has pointed out, we must allow for multiple meanings of a single name. For example, a single term like *conductor* can have at least the meanings of "one who directs an orchestra," "an official collector of tickets on trains and buses and so forth," and "something that transmits electricity, heat, sound, and so forth." Conversely, a single or a similar sense can be conveyed by differing words, as in *oculist* and *eye doctor* or in *little, small, tiny, wee,* and *undersized.*

More often than not, however, word and meaning, or name and sense in Ullmann's terms, are interwoven into a complex network of relationships that are set off by having similar synonyms, by sounding completely or partially alike, by belonging to the same part-of-speech class, or by having any one of a number of ties possible for words and their senses. Any number of possible relationships are cued by the sound of the item, its meaning, or a combination of the two. Once the framework includes the further relationships these items may have, even more semantic and phonological ties are possible. As in ad hoc categories of other types, one item can suggest any one of a very large number of other possible items through the intersection of such relationships. And the larger the frame of reference, the larger the number of relationships that can then be established under its ad hoc guiding principle. For example, *table* and *chair* are obviously cues for each other, and so, perhaps, are *bed* and *dresser*. But it does not seem likely that their presence in the same category would be felt as strongly as their immediate ties to each other until the superordinate category of *furniture* is added.

Such organizational shifts consistently occur when the frame of reference is changed. To use a common example, read the following list one word at a time by using a piece of paper to cover up all the rest of the words. Quickly read the word and let words and thoughts associated with that item flit through your linguistic consciousness. Then move the paper down one space so as to be able to read the next word.

gravity
seriousness
death
grave
specific gravity
weight
kilogram
pound
dollar
yen
desire
passion
emotion
gravity

With each successive move, new horizons are opened and others closed. Those terms with several different meanings (**polysemy**) are seen as belonging to one or another frame of reference, which shifts as new information is added. The lingusitic situation is not unlike the optical illusion that appears as first one thing and then another. However, these optical illusions usually present only two possibilities to the perceptual apparatus; polysemy and word associations present multifaceted possibilities.

This is reminiscent of the "tip-of-the-tongue" phenomenon reported by Brown and McNeill (1966). Having individuals search for some word that is on the tip of the tongue but cannot be immediately recalled is felt to give some idea of how words may be stored in the memory. For example, subjects might be given a definition like "navigational instrument used in measuring angular distances, especially the altitude of the sun, moon, and stars at sea," and be asked to recall the word. Chances are that the individuals cannot, and instead come up with words like *astrolabe, compass, protractor, secant, sextet,* and *sexton,* not the correct *sextant.* The terms *astrolabe, compass,* and *protractor* all might have been suggestive of the function performed and thus similar to the desired word in content, while *secant, sexton,* and *sextet* all might have been suggestive of the word in their phonological shape (the first syllable).

Another kind of word-association study involves presenting a stimulus word to subjects and asking them to respond with the first word that comes to mind. Thus, the experimenter may say *table* and receive *chair* in return or say *bread* and receive *butter* in return. A large number of such presentations is made in order to assess the uniformity of response across members of the sample linguistic community and the frequency with which the responses occur. The word-association method has been employed since after the turn of the century as a means of illustrating the kinds of meaning networks that exist for lexical items in a language.

In the word-associationist view of meaning, words are stimuli that evoke reactions. The reactions are a function of the domain ties individual words have with other words in the network of language in the mind. These associations obviously offer some commentary on how vocabulary items are stored in the mind. They appear to be almost like little switchboards, with ties running off to various other lexical items related by some similarity in meaning or phonological shape, opposition by antonym, membership in the same subclass or part-of speech class, or any one of a number of frequently occurring features. It would appear even at a casual glance that more frequently occurring vocabulary items are more likely to elicit more speedy responses and that the responses will be more uniform across the linguistic community. *Table* may elicit *chair* from a large number of speakers, but it is unlikely that *aardvark* or *puffin* would prompt either speedy or uniform responses.

Some researchers, such as Noble (1952, 1963) and Deese (1962, 1965), have attempted to use the associational qualities of vocabulary items as a measure of meaning. For example, Noble listed the number of associations given to a specific word by a representative sample of speakers during a given time interval; meaningfulness thus takes on a quantitative sense. In such studies, the meaningfulness quotients of words are presented by averaging or relating the associations given by subjects. As with all other such averaging methodologies, it is difficult to say just what the result reflects other than a leveling of the actual data. Still, the method does commend itself as a cumulative value for the kind of meaning-bearing relationships between vocabulary items shown by word-association studies. The interesting aspect of tests of time-period association is that they do reveal some of the facets of polysemy, or multiple meaning, that characterize most words in the language. Rather than providing a single response to a single stimulus instantly, a hazy picture of the different meanings of the word and their weblike relationships to other items can be shown, or at least this is part of the intention.

For an account of the possible relationships between word associations and linguistic theory, see Clark (1970) for a position that views word associations as more of a side-product consequence of the ability to produce and understand sentences. Clark implies that such associational ties between words do not play any fundamental part in the acquisition and use of language.

One thing is clear though. The same reference problem that plagues a simple dualism in the view of meaning as the relationship between the sounded name and the actual thing is also true for associations. It seems clear enough that the associations a word has cannot be the meaning of the word. If this were so, the word would not symbolize some referent but would stand for the associations linked with it. Instead, associations seem to provide a set of verbal clues to the manner in which they appear. The basic notion is that both the single association and the massed time–number continuum of associations represent some amount, greater or smaller, of the meaning a word has. But it would appear that such association methods do not reveal the nature of meaning itself, though they are indeed telling us some very important facts about the realization of meanings for words.

The Semantic Differential

Osgood and his colleagues present an excellent example of those who view meaning as an internal mediating process. This concept of meaning is, of course, congruent with the mediational attitude toward the nature of language itself, which was discussed in Chapter 2. In their attempt to establish concrete ways of measuring such internal processes, Osgood and his colleagues developed a measuring device called the **semantic differential.** Essentially, the semantic differential represents an approach to the investigation of the connotative aspects of meaning. **Denotative meaning,** of course, refers to the object or range of objects that a verbal label actually stands for, while **connotative meaning** refers to the attitudes and emotional reactions speakers have toward a given verbal label.

The semantic differential is consistent with Osgood's efforts to answer objections to more simplistic versions of learning theory that attempt to explain all behavior in conditioning terms. The question is a crucial one in the analysis of meaning, for it would appear that here and in the matter of acquisition the learning-theory approaches face their biggest tests. Skinner's functional analysis, as was discussed, would be categorically disposed to omit any mentalistic considerations in dealing with meaning, for these are not congruent with direct stimulus–response relationships and with the concepts of reinforcement, extinction, and so forth. This is unfortunate, since the meaning side of language seems to be the most striking in our daily interactions. Osgood does admit mentalistic considerations and maintains that meanings are the central mediating processes between the word and any possible external related behaviors. The meaning of a given item is an internalized subset of the total behavior repertoire for that item. Thus, for Osgood, meaning is an acquired entity, and the way in which it is acquired is a reflection of the process of conditioning. But this is not the kind of conditioning that one has been led to expect in experimental cases of conditioning salivating dogs and maze-meandering rats. This is a kind of conditioning more like the unobservable response that some stimulus might elicit from the central nervous system—quiet and covert but nevertheless real and present. Meaning thus serves as the breaking point between the stimulus itself and the response behavior it might have been associated with in more classical terms. In this view, what is conditioned is actually a partial response to the item or experience, and this partial reaction is attached to and becomes the meaning of the word for the item or experience. Such reactions are thus responses, yet they can become stimuli in their own right, so that they are at once the reactions of speakers to lingusitic events and a spur to other kinds of behavior in response to the reaction aroused by the initial utterance of the word. Meaning is the go-between stage, or, in Osgood's terms, the mediator.

One must take care not to expect knee-jerk or lever-pressing responses. The mediating responses here are of a more subtle nature and take shape as the mental reactions that speakers have to the words they acquire. The problem is an individual one, since individuals acquire words and reflect internalized values of such language experiences. To tap this lodestone of meaningfulness, Osgood and his colleagues proposed the simple but charmingly ingenious device called the semantic differential.

The semantic differential is a convenient measuring device to work with because, like other statistically oriented devices, it offers easy data-gathering methods, an air of objectivity, relatively straightforward tabulation methods, and the possibility of comparative profiles. Subjects are presented with a word, concept, or whatever and asked to record their judgments of that item along a seven-point scale. The scales represent a number of continua that Osgood and his colleagues have found to be reliable indicators of such meaning approaches. The continua are usually three in number: the **evaluative** dimension, shown by such oppositions as good–bad, kind–cruel, pleasant–unpleasant, and heavenly–hellish; the **potency** dimension, shown by such oppositions as hard–soft, strong–weak, large–small, and heavy–light; and the **activity** dimension, shown by such oppositions as slow–fast and active–passive. There are other possible dimensions, and semantic differential scales can be established using any number of possible oppositions for whatever purpose desired, but Osgood and his colleagues have found that the three general factors of evaluation, potency, and activity account for an important percentage of the meanings of most words.

Procedurally, subjects are requested to mark their impressions of a word on the seven-point scale according to whether they view them as being, for example, extremely good, very good, good, neutral, bad, very bad, or extremely bad. Thus, if one had no feelings one way or the other about a word, one would mark the middle slot, indicating neutrality. Take, for example, the word *mother*, and mark it according to the way in which the word strikes you as being meaningful on the following sample semantic differential.

mother

good ___ : ___ : ___ : ___ : ___ : ___ : ___ bad

kind ___ : ___ : ___ : ___ : ___ : ___ : ___ cruel

weak ___ : ___ : ___ : ___ : ___ : ___ : ___ strong

beautiful ___ : ___ : ___ : ___ : ___ : ___ : ___ ugly

nice ___ : ___ : ___ : ___ : ___ : ___ : ___ awful

active ___ : ___ : ___ : ___ : ___ : ___ : ___ passive

positive ___ : ___ : ___ : ___ : ___ : ___ : ___ negative

heavenly ___ : ___ : ___ : ___ : ___ : ___ : ___ hellish

reputable ___ : ___ : ___ : ___ : ___ : ___ : ___ disreputable

large ___ : ___ : ___ : ___ : ___ : ___ : ___ small

One can immediately see the usefulness of such a measuring device and its easy applicability to a variety of situations in which definitions and measurements of attitudes were previously impractical, if not impossible. The scale has also been used in concept evaluation, music appreciation, and other equally diverse activities. Once the oppositions are tabulated, one can locate the particular meaning of a specific word, concept, or experience on a semantic space determined by the three dimensions of evaluation, potency, and activity. The reactions of different groups to different words can also be measured, providing some indication of differential attitudes toward given subjects. Still another application of the device is the measurement of the evaluative use of different dialect varieties—that is, the assessment of the differences between one group's reaction and another's. This application, of course, applies to individuals as well, so that the technique can be used to trace the chronological history of a given individual's evaluation of a given word or concept. One of the more dramatic applications of the technique was its early use by Osgood and Luria (1954) in assessing personality evaluations in a case of classical multiple-personality split later publicized by the best-selling book *The Three*

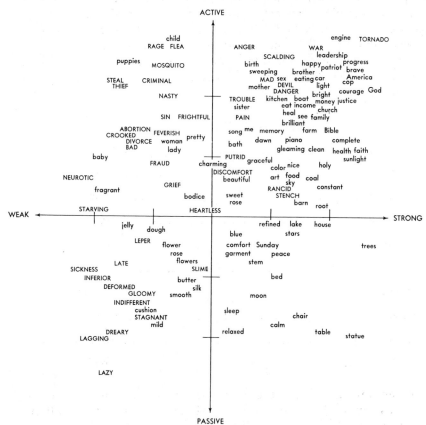

Figure 7.1 An example of semantic profiles for some English words. [From J. B. Carroll, *Language and Thought*, © 1964. Reprinted by permission of Prentice-Hall, Inc., Englewood Cliffs, New Jersey.]

Faces of Eve and the related Oscar-winning movie. The three personalities that characterized the young woman's emotional states differed dramatically in the evaluations by the semantic differential technique as applied to self-concepts.

Since the appearance of a wide scale of the semantic differential technique in the early 1950s, it has been frequently used in both unicultural and cross-cultural (see Osgood, 1964) investigations of meanings and concepts. Cross-cultural comparisons are difficult enough when dealing with material traits, and so the suggestion of a universal framework underlying affective, or connotative, aspects of language was most welcome. Moreover, the semantic differential, because of the manner of its construction, offered a way of getting around the language barrier usually involved in such studies. Atlases of semantic profiles have been available for some time (see Jenkins, Russell, & Suci, 1958), and an idea of the tremendous number of studies the semantic differential has either influenced or generated can be gained from a glance at Bobren, Hill, Snider, and Osgood's (1968) impressive interim bibliography.

Figure 7.1 shows Carroll's (1964) presentation of the semantic profiles reported by Jenkins *et al.* (1958). It lists the locations of the concepts relative to the two polar dimensions of active–passive and weak–strong. The concepts are also rated in a third dimension, good–bad, with the words in lower-case letters rated as good and those in capitals rated as bad.

Semantics and Linguistic Theory

The semantic differential approach measures the connotative meanings of words for individual speakers of a language. Individual speakers have differing emotional and intellectual reactions to words and what they stand for, and the semantic differential affords a method of measurement that throws such individual differences into sharper focus than they were before. However, the method does not tell enough about what it is that language has in a unified sense. As was the case with the associational aspects of meaning, the connotational aspects of meaning cannot be simply equated with meaning. We must look elsewhere for some kind of description of the denotational aspects of language—that is, what all speakers have in common with respect to the semantic content of language. We may also have to include some account of how such semantic knowledge is reflected in the universal theory of the structure of language. One method of solving this dilemma has been evident in the extension of generative grammatical theory into the area of semantics (Katz & Fodor, 1963; Katz & Postal, 1964; N. Chomsky, 1965).

Generative grammarians see the investigation of meaning as inextricably tied to the examination of grammatical abilities. The grammatical structure of the language is the finite set of rules that allows an infinite range of ideas to be expressed through a potentially infinite number of sentences. Thus, the essence of meaning, in such terms, is the relationship between that infinite set of ideas and that infinite set of sentences. However, in language the best we can do is to admit lexical items as representative of some such ideas and find the structure of these. So the task is, first, to find out what the inherent structure in that world of lexical items representing ideas is and, second, to figure out how such notions are then mapped onto grammatical structures in the language. Generative grammarians already seem to have a fairly good idea of how the infinite range of sentences is to be described, or at least how it should be described. The problem has been to find an analogous system for tapping the infinite range of language-appearing notions and describing them in similar fashion by a finite set of units and rules governing those units.

Such attempts to synthesize the nature of meanings have been linked to an approach to semantics that is congruent with the general theory of language embodied in generative grammar. This sort of theory fills in the gaps left after a complete syntactic description of the language has attempted to exhaust the abilities that must be included in a formal description. Obviously, speakers have other abilities regarding sentences that were not covered by the conventions established by N. Chomsky's earlier discussions.

In this approach, meaning is defined and described much as Chomsky's syntactic component in a generative grammar is, purely in terms of the operations within the language itself. A set of rules attempts to portray the universal aspects of meaning in language and depicts the actually occurring surface-structure collocations of the atoms of meaning in specific languages. Such an approach clearly includes in the scope of its concerns what speakers must know about the meanings of the constituent words of sentences to be able to interpret sentences correctly. Thus, in this view, the meaning the analyst is concerned with is the one derived from its syntactic context—that is, the one arising from the permissible collocations it appears in and excluding the ones in which it does not appear. Such a concern clearly lends itself to a feature-oriented analysis, for all one must do now is to find out what the feature-like units that match or do not match in the process of collocation are.

Moreover, this direction nullifies previous attempts to keep the study of grammatical features of language separate and distinct from semantic concerns. The question is no longer whether semantic rules are rules that relate languages to the real world and whether grammatical rules are rules that only relate linguistic items within the confines of language structure itself. The notion of such rules and what they encompass can best be prefaced by referring to a discussion by McIntosh (1961). On the level of phonology, rules of sequencing permit strings like *thistle, heed,* and *flint* as well as *histle, geed,* and *plint.* The rules are not specific in which blanks are to be filled in or not filled in; they merely specify the shapes that words in a language normally take. By the same token, the rules prohibit certain shapes like **pdilb* and **brdliou.* Perhaps this is what is so poignant about Al Capp's Dogpatch character Joe Btfsplk—even his name suggests the unspeakable fate that seems to follow both him and whomever he touches.

The rules of syntax are similar in this respect. They provide for sequences like *The old man seems to have gone out of his mind* and *I'll meet you for lunch at twelve tomorrow* as well as for sequences like *The flaming wastepaper basket snored violently* and *The spectacled lollipop ate the molten armadillo.* The rules prohibit sequences like **Twenty because tomorrow the had a it* and **Inherent paint the in wild actually chariots windfall.* However, sentences of the type dealing with burning wastepaper baskets and short-sighted lollipops do seem a bit odd and not just from their not having occurred before; sentences like *Thirty-nine linguists invested in an old abandoned salt mine* and *My mother-in-law retired to a resort at the perimeter of the South Pole* are equally original, but they do not share the same kind of eccentricity. The former type seems to violate some kind of restriction that must be coded in the way the language operates for all speakers, and this restriction must be taken as part of the abilities of speakers in assessing their competence.

Speakers know, for example, that certain sentences are ambiguous in ways that syntax does not explain. Katz and Fodor's example (1963) of *The bill is large* is indicative of this ability. If non-native speakers are presented with such a sentence, they cannot possibly account for the ambiguity even if they are provided with a complete grammatical description of the language. Native speakers, on the other hand, instantly recognize the ambiguity inherent in the sentence and obviously exhibit interpretative abilities in resolving it. Apparently, a grammatical description is insufficient in its account of certain aspects of speakers' interpretative abilities, so that such cases of ambiguity are resolved on the basis of other information. Moreover, given additions to the sentence like *The bill was large, but the meal was worth it; The bill was large, but fortunately the cabbie was able to change it;* and *The bill was large, which is a characteristic of all toucans from this part of Amazonia,* speakers immediately refer back to the initial part and resolve the problem of ambiguity on the basis of such additional semantic information.

Native speakers are also able to recognize anomalous sentences, sentences that somehow differ from the normal, expected type but are clearly exponents of properly coded higher-order grammatical rules. *Silent paint, the flaming wastepaper basket,* and *The giggly eraser sidled up to the voluptuous pipe cleaner* are all examples of anomaly. They are all well formed from a grammatical point of view, though they do indeed deviate from some rules of which speakers are only too aware.

Finally, speakers are able to paraphrase sentences as well as individual words. Not too much has been made of this ability, for much of the feature development of semantic theory along the lines suggested by early generative grammarians has taken the first two abilities as the setting-out point for the creation of rules. To some degree, the problem of paraphrase is accounted for by lexical items that have extremely similar feature representations. For example, one would expect pairs like *eye doctor–oculist, old maid–spinster, boxer–prize fighter,* and so on to be shown as similar in their representation in the lexicon. However, the problem of sentence paraphrase is answered only in those cases in which the individual lexical items are similar in this respect and in which sentence paraphrasing can reflect this fact.

Speakers are thus characterized as having some internalized lexicon that is employed in the production of sentences. Moreover, there must be a set of rules for combining such entries in the lexicon in ways that correspond to the sequences that comprise the grammatical sentences of the language. Consider the word *bachelor.* Figure 7.2 indicates the way in which defining semantic markers delimit the boundaries of meaning for such an item. The unenclosed marker gives the grammatical category to which the item in question belongs; in this case, *bachelor* is a noun. The further feature of count might have been added, indicating that *bachelor* occurs in certain syntactic phrases like *some bachelors.* Other words, however, do not; the phrases **some confettis* and **some rices,* when speaking of the generic term, are ungrammatical. There are also semantic markers like animal, human, and male, which serve to distinguish the meaning of the word by referring to that specific part of the word that is vital in making the distinction. Finally, specific and idiosyncratic meanings of the word itself (enclosed in brackets in the diagram) are listed for each individual word.

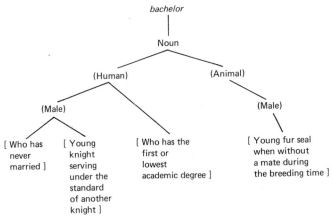

Figure 7.2 An early example of a semantic theory. [From J. J. Katz and J. A. Fodor, "The Structure of a Semantic Theory," *Language* 39 (1963): 170–210. Reprinted by permission of the authors and the Linguistic Society of America.]

The grammatical and semantic markers obviously correspond to what is regular and systematic in the language, and the distinguishers refer to that which is not and which varies form word to word.

This approach to semantic theory takes up the slack in Chomsky's earlier treatment (almost entirely devoted to syntax) as an integrated whole, and it is not surprising to see aspects of this view of semantics incorporated into Chomsky's later version (1965) of language theory. Essentially, providing for such abilities as sentence interpretation on the basis of synonymy, ambiguity, anomaly, and so forth had made possible the systematic listing of all the semantic components that make up the meanings of words. It is an interesting complementation and one that cannot be overlooked, for just as a knowledge of the meaning of individual words gives no clue to the meaning of sentences, a knowledge of sentence production gives no clue to the meaningful end product of true sentences in language.

The structure of a semantic theory in this view is, then, one concerned with discovering the atoms that make up the semantic identities of items in the lexicon of the language. Just as distinctive features in phonology reflect a small number of universal features that can be used to describe all sounds in all languages, semantic features can be viewed as a restricted set of semantic atoms that are at the heart of meaning in language. This approach is based on feature analysis and reflects a past trend in descriptive methodology in anthropology, linguistics, and related fields.

It may be instructive to assess the use of the concept of feature analysis in both linguistics and disciplines related to lingusitics, for the notion of feature analysis is at the basis of the view of semantic structure presented by Katz and Fodor's earlier treatment (1963) and Chomsky's later discussion (1965). It also finds its way indirectly into some aspects of later generative semanticists' views and branches out from the treatment of semantic categories in languages to the analysis of single words themselves. In fact, the analysis of meaning by semantic features is very similar to distinctive-feature analysis of speech sounds in generative phonology and the use of componential analysis in anthropology.

Earlier work by Goodenough (1956) and Lounsbury (1956) provides clues to the future of feature-oriented componential analysis. Goodenough's study (1956) was essentially an ethnoscience treatment of Trukese-kinship analysis, but it was presented in a fashion intended to call attention to the problem of deriving significata from kinship terms and determining which of these forms go together in semantic systems. Meaning in this respect is to be considered as **signification,** completely distinct from connotation. Such an analysis would answer what one would have to know about two persons to say that one is the other's brother or cousin or aunt. Obviously, individuals must have certain criteria by which they judge, for example, that a given person is or is not another's cousin in the particular kinship system under consideration. Meaning in the signification sense is thus the particular set of criteria by which judgments like this are made.

Moreover, as Lounsbury (1956) points out, the categories need not be overt but may be covert, though nevertheless real. For example, in comparing the following partial kinship sets, in English and Spanish,

uncle–aunt	*tio–tia*
son–daughter	*hijo–hija*
brother–sister	*hermano–hermana*

one immediately notices that both language sets have distinctive terms for the male kin term and the female kin term. That the male kin term is signaled in Spanish by an *–o* ending and the female kin term by an *–a* ending does not in any way alter the fact that both languages differentiate between male and female kin terms in the kinship paradigm. The overt manifestation in Spanish is a feature of that language and can be considered an overt category, but the situation in English is no less real because it is not signaled overtly. Rather, it is simply a covert category. In addition to drawing this conclusion, we have extracted a single atom of meaning, male as opposed to female, with which we can define the differences between *uncle, son,* and *brother* as a group, as opposed to *aunt, daughter,* and *sister* as a group.

This notion of feature analysis was elaborated into a sophisticated method of dealing with compact and tightly defined systems like kinship in which the boundaries of a given semantic field within a given language–culture setting can be defined by means of a small set of variable features. Each term—such as kin terms—can be defined within that field by listing the features that define it. Each term has a feature in common with the meanings of all the other items in the set, and yet each term differs from each other form by at least one feature. Thus, we can point out similarities between all the terms that share a given feature, such as "male," which relates to all the members of the set *father, son, uncle, brother, grandson,* and so forth. Or we can specify "ascending generation" to mark *father, mother, uncle, aunt,* and so forth, as distinct from its opposite feature, "descending generation," which might mark *son, daughter, grandson, nephew,* and *niece.* The common feature of kinship is what relates all the members of this particular semantic field, and the notion of separate atom-like features of meaning is what enables us to define each term in relation to every other term in a way that allows us to point up both their similarities and their differences within that field. For example, Figure 7.3 illustrates how the eight kinship terms *father, mother, uncle, aunt, son, daughter, nephew,* and *niece* relate neatly along the continua of generation, sex, and lineality.

Such descriptions of meaning by feature analysis are clearly denotational enterprises, as opposed to the description of meaning by, say, the semantic differential. The starting point is the notion that components can be factored out as a set of defining features providing critical information about the attributes by which such terms are recognized within the field they inhabit. The problem, of course, is whether such concepts as feature analysis can be applied to nonrestricted fields like language at large. Ethnolinguistic investigations successfully using the device of componential analysis have usually been limited to relatively restricted areas of cultural experience like kinship, color categories, ethnobotany, disease, and so on. Generative grammatical theory's application of the concept of feature analysis is to a far broader field, the semantics of natural languages.

This interface between the supposedly separate levels of syntactic

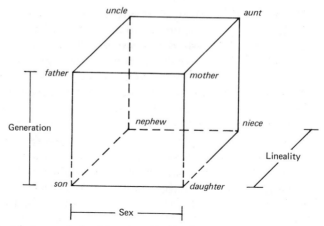

Figure 7.3 A feature analysis of American kinship. [From R. Brown, *Social Psychology*. Reprinted by permission of the author and Macmillan Publishing Co., Inc., New York. Copyright © 1965 by Macmillan Publishing Co.]

rules and semantic rules simply reunites them into a continuum of rule-oriented structures within the organizational framework of language. However, it should be noted that there are limits to this kind of semantic investigation, for it answers only certain questions about the nature of meaning that are contained within the nature of syntactic collocation. We can establish semantic rules that provide subclasses for the part-of-speech categories, thus outlining which subclasses may occur with which other ones. For example, *spectacled lollipop* violates the constraint that *spectacled* is an adjectival normally occurring with nouns of an animate human subclass; *wastepaper basket snored* appears to violate the constraint that permits only animate nouns with intransitive verbs like *snore*; and *John found sad* appears to violate the constraint that calls for nouns as objects of transitive verbs like *found*, while *John seems sad* is satisfactory in its collocation of a linking verb like *seems* with an adjective like *sad*. The rules can be of a higher-order syntactic type, as in the last example, or they can be even more fine-grained and deal purely with collocation, as in the first two examples. This is obviously one facet of meaning in language, and it provides for our interpretations of certain linguistic sequences as being special. It also provides a basis for some kinds of literary analysis and metaphor, since some aspects of such investigations of language involve analysis of the way in which utterances are creative, original, and flamboyant. A deviation from the expected collocational norm is certainly one way to achieve all three, and such syntactic–semantic rule analysis provides an objective method of dealing with them.

If each individual word is seen as having unique dictionary definitions and yet is to be encompassed within a uniquely restricted lexical
field, such definitions will have to be dependent on a sort of
componential-analysis breakdown of meanings of words by reference
to atoms of meaning. These atom-like units were termed semantic
markers by Katz and Fodor and appear as selectional features in
Chomsky's discussion. Such markers, or semantic features, express a
characteristic shared by an entire group of words and set it off from
other groups of words, which presumably are characterized by similar
defining features. Examples include animate–inanimate, human–nonhuman, count–noncount, male–female, and so on.

It is not entirely clear what constitutes an objective method of
choosing among those features that should be included in the description, for some features are clearly semantic in origin, such as
human–nonhuman, and others, such as count–noncount, may reflect
grammatical parallels as well. The latter feature more or less reflects
whether items like *dog, cat, boy, hen, wagon, dirt, sincerity,* and *slime*
take overtly manifested plurals. *Dogs, cats, boys, hens,* and *wagons* do,
but *dirt, sincerity,* and *slime* do not.

Another factor is that nouns that are specified for such lexical features are to be marked for a cluster of these in a complex symbol fashion, for this is what constitutes their semantic identity in the lexicon.
However, the manner of presentation in hierarchical fashion is not the
method best suited to this situation; it would appear that nouns and
other such lexical entries are better cross-classified in their presentation. The problem is not unlike a card-sort in which items are marked
for their distinguishing characteristics on a number of points. When
one wants to recall all those items marked for having a specific characteristic, it is easy to recall just those items by poking a long needle
through unpunched holes in the cards, activating electronic sensors on
a computer, or whatever. For example, for just two features, four possibilities may occur in a two-item set. They may both have the characteristics in question (+ and +), or neither may have them (− and −),
or they may each have one but in different combinations (+ and −; −
and +). Thus, it is possible to see immediately just which of the characteristics are present, which items show these characteristics, how
large is the population of items (in a sample set of more than two
items) that shows the characteristic, and so forth. Adding another
characteristic produces groups of varying sizes according to their similarities and differences along the dimensions employed in the definition of the items.

Applying these notions to the lexical description of nouns like *John,*

Egypt, boy, and *book,* we can specify their entries in the lexicon in the following fashion (see Chomsky, 1965):

John:	+ proper, + human
Egypt:	+ proper, − human
boy:	− proper, + human
book:	− proper, − human

The feature of plus or minus (±) proper refers to whether the noun belongs to a set of proper names (with consequent restrictions on occurrence with determiners like *the, a, some,* and so forth, plus capitalization features if one considers the orthographical version in the rule output). The feature of ± human signifies whether the noun refers to a human referent. This convention uniquely specifies our four sample nouns as having or not having this pair of semantic features and also points up their similarities and dissimilarities in this respect. *John* is similar to *Egypt* in being marked + proper but similar to *boy* in being marked + human. *Boy* is similar to *book* in being marked − proper but different from *book* in being marked + human. *Book* shares the feature of − human with *Egypt,* and so on. Each form is uniquely identified, but it is defined with respect to the other nouns that constitute the class.

If we add several other nouns like *dog, slime,* and *sincerity* to the example, we will have to add several more features to refine our lexical description to approximate a larger and more complex system. One of those that we will have to add is the feature of animate to account for the *boy–dog* distinctions. The feature of animate is a step above the feature of human, for everything that is marked + human is automatically + animate. But the reverse is not true; not everything that is marked + animate is automatically + human. Reduction in the actual entry form for each noun can be achieved by recourse to rules that take into account such redundancy factors. Thus, all items that are marked + human can automatically be taken as being also marked + animate. This may seem an idle comment at this time, but if one thinks of the task of identifying all of the thousands upon thousands of possible nouns in the language by their feature specifications for inclusion in the dictionary-like lexicon attached to the grammar, it will be clear that this one redundancy rule saves an enormous amount of time, space, and effort, yet provides exactly the same information.

We will also have to add the feature of count to our description to account for the fact that items like *slime* and *sincerity* are not pluralizable but *boy, book,* and *dog* are. We might even wish to add the specification of abstraction and list *slime* as − abstract and *sincerity* as +

abstract. Our sample of − proper nouns might now look like the following:

boy:	− proper, + count, + animate, + human, − abstract
book:	− proper, + count, − animate, − human, − abstract
dog:	− proper, + count, + animate, − human, − abstract
slime:	− proper, − count, − animate, − human, − abstract
sincerity:	− proper, − count, − animate, − human, + abstract

Once again, each item is uniquely specified in a manner that provides its own lexical identity by selectional features that can also be expected to mesh with appropriate grammatical rules or semantic collocational rules or both. For example, transitive verbs like *frighten, terrify, kill, wound, pursue,* and so forth could be marked as occurring only with nouns marked + animate, such as *John, boy,* and *dog.* One cannot *frighten a book, *wound the slime,* or *terrify sincerity* except in a metaphorical sense. What gives metaphor its poignancy is that it is somehow once removed from the first level of priorities of how items collocate in sentences. Thus, the phrases *antique gentleman* and *elderly armchair* are clever turns of phrase simply because they are not common and hence not trite.

Similarly, one can mark verbs like *persuade, convince, marry,* and *invite* as occurring only with direct-object nouns that are marked + human. One can have sentences like *He persuaded John, He convinced the boy, Jill married Jack,* and *Sue invited Cathy to the party,* but not sentences like *He persuaded sincerity, *He convinced the slime, *Jill married the armadillo,* and *Sue invited the tomato to the party.*

Part-of-speech categories are seen as large categorical units that occur in specific grammatical positions and are developed later in the grammar as being populated with individual lexical items uniquely specified in terms of characteristics that can easily be applied to the description of collocation privileges. That part-of-speech categories are now marked for such features makes the problem of collocation with other part-of-speech categories less difficult than it seemed and clearly puts the treatment of semantics within the boundaries of language behavior treated by a comprehensive linguistic theory. Providing a systematic answer to the description of collocational privileges in the language also provides a systematic answer to the problems previously raised by ambiguity, anomaly, and paraphrase.

However, certain other questions that do imply a knowledge of the relationship between meaning and our knowledge of the real world are not answered in this fashion. Sentences like *Most men have three eyes* and *Most Hindus are fond of rare roast beef* provide a facet to the study of meaning that is not covered by the semantic-feature and collocation type of analysis offered by Chomsky and Katz and Fodor. Such utterances can be meaningfully interpreted, but they run counter to our knowledge of the universe. True, one can find contexts in which they might occur, but one can do the same for the sentences previously listed as being somehow odd or unique. It is a matter of first priorities, and on that level of priorities, it would still appear that more is involved in our assessment of *Most men have three eyes.* This is also an area in the study of language that will have to be explored in our study of semantics; it involves presupposition, entailment, and so forth.

The semantic theory discussed here does not deal with the language user's knowledge of his extralinguistic surroundings. Sentences like *Most men have three eyes,* which appears to violate our knowledge of human physiognomy, or even sentences like *Most Hindus are fond of rare roast beef,* which violates what many of us know vaguely about India and Hindu reverence for cattle and life in general, appear to be well formed grammatically and even semantically according to the structure of the theory and the domains with which it is concerned. The theory is concerned only with what all speakers of the language know as a reflection of their common knowledge of the way the world of conceivable meanings is reflected in actual language. No attempt is made to explain why certain interpretations are given to sentences in one context as opposed to another. The theory takes as its main objective the task of accounting for the possible semantic reading or readings of grammatically well-formed sentences; the purpose of the theory is not to explain why a sentence is uttered or what its interpretation is according to the situation or the current state of knowledge. Thus, the system would appear to be entirely bounded by linguistic criteria themselves, though the question does arise as to just what the semantic features comprising the identifying set are based on, if not the real world itself. Still, the accomplishment is a noteworthy one, for no previous theory was able to account for the interpenetration of such semantic and syntactic information in such a systematic way.

At least one kind of analysis that tackles the problems involved in both paraphrase and speakers' knowledge of the real-world relationships expressed in sentences is Fillmore's (1968) discussion of **case** in language. Fillmore is perhaps not directly interested in paraphrase possibilities, but such relationships are implicitly pointed out in his demonstration of invariable caselike relationships in language. For example, in a set of sentences like the following, the relationships underlying the sentences themselves are invariable: *The door opened, John opened the door, The key opened the door, John opened the door with the* *key*, and *The door was opened by John with a key*. It is always John who is the initiator of the action, and the agent whereby the action is effected. It is always the door that is the recipient of the action and that which is opened. It is always the key that opens the door as an instrument by which the action takes place. The actual surface-structure manifestations of the sentences do not matter, since these case relationships are invariable and underlie the interpretation of each sentence. Fillmore has labeled these relationships case, possibly for the likeness they suggest to the caselike relationships of nouns to the verb predicate in the traditional analysis of classical languages. In those languages, as well as in some modern languages of our Indo-European group, surface-structure case is shown by affixes attached to the nouns in question that clearly mark their manner of participation in the sentence. In English, and probably in all languages, the relationships are invariable, Fillmore would argue, and the actual surface manifestation of a sentence is not necessarily a clue to the real case interpretation that underlies its formation.

In sentences like *John broke the window* and *A rock broke the window*, the deep-structure case analysis of the relationships is constant despite the superficial similarity of the sentence structures. John is the agent in the first sentence, and the rock is the instrument in the second. Conversely, sentences like *John fought with a knife, John fought with a hoodlum*, and *John fought with a friend (at his side)* can all be seen as representing different case relationships.

In a sense, one can still maintain that syntactic rules and semantic rules are to some degree interwoven, with semantics being on a continuum with syntactics. But this applies only to the manner in which such case relationships are actually shown by the mechanisms in language and does not necessarily refer to the semantic knowledge underlying the interpretation of such sentences. This can be illustrated by the fact that there are other kinds of knowledge underlying such interpretations, as in the ambiguity underlying the sentence *John paints nudes*. The ambiguity in this case refers to prior existence before the activity. John may be either a modern painter who paints designs on nude bodies or a classical buff after the style of Modigliani or Utamaro. The same thing could be said of the differences between the verbs *smash* and *build* in sentences like *John smashed the table* and *John built the table*. What is implied is a knowledge underlying the interpretation of language utterances that surpasses what can be presented in the two-dimensional models of semantics already presented.

An even more semantically oriented description is presented by Chafe (1970), in which the nature of semantic ordering and semantic knowledge is considered first, and the overt manifestations of language second. In other circles, generative semanticists also appear to be moving toward an alternative approach in which such semantic considerations are the most important in any description of the relationships within language. In fact, some approaches have simply considered semantics as not only the starting point of linguistic analysis but also the central focus of linguistic theory.

Some hint of this shift can be seen in the work done on such semantic notions as **focus** and **presupposition**. The focus of a sentence is the part that contains the intonation center or that presents some new information; presupposition, on the other hand, involves those conditions which the sentence presupposes to be true. Obviously, such incursions into definite semantic realms are removed from the narrower view of semantics characterized by Katz and Fodor (1963). Some, like Fillmore (1971), would also maintain that the lexicon should also contain information on "happiness conditions" that must be satisfied before the lexical items can be used properly. This kind of approach is congruent with arguments advanced by philosophers of language like Searle (1969), who demand that consideration of speech acts be an integral part of any theory of language. One result of this tendency toward incorporation of this kind of "semantic" information in the description of the language is to blur the distinction between performance and competence, a tendency likely to be applauded by many.

What such approaches can mean in the description of language is yet to be seen, but they may portend a split in the analysis of the different levels, with one kind of linguistic knowledge being contributed by the analysis of the overt side of language and another kind by the analysis of the suppositions and conditions underlying language expression. This split is reminiscent of the time when the provinces of disciplines like linguistics and philosophy were viewed to be similar to the above, though it also seems to portend a melding of the two areas of semantic knowledge in a comprehensive theory of their relationship not yet entirely worked out. It may be that the two areas are in fact one and the same, but it is one thing to write rules that portray the grammatical and semantic constraints operating within language and another to equate this with the natural processes involved in meaning and the production of sentences to carry that meaning. We may be left, after all, with describing two separate faces of meaning, one that involves the relationships that exist between the linguistic units themselves and another that might take into account the relationship of linguistic expression to phenomena occurring outside language itself.

Language Statistics and Stylistics

Probability, Redundancy, and Information

Statistical models of language analysis have been used to make inferences about language, particularly style. The application of mathematical and statistical views to language is perhaps not as common now as it once was. Two decades or so ago, statistical methods and applications were suggested as keys to the understanding of language in some quarters. Some suggested that at least such statistical methods could tell us a great deal of what actually happens in the structure of language itself. It has been applied most successfully to the analysis of information-transferral probabilities in communications codes and in the investigation of style.

The application of methods of mathematical statistics can provide interesting insights into the performance side of language as well as ways to assess the internal relationships of items and structures in language as a system of recurring parts. However, mathematical measurement does not automatically provide one with the key to what language is about. It merely tells what the frequency of occurrence of these items and arrangements may be with respect to other items and arrangements. Such observations are based on a random sampling of the data, from which one constructs frequency distributions. Dependent on the size and quality of the sample, one can attempt to generalize about the characteristics of linguistic features and infer probability measures of their appearance in other language manifestations. Probability in this respect is hardly more than an observation that if one's sample is a reflection of all natural-language instances in this linguistic system, a given item will have the same or a similar frequency of distribution in language in general. Such is rarely the case, and such judgments are approximations. An excellent example is the commentary made by Cherry (1966) on a statistical count of 25,000 words of British telephone conversation in which *mudguard* was one of the most frequently used words. *Mudguard* is not one of the all-time frequent choices of English speakers, of course; it is a result of the sampling itself.

The other possibility is to use such statistical measures to analyze individual samples of language to derive measurable parameters of identification. Thus, in a literary analysis one singles out a number of variables to investigate one author's work or changing styles in a single author's career. Previously, such analyses have been mostly intuitive. Moreover, such techniques can be applied to language samples from a wide range of linguistic sources, from suicide notes to instances of disputed authorship.

In their origins, such mathematically formulated approaches may have nothing to do with theoretical speculations about language probability and frequency structure, but they may be of interest in specific fields. For example, an earlier model that held great promise in psychology, linguistics, and consequently psycholinguistics was information theory, the brain child of communication engineers designing such communications systems as the telephone and telegraph. They used probability to assess predictability within a system and hence the amount of information actually conveyed by any single event within a given system. There was some similarity between information theory as developed by Shannon and Weaver (1949) and the behavioristic theory transplanted in early psycholinguistics, which is probably why it figures so importantly in earlier psycholinguistics discussions. As a theory of the nature of language, its main use has been as the Markov process models that N. Chomsky (1957) attacks as being less adequate than phrase-structure and transformational grammars. Still, the theory and methodology is of some import for the part it plays in psycholinguistics as well as other sciences; its general approach continues to suggest tactics for handling bounded samples of data characterized by transitional probabilities.

All systems must by their very nature have some degree of organization, and where there is organization and regularity, there is predictability. If a system is perfectly organized and perfectly regular, there would be perfect predictability, and from the point of view of chance, there would be none but a set and given alternative for each event in the system. Think of a train company that runs a train regularly at 8:15 AM every day. This train is never early, never late; the Bullet Express is always on time. In information theory the train's departure every morning offers no alternatives and hence conveys no information. Only when the train runs at random times, say, 8:14, 8:13, 8:17, 9:05, 9:27, and so forth, without predictability, is information conveyed. True, it is information of the most irritating sort. Nothing in our culture is so irritating as waiting for unpredictable transportation. One has a system with complete predictability (the trains always run on time) and hence no new information in the technical sense, for one knows a priori that the train runs invariably at 8:15. Each time one lines up for that 8:15, one is learning nothing new, for we knew by the very nature of the organizational system that it would leave at exactly that time and only that time. However, when the train runs at slightly varying times, it is only when the event happens that we are assured of its actually happening, and we are learning a new piece of information each time that the train actually sets out on its runs. There is no predictability within this system, and, consequently, there is a maximum amount of information each time.

To move the example a little more into the realm of chance, toss a coin. A coin can go only two ways, and the result of the toss does not in that sense tell us as much as it might have if we had been dealing with a 32-sided Venusian coin. A system with 32 alternatives, random in occurrence, provides us with more alternatives and hence greater uncertainty than a system with two randomly occurring alternatives. The amount of uncertainty is greater, and the reduction of uncertainty is of a greater magnitude when measured statistically. Thus, **information** in the sense used in information theory refers to the reduction of uncertainty and its measurement.

Information is a measurement term. It cannot (Miller, 1953) be directly equated with meaning, or even with notions of truth or content. It is simply a reflection of the actually occurring states in a system of events or states as measured in respect to what could, within the limits of that system, actually occur. A checkerboard has 32 squares.

Assume that I am thinking of one of these squares. The observer must guess which of these 32 squares I have in mind. One can proceed by trial-and-error guessing which of these squares is actually the one. One could guess 32 times before hitting upon the particular square, or guess on the first or tenth try. However, if one proceeds by a process of binary divisions, cutting the alternatives by half each successive time, the number of times one will have to do this is only by five such binary divisions. Let us say that the square in question is the square marked with an X, as in the following diagram.

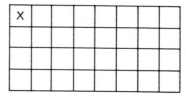

One can immediately proceed by asking whether the square is in the right-hand group of 16 squares. If the answer is no, this group is immediately eliminated from further consideration. If the square had been in that group, it would conversely have eliminated the opposite set of 16 squares instead. Thus, we are left with our left-hand group of 16 squares:

We can now ask whether the particular square is in the right-hand group of eight squares. Again, if the answer is no, as it is, these eight are eliminated from further consideration, and we are left with eight squares.

Again, we can ask whether the square is in the right-hand grouping of four squares, and if the answer is no, we again eliminate these from further consideration, leaving us with the following set.

We can now ask whether the square is in the top group of two squares, and if the answer is yes, we eliminate our bottom grouping of two squares, and we are left with the following.

Our last question might now be whether the square is the top one, and if the answer is yes, we have eliminated the bottom square and have at the same time arrived at the square in question by no more than a total of five choice points. The guessing was not random but directed, and it can be repeated on any system or set of 32 equally occurring random alternatives. We have accomplished this by reducing our uncertainty by half each time, and the number of times we have been able to do this has been five times before reaching the appropriate alternative. Thus, this particular fact has conveyed five pieces of information, or as the technical term has it, five **bits** of information, on the basis of a single alternative within a 32-alternative system. Each time the number of alternatives is cut by half, one bit of information is gained. The implication is obvious. We are now in a position to measure information in a mathemetical sense and to make observations and comparisons about the amount of information carried by different systems. We can also make technical observations about what may enhance or disturb the transmission of information now that we have an objective measurement.

This same reasoning is also what makes the game "Twenty Questions" workable. "Twenty Questions" allows the guesser to progress through successive choice points, beginning with animal, vegetable, or mineral, until he narrows the range of possibilities to the likely one. Information theory thus puts together two familiar concepts. Chance is familiar to all, algorithm less so, but both are at the basis of this assessment technique.

However, systems are never completely randomly occurring. For example, someone may know from playing the checkerboard game with me that I always choose a square from the left-hand grouping of 16 or that I have a predilection for choosing a square on the far outside line of squares on the left-hand side of the board. Though the number of alternatives remains the same, the probability of their occurrence is definitely not the same, and one can predict with some reliability that certain states will occur more frequently than others. Clearly, certain events are more likely to occur than others, and the more information we have about the states immediately preceding a choice point, the more likely it is that we will be able to predict accurately which states will occur. This can be applied directly to language, where it would appear that the system of events we call verbal communication, either spoken or written, is in general not a chance sequence of events but a series of events with differing probabilities. And given that one linguistic item occurs, it to some degree predicts or narrows the possibilities for what the next linguistic unit will be. Natural languages, it has been said, generally appear to hover about the 50% redundancy level in this respect, though specific aspects of language may go above or below this level.

The writing system of English is an example of the conditional probabilities implied in redundancy. Given the nature of orthographic redundancy in English writing and the conditional probabilities of the 26 letters, plus the open space between words (a total of 27 possibilities, excluding punctuation), one can predict the choices that may occur. The first spot may be filled with the letter symbols. A likely choice might be T, but not so likely is X. Still, any one of the letters may occur, but it is more likely that T will be the choice, not X.

According to the orthographic conventions in English, having filled in the first letter slot with T, X is definitely not a candidate for the next slot, nor are Z, K, P, and a number of others. However, H is a likely candidate, as are A, E, I, R, and others. Say, for example, that H fills the slot, and one now has the sequence TH and ponders the occurrence of the next item. Again, certain items are ruled out: Z, K, P, and a number of others. Each new choice point presents a series of possible alternatives conditioned by what immediately preceded. Here one might choose A, O, E, R, and several others, but the choices are again restricted.

Let us use Gleason's concrete example (1961) and say that we have actually taken a sample of English writing and have found that the 26 letters of the alphabet have the following frequencies initially:[1]

---

[1] From H. A. Gleason, *An Introduction to Descriptive Linguistics*, 1955, 1961. Reprinted by permission of Holt, Rinehart & Winston, Inc., New York.

T	.23		R	.02
I	.13		C	.01
A	.10		Y	.01
H	.08		D	.01
S	.08		E	.00
W	.07		G	.00
B	.06		J	.00
M	.04		U	.00
F	.04		V	.00
N	.03		Q	.00
O	.02		K	.00
P	.02		X	.00
L	.02		Z	.00

Letters with .00 frequency do occur initially in the language. This set of frequencies stands only for **our** language sample, which is not the same as the entire language. Probabilities are direct reflections of the number of times an item will occur. Probability measures what occurs, not what could occur.

Also, if the 26 letters in the alphabet had the same occurrence frequencies, their frequency would be .038 for each letter. But if a small number of letters exceeds that figure, the majority falls below. Redundancy is thus already present in the first choice, for certain letters are more likely to occur in initial position than others. Some letters, like T, are well above the average; in fact, T is 6.1 times more frequent. Other letters are well below the average, occurring infrequently in this position. If all the letter alternatives were equally possible, the information value conveyed would be 4.70. As it is, only 3.10 bits of information are conveyed by sentence-initial letter choices in this English sample. The average redundancy in Gleason's example is thus 34% for the first choice point in the appearance of sentence-initial letters.

If the first letter is T, likely according to the previous figures, then the freedom of choice is again restricted, even more so than for the initial slot. One must work out an entirely new set of contingency probabilities to take into account one preceding slot filled with the letter T. The letter H in this sample has a probability of 88%, O about 6%, and letters like A, E, I, U, W, R, and so forth less. The redundancy for this slot now rises to 83%.

Say the slot is filled by H. The third slot will likely be filled by E with 83% possibility, I 8%, A 3%, and so on. One now has a sequence THE and another choice point. If the sentence begins with THE, the empty space setting off word boundaries (and counting as a unit) has 53% probability of occurrence, Y 18%, N 14%, R 12%, and so on. Redundancy is essentially repeated, or predictable, information; sometimes the redundancy is 100%, as in English with U after Q, but this is not the rule.

Generally, the more choices that precede a point, the more restricted is the probability of an item's appearing in that context. For example, given *HE WAS THE MAN I SAW AT THE BEAC_*, the choice is obviously limited to H and O, as in *beach* and *beacon*. And in *HE WAS THE MAN I SAW YESTERDA_*, there is only one choice, Y. Moreover, there appear to be differences between the signaling capacities of certain items within a system, as, for example, between consonants and vowels. The sequence

$$A \mid \_ O \_ \_ I \_ \_ \mid \_ \_ O \_ E \mid \_ A \_ \_ E \_ \_ \mid \_ O \mid \_ O \_ \_$$

conveys very little redundancy information, while its consonant counterpart exhibits considerable redundancy:

$$\_ \mid R \_ LL \_ NG \mid ST \_ N \_ \mid G \_ TH \_ RS \mid N \_ \mid M \_ SS.$$

The same can be said of other such choices, for example, words in sentences. A sentence in the closing paragraph of a letter might run, *I am certainly hoping that we will see you very* _____. The slot might be filled with *soon*, perhaps *often*, and a few other possibilities, but not with words like *rabbit, thankful, truth, the, and*, and so forth. To some degree, this is what was implied in the discussion of collocational features of semantic readings of sentences, in which the first order of normal collocational priorities helps indicate which categories occur with others and which features normally occur with other subclasses. The grammatical structure of language reflects rules of order and arrangement. Language is not random; it is patterned.

The checkerboard example indicates that information is conveyed each time uncertainty is reduced. Context also provides us with some idea of what items are likely to occur next, reducing the range of alternatives. Uncertainty is reduced and information conveyed. When an item thus appears it confirms some of the information already available from context, and in this sense is repeated information. This kind of redundancy is often desired in communication systems in which accuracy of the message is paramount. Efficiency here is the capacity to ensure rapid and accurate transmission of messages, not how to ensure equal probability. This is why *Able, Baker, Charley*, and so forth stand for the letters A, B, and C in radio messages; /t/ can sound very much like /k/, and /f/ very much like /v/. However, in words, the chance of confusion is greatly reduced.

Similarly, Morse code takes advantage of naturally occurring redundancy in English. It is no accident that E, I, and T are represented by a single dot (·), double dot (··), and dash (–), respectively, while less frequently occurring items like Q and X are represented by the more complicated dash–dash–dot–dash (––·–) and dash–dot–dot–dash (–··–). (One might even improve on the system by not requiring a symbol for U after Q, since in written English U automatically appears after Q, as all hard-pressed "Scrabble" players will attest. However, this might unduly burden the code by adding an extra rule of memory for a small number of words.) Before secret codes were based on other than natural language, cryptographers tried to decode secret messages by applying rules of language frequency. It is difficult to speculate on the reasons for high redundancy in natural language. Of course, redundancy is a safeguard against the possibility of error and ensures some high degree of accuracy. After all, as Miller (1953) has suggested, we are not the best "information-handling" system available and are far from competing with the sophisticated systems of calculators and computers.

In sum, the techniques applied above can be applied in general to language structure and performance. Such applications should deliver important information about structural components of language and how language is used in speaking and writing.

Information Theory as a Theory of Language

One can easily see how behaviorist psychology, with its partial concern for left-to-right dependencies, found a powerful tool in information theory. The measurement of an item's information should directly reflect the item's probability of occurrence. Thus, if one views the alternatives as responses, as one must in language, which alternative arises in response to a preceding stimulus? How often does a particular item occur? Take, for example, the following strings of English words. Such strings match up with the frequencies displayed by generating words through stages from entirely random generation of words to the highly restricted generation of words actually displayed by English sentences. The following, derived from Miller and Selfridge (1950), represent different orders of approximation of 10-word sequences in English:

zero-order: *byway consequence handsomely financier bent flux cavalry swiftness weather-beaten extent*

first-order: *abilities with that beside I for waltz you the sewing*

second-order: *was he went to the newspaper is in deep and*

third-order: *tall and thin boy is a biped is the beat*

fourth-order: *saw the football game will end at midnight on January*

fifth-order: *they saw the play Saturday and sat down beside him*

seventh-order: *recognize her abilities in music after he scolded him before*

text: *the history of California is largely that of a railroad*

Zero-order of approximation strings like *byway consequence handsomely financier bent flux cavalry swiftness weather-beaten extent* is entirely random. A string like *abilities with that beside I for waltz you the sewing* is chosen for relative probability of occurrence in the language, but without reference to preceding context. Lower orders reflect varying degrees of contextual restriction. One eventually reaches the actual text sentences generated by probabilities of words in English sentences.

Such a point of view is ideal for investigating left-to-right dependencies in a language, but as strings more closely approximate sentences, hierarchically dependent grammar plays a more important part in our understanding. Miller and Selfridge found that the recall of strings improved as the order of approximation to English increased and that there was no great difference in recalling text sentences beyond fifth-order approximations.

However, although such considerations may be useful for understanding certain aspects of language, N. Chomsky (1957) points out that they cannot completely explain the nature of language. Natural language is not limited by statistics, nor can it be analyzed by probability. Native competence provides an infinite variety of well-formed sentences. Probability theories require data. Excluding practical performance considerations like memory and life span, state of the speaker, and so forth, there is no theoretical limit to the length of a grammatically well-formed sentence. It is possible to make any sentence longer by expansion or embedding. *I saw John* can be expanded to *I saw John yesterday, I saw John yesterday on the corner, I saw John yesterday on the corner by the candy store, I saw John yesterday on the corner by the candy store that burned down,* and so forth.

Miller (1964) also points out that a simple and by no means uncommon sentence in English can run beyond 20 words. For example, *The little girl who was waiting on the corner waved merrily at me as I passed by on the bus.* There must be at least 10^{20} such sentences that English speakers can comprehend and produce. Miller says that it would take 100 billion centuries, or 1000 times the estimated age of the earth, to produce all possible 20-word sentences in the language. Thus, unless the sentence is frozen or a cliché like *Hi, how are you?* and *What're you having for lunch?* the chances of having heard a particular sentence before are low indeed. The example becomes even more interesting when we include 19-word, 18-word, and 17-word sentences. This fact offers an interesting commentary on learning-theory proposals regarding the acquisition of language by children through mere exposure to language instances, as well as an interesting commentary on the possibilities for a theory of language that relies exclusively on statistical-probability measures to explain and predict language behavior.

Even without the infinitely long sentence, mathematical probability does little to enhance our understanding of why sentences like *I saw a fragile whale* are grammatical and why sentences like **I saw a fragile of* are not. Both have zero probability in normal English, but the first is well formed in syntax, while the second is not. Moreover, *I saw a fragile whale* could acquire an acceptable semantic reading or at least appear in genres like poetry, fairy tales, Ogden Nash verse, and the like.

Such performance considerations, reflected in what is actually said and when and how, are of course vitally important in studying language. But for a theory of language as competence, not performance, such probability considerations are neither complete nor necessarily fruitful. Probability theory depends on a closed system. If the system is closed and unchanging, one can expect specific events to exhibit the same probability of occurrence when the system is operating. However, language does not operate this way.

The other practical alternative is to base one's investigation on a corpus and this is characteristic of structural studies. But one can only generalize from the regularities of samples. However, the probabilities themselves have probability. They reflect language, but they are not categorical statements. The larger the sample, the more secure the analyst feels. This may be why some do not trust statistical applications out of context.

When considering these implications for language analysis, a sample corpus for a language is insufficient to build an entire language theory. Like other statistical samples, it is a handy tool, perhaps the only tool available. Samples of language provide convenient entry points but cannot provide the basis for building a complete theory of language. We may again raise the question of those abilities submerged beneath the actual language manifestations which constitute the sample. As has been seen, speakers are characterized by abilities that cannot be fathomed inductively. Such abilities, can be described only deductively. Operational processes like transformations cannot be induced from any overt markers in a given set of data; they must be postulated by the linguist to account for the manner in which language functions.

For similar reasons one cannot seriously accept conditioning theory and behaviorism as the answer to acquiring language. The number of utterances in a language is infinite, and children can never have had direct experience with enough utterances to condition them to acquire their language abilities. Even so, children have different language experiences in their acquisition of English, yet they manage to arrive at the same grammatical competence that signals them as speakers of English. One would have a least expected such a result to have been derived from the same or similar experiences. Nevertheless, certain aspects of such statistical considerations of language can be retained as useful tools in the analysis of performance features of language. It appears to be a matter of having one's priorities straight regarding what explains what and in the most adequate manner.

Information theory may still find a place in assessing speakers' interpretations of performance variables, for speakers and listeners obviously react not only to what is uttered but also to what their expectations may lead them to believe has been uttered. In many instances, what is actually heard and what the hearer thinks he has heard are not the same and are dependent on what **must** have been the message. For example, we know a great deal of what is likely to follow at any given point on the various levels of language; the **most important** thing we know is that we expect it to make sense, and sense it makes. For that reason, mistaken telegrams or quickly scribbled messages like *JOHN SAID TNAT YOH SHOLD NEET HIX AT THE COSNER MAXKET* offer sufficient clues about the intended message.

Stylistic Analysis

Is style amenable to quantitative measures? Or, as in the past, must we rely on the intuitions of a highly literate few? Are variables of style easily quantified, easily discussed? Are such mechanical variables, the cutting edge of stylistic expression, profitably studied in this way?

We can distinguish one kind of writing or speaking style from another. Such concerns overlap literary criticism, and it is true that there has been cross-fertilization of the disciplines. Without demeaning the goals and method of literary criticism, it seems that the social sciences have been influencing the humanities in the recent use of seemingly objective techniques of analysis and measurement to aid or sometimes supplant the traditional subjective evaluations made by competent scholars. The questions here is whether there are demonstrable variables for all to see and agree upon, and whether such variables can be compared with other variables along a set of continua.

However, the concern for style and content analysis is somewhat different in psycholinguistics. There is no question of aesthetic judgments here, only the measurement of objective variables that can provide meaningful parameters for style in specific instances. Or perhaps the hope is vain and cannot be answered by the empirical attitudes of the calculating social scientists. Perhaps one can no more measure style than calculate a daisy or formulate the feeling of morning fog on one's cheek. Putting the efforts of scholars aside, and yet agreeing that appreciation of particular styles cannot be entirely explained with measuring devices, we can nonetheless say that certain aspects of language must have overt characteristics. After all, appreciation of style is based on something we like and something we do not like. If that is true, and we can measure such indicators accurately enough to be able to express our opinions about a given sample to others, then we have in fact taken some device, internal and personal though it may be, and have applied it in a measuring sense.

The analysis of style, then, is the selection of certain observable variables as characteristic of different language outputs. Such features may tell something about the type of style or about the speaker or writer. Bearing in mind regularity and redundancy, one sees the implications of a departure from expected frequencies—a highly creative style or possibly a linguistically unexpected or bizarre behavior. The very notion of a regular set of patterns in competence as well as in performance sets the stage and provides a framework for describing creative style.

Any language contains obligatory features and variable features on the various levels that comprise language. Even though there is no absolute constraint, some predictability exists as a result of the differing statistical properties of the actual choices made in specific styles. The same is true of a particular individual's style. If we take into account the approaches to meaning discussed, especially the generative point of view of incorporating the semantic component into a grammar by rules of collocation as specified by features, style becomes both syntax and semantics. Content is not the essence of style, but it is the medium. Style has different possibilities on language's various levels, according to the size of the linguistic unit class. Thus, the larger the unit class, the more the possibility of choice, and hence the more fruitful the possibilities for building specific characteristics into style. Conversely, the smaller the unit class, the fewer choices possible, and the more constrained one is by the rules of the language. However, that very fact of constraint offers an outlet for style in the possibility of deviating from the norms immediately and with a resounding stylistic flair. But the constraints must not be too much tampered with, or the language intent itself becomes obscured.

There can be little doubt that one of the key factors in approaching style is choice. Language constrains its users to make use of the devices available within its repertoire, yet at the many choice points available within that repertoire the user is to some degree free to employ whichever tokens of a type class he deems appropriate to his stylistic ends. Moreover, departing from the original restrictions of language is a style too, but it is best covered in a discussion of styles as entire paradigms of organization. Certainly there is a similarity in the history of art, music, poetry, and prose that bears out such suggestions. When a particular procedural paradigm becomes too common, and to the radical artist, musician, or writer, too trite, one means of establishing an entirely fresh perspective is to change the rules of the game altogether. Thus, instead of painting in a manner that reproduces nature in landscapes and portraits, an artist may view it in a surrealistic or cubistic sense, and the result is an entirely new mode of artistic expression. Or an artist may devise new techniques of painting, with large or small dots to reproduce the image, or even introduce new techniques by using the palette knife instead of the brush. So also with the traditional writing styles in prose and poetry. However, this is infringing on the concept of style in the manner of a typology of style. The style considerations we have entertained up to this point are more of the nature of possible avenues of investigation of individual styles within the framework of a style type.

This is also different from the style one may equate with content itself, for to some degree content will influence presentation. Those elements of prose style, however, resulting in shifts of content should also be amenable to the statistical techniques of content analysis. There is thus an important distinction between such linguistic phenomena as words and sentence structures and their usage in a mathematical sense. As Saporta and Sebeok (1959) point out, the linguistic data most amenable to content analysis are information about the various ways in which a given idea can be expressed. Content analysis then becomes a series of statements about the relative frequencies of the various ways in which these ideas are expressed—for example, the use of a specific device like the active and the passive in English.

Some suggest that certain inferences may be made about the intentions of the state of the encoder–originator of utterances. Style is viewed as dependent on and thus reflective of individuals' habits, motivational and emotional states, and attitudes at the time of encoding or in general. One of the more interesting attempts to assess style as an indicator of the inner emotional states is Osgood and Walker's (1959) content analysis of suicide notes. For them, style was a measure of the individual's deviations from situational norms. If we assume that suicide note writers are working in an atmosphere of heightened motivation and emotional energy, this was indeed an excellent place to assess the effects of motivation on language behavior. The researchers assumed that anxiety would be evidenced in a number of ways. One would expect that the greater the anxiety, the greater the stereotypy of encoding. Complexity would be diminished, and the high proportion of adjectives and adverbs to nouns and verbs would dwindle. There would also be a tendency toward repetition of stereotyped phrases and unelaborated basic sentence types. One might also expect that some disorganization of language skills might appear and that some choice points would reflect the content of the speaker's distraught state and his need for reassurance and reaction. Last, of course, one would expect that where there are competing anxieties, clues to the conflict of anxieties would appear in the choice of phraseology, and perhaps evidence of compromise between the anxieties. Osgood and Walker compared actual suicide notes with faked ones, to see if encoders of the latter could somehow intuit the states of the actual suicide notes and produce facsimiles. Certain features of the suicidal style could easily be reproduced. But the emotional ambiguity, the disorganized state of mind, and the pleading tone of the suicide's cry for help could not be entirely reproduced. Some states, it would appear, cannot be completely appreciated until experienced. Be that as it may, the important point of the study is the application of principles of stylistic analysis that depend on external variables as the basis for the evaluation and definition of a given style. It would appear that such styles as the extreme example presented by suicide notes do lend themselves to a description by such a set of external variables.

Other studies have concentrated on style and content in less grim settings. Gilman and Brown (1966) contrasted the literary styles of Emerson and Thoreau. They found that the passages written by each author were distinctive in their use of conjunctions (*but, even, though,* and *yet*), negatives, first-person pronominals, nouns and verbs with abstract or metaphorical meanings as opposed to nouns and verbs with concrete and tangible meanings, and so forth. Gilman and Brown claimed to differentiate the two men, although they shared much in ideology, environment, and education.

Similar work has been done on the authorship of the Alexander Hamilton–James Madison *Federalist Papers,* 1787–1788. The authorship of some of the papers is in question and is neither documented nor admitted to by Hamilton and Madison. After the papers were written, Hamilton and Madison took political positions considerably different from the views expressed in the disputed papers. Old writings, available for posterity in formal black and white and frozen for eternity, can be a source of embarrassment, and since these papers were written specifically as propaganda, they were strongly stated positions. Mosteller and Wallace (1964) suggest that Hamilton and Madison used certain words at different rates, so that Madison is the likely candidate for authorship of the disputed 12 papers in *The Federalist Papers.* Similar statistics have been used upon the Old Testament, the Homeric epics, and Thomas à Kempis's *The Imitation of Christ.*

Generative grammatical theory has also been the basis for the discussion of stylistic differences. Thorne (1970) and others have speculated that some of the traditional stylistic terms like *loose, terse, emphatic,* and *complex* may actually find their origins in deep structure. Such terms may not necessarily be impressionistic, as often assumed; there may be a correspondence between them and formal grammatical properties. With increasing ties between disciplines, innovations in the study of grammar and structure may have corresponding applications for stylistics.

The notion of degrees of grammaticality could well serve, as Thorne points out, as examples in a treatise on style dealing with how to recognize and evaluate certain sentence structures. Or, conversely, one might expect that, depending on the stylistic effect one might wish to achieve, one might count such structures as examples of how or how not to achieve exactly a particular stylistic effect.

Of course, some fruitful carry-over into the analysis of style might be expected from the work in grammatical studies. There is now appropriate terminology for discussing such categories: grammaticality, degree of grammaticality, acceptability, collocation, subcategorizational features and selectional features, left-, right-, and self-embedding, and many more. Such terms are attractive in their easy application to much of the prose that constitutes the subject matter of stylistic analysis. Moreover, by the manner of their incorporation in the grammar, they also provide a basis for deciding on a hierarchy of stylistic innovation, if deviation from the norms is taken as the avenue of stylistic expression. Individuals recognize and, in many instances, construct stylistic parodies in music, painting, and language. Such variables may be very well handled by the objective descriptions of language in statistical models.

Experimental Psycholinguistics

Linguistic Theory and the Notion of Psychological Reality

Experimental psycholinguistics is concerned with the investigation of encoding and decoding processes in language. At one time experimental psycholinguistics encompassed an amazing variety of topics, but during the past 15 years the emphasis has been on questions suggested by the various models of linguistic theory based on the earlier or later model of generative transformational theory. The consolidation of this aspect of psycholinguistics can best be seen in the progression of reviews of psycholinguistics in the *Annual Review of Psychology*. Rubenstein and Aborn (1960) view psycholinguistics as a less than well-integrated field of study, without the helmsmanship provided by a single steady trend, while Ervin-Tripp and Slobin (1966) narrow it to the investigation of the acquisition and use of structured language, with a particular focus on syntactic organization. Fillenbaum (1971) concentrates on syntax in his discussion of experimental psycholinguistics, both because of its centrality to linguistic theory and because of its investigative popularity. Johnson-Laird's point of view (1974) is even more straightforward; he sees the fundamental problem in experimental psycholinguistics as simply the question of what happens when we understand sentences.

Rather than surveying all the areas of language mentioned in discussing linguistic theory and the nature of language, this chapter concentrates primarily on syntax. Syntax has been the focus of many recent psycholinguistic investigations because of the degree to which Chomsky's syntactic theory has been translated into psycholinguistic concerns. Other topics, such as phonological skills, have, of course, been researched, but a sizable amount of research time and journal space has been devoted to syntactic and related semantic investigation. Even some investigations of other aspects of language have been motivated by formulations in generative theory. Examples are the Steinberg (1973) and Moskowitz (1973) commentaries on the suggestion (N. Chomsky & Halle, 1968; C. Chomsky, 1970) that conventional English orthography is much closer to the sound structure of the language than is ordinarily assumed.

One basic question in experimental psycholinguistics has been whether a linguistic theory of competence explains the way in which the mind produces and understands sentences. Does it at least parallel the way speakers of a language generate sentences and the way hearers of a language understand sentences? This controversy over the concept of "psychological reality" is vaguely reminiscent of Householder's division (1952) of linguists into two camps on the basis of their attitudes toward the "reality" of their linguistic descriptions of languages. On the one hand were the "God's truth" linguists, those who believed that languages have a real underlying structure and that their task was to discover and describe it. On the other hand were the "hocus-pocus" linguists, those who felt that the language data could be handled and presented in whatever way was practicable, efficient, or economical and that their linguistic descriptions allowed whatever machinations necessary to present a tidy analysis of the data. Of course, no one ever really belonged entirely in one camp or the other, but the characterization is illustrative.

The concept of psycholinguistic reality faces similar problems. The question is basically whether a linguistic theory of language is simply a theory to account for linguistic competence or whether it also explains language behavior. The problem is, moreover, not as simple as this. On the one hand, we can ask whether the theory of linguistic competence matches up in some way with the speaker–hearer's mental processes. On the other hand, we can also ask what relationship a theory of linguistic competence has to a theory of linguistic performance. There is moreover, the basic problem of testing and proof, difficult enough in any setting, but complicated by the basically rationalist formulations underlying generative grammar and the empirical foundations of most experimental psychological investigations.

N. Chomsky's basically rationalist approach postulates innate organizing principles and operations for language, but not as the result of experimental investigation or as areas that can be profitably explored by experimental techniques. Competence cannot be inferred from performance, though Chomsky does envision the description of competence as an important factor in the investigation of performance. Since performance is not a mirror reflection of competence, investigations of performance variables may not tell us anything after all about the nature of competence. One is left wondering whether this model of grammatical theory is even amenable to empirical verification, let alone encouraging it. This is again a manifestation of the basic gap between the traditions of rationalism and empiricism, and we are left with an impasse. In addition, the expanding history of generative grammar has made experimental investigation of the psychological reality of some facets of earlier linguistic formulations obsolete in view of changes within linguistic theory.

Grammaticality

Do speakers actually exhibit notions of grammaticality in response to sentences or would-be sentences in the language? Are there differences in grammaticality such that one can characterize degrees of deviation from well-formed sentences? If so, what are these degrees of ungrammaticality, and how do speakers of the language actually respond to and rate them?

Sentences are remembered with greater ease and accuracy than random strings of words. In turn, deviant sentences are not recalled with the same ease and accuracy as fully grammatical sentences, but they are recalled with greater facility than entirely random sequences of words. Marks and Miller (1964) had individuals recall sentences of equal length but different grammatical status. The sentences were of four types: (1) grammatically well-formed, semantically acceptable sentences (*Rapid flashes augur violent storms*); (2) grammatically well-formed, semantically unacceptable sentences (*Rapid bouquets deter sudden neighbors*); (3) randomized versions of category 1 (*Rapid augur violent flashes storms*); and (4) randomized versions of category 2 (*Rapid deter sudden bouquets neighbors*). Recall depended on the grammaticality of the sentence, with category 1 being best recalled, category 2 the next best, category 3 the next best, and category 4 the least best. In general, the more disruption in the sentence, the poorer the recall.

Miller and Isard (1963) had similar results in an earlier study that required subjects to listen to sentences under both quiet and noisy conditions. Only three types of sentence were included, sentences similar to those in categories 1 and 2 and a randomized list. Thus, sentences like *Total chaos follows nuclear attacks, Total coffee loses eternal spots,* and **Follows coffee games romantic ugly* were understood in exactly that order. The clear contribution of the semantic factor in these findings is in line with later findings by Rosenberg and Jarvella (1970). There may also be degrees of deviance in terms of expected collocability for the semantic relationships in sentences, so that sentences like *The doctor cured the patient* are better remembered than sentences like *The doctor shook the author.*

Phrase Structure and the Sentence Constituent

Relationships are hierarchically ordered in sentence structure. This fact is in sharp opposition to the motion of linear ordering and linear relationships as being primary. The results of the following experiments are clear—as in the Gestalt notion that we perceive in terms of wholistic units, there are units in sentence perception, and they are the sentence constituents.

Fodor and Bever (1965) found that when clicks were superimposed on tape-recorded sentences and subjects were asked to reproduce the sentences in writing and show where the clicks were, the subjects invariably reproduced the sentences with the clicks occurring at major syntactic boundaries between the constituent phrases of the sentences. For example, in the sentence *That he was happy was evident from the way he smiled,* the first major constituent break separates *That he was happy* and *was evident from the way he smiled.* Thus, one might superimpose clicks on *was, happy, was, evident,* and on the boundary between *happy* and *was* itself. Even though a click was sometimes actually superimposed on words a word or two before or after that major syntactic boundary, the subjects moved it toward the boundary in their interpretation of where it had occurred. When the click actually did coincide with the boundary, the subjects reported nearly unanimously that it had appeared there.

In an effort to ensure that such findings were not merely the result of other cues, such as intonational contours, pauses, or vowel lengthening before pauses, Garrett, Bever, and Fodor (1966) spliced the exact same segment of speech onto other sentence fragments to produce two complete sentences, each with the spliced segment in a different position. For example, taking a sequence like *hope of marrying Anna was surely impractical,* they proceeded to splice this to other segments like *your* and *in her* to produce sentences like *Your hope of marrying Anna / was surely impractical* and *In her hope of marrying / Anna was surely impractical.* Since the spliced segment was identical, intonational cues were constant and identical. In general, the results support the study just discussed; speakers still interpreted click placement in terms of syntactic boundaries. It would seem that constituent structure is a primary criterion in the interpretation of sentences, one that substitutes for absent intonational cues and possibly even over-rides present ones.

Another instructive experiment is Johnson's attempt (1965) to assess the manner in which speakers store sentences and reproduce them during recall. Johnson was interested in investigating whether words within specific groups of words are more likely to be associated than other words. To find out whether words are recalled on the basis of equal association with all the other words in a given sentence or on the basis of units or constituents, Johnson devised a measurement of the errors in the transition from word to word in sentences. This scale, the transitional error probability, provides the probability of a word's being recalled correctly once the word before it is provided. One would obviously expect that the more the errors in going from one word to the next, the less the association between them, and that the fewer the errors, the higher the association. Johnson did find that there were differences and that those differences paralleled the syntactic constituent boundaries of sentences. Wherever major syntactic boundaries occurred, so did the highest proportion of transitional error probabilities. For example, in the sentence *The tall boy saved the dying woman* the highest transitional error probability occurred between the subject NP and the predicate VP, or between *The tall boy* and *saved the dying woman.* Similarly, the sentence *The house across the street is burning* exhibited the highest error probability before *is burning,* the first major break, and the next highest error probability before *across the street,* the next most important break.

The results reported by Maclay and Osgood (1959) also support the notion of constituent breaks used by the encoding speaker. Hesitation phenomena in spontaneous speech are not random but come at decision points that correlate significantly with syntactic boundaries. In this sense, hesitation phenomena can be viewed as the encoding parallels to the decoding seen in the results of the click-paradigm experiments. Syntactic boundaries offer convenient points for chunking in handling incoming speech signals, and they constitute decision points in encoding the speech signal. This conclusion seems to jibe with Goldman-Eisler's early observation that pauses seem to precede the least redundant items in spontaneous speech, though not necessarily with her later observation (1968) about their relationship to complexity of content. She has also found that individuals make fewer such pauses when reading aloud (indicating that when choice of semantic content is limited, so is pausing), but that when they do, the pauses usually come at syntactic boundaries.

Intersentence Relationships

What is the nature of the relationship between sentence types? Can one sentence type be considered basic and underlying all other variants of that particular type? If so, are all the sentences derived from this basic type more complex in terms of processing, implying that memory storage and retrieval are somehow tied up with reduction to basic sentence types? Does this also imply that such derived sentences will also exhibit variations in measurable terms, so that derived sentences take longer to understand, interpret, and match?

By and large, early experiments on the psychological reality of transformational grammar concentrated on the optional transformation aspect of Chomsky's early theory (1957). Such experiments attempted to match perceptual or processual complexity with grammatical complexity—that is, the more grammatical steps transformationally, the more difficulty in understanding or recalling, the more time involved, or the more storage space in short-term memory taken up. These experiments concentrated on the kinds of optional transformations that change kernel sentences (the simple, active, affirmative, declaraative types) into other types. Not much attention was paid to the obligatory transformations that make sure the output of the grammatical rules ends up looking like a real sentence. These obligatory transformations are more obviously analytic manipulations of the system and did not seem to be a fruitful area of investigation. The assumption was that kernel sentences are more than just a starting point for the purely mechanical aspects of the language description. Kernel (K) sentences were also assumed to have some kind of primacy in actual performance involving transformations into the question (Q), the passive (P), the negative (N), and the passive negative (PN)—for example, transforming *Bill hit the ball* (K) into *Did Bill hit the ball?* (Q), *The ball was hit by Bill* (P), *Bill did not hit the ball* (N), and *The ball was not hit by Bill* (PN). It was predicted that a single transformation like the passive or negative would take a certain amount of time. A complex structure like the passive negative would involve two transformational steps and a passive negative question three steps, so that both could be expected to take longer. Note how the PN is two steps away from the K in the following diagram.

Miller (1962) attempted to test the reality of the kernel sentence in a psychological sense as well as the concept of optional transformations that produce derived sentences. He assumed that each such transformational derivation can be viewed as an operational step that takes a certain amount of time to perform. He also assumed that in sentence derivations involving several steps—for example, the passive negative—the time taken to perform these steps is additive. Thus, in some gross fashion the time needed to produce a passive negative should approximate the individual times needed to produce the passive and the negative. To test these assumptions, Miller used sentence-matching tasks in which the same sentence appears on two lists but in a transformed version. Thus, in one matching task on one list you might have a kernel *Bill hit the ball* and on the other list (amid other sentences to be matched) the passive *The ball was hit by Bill.* Again, in another matching request, you might have the passive *The ball was hit by Bill* on one list and the negative *Bill did not hit the ball* on the other. The point was to calculate the average amount of time it took to match one sentence type with another. In general, it took longer to handle two transformations in the sentence-matching tasks than it did to handle single transformations in matching up sentences; that is, it took longer to get from K to PN than from K to P, K to N, or P to PN.

An interesting variation on this theme is offered by Mehler (1963). Mehler had subjects learn and recall sentences, but the sentences were of varying transformational types. Obviously, the more complex the sentence transformationally, the harder it should be to learn and subsequently recall. Mehler did find that kernel sentences were the easiest to learn, but he also discovered an interesting fact about the recall of more complex sentences and, by implication, about their storage in memory. When more complex sentences were recalled, they were often recalled in such a way that the recalled structures were less complex, or in transformational terms, in a way suggesting the loss of one or more transformations. Mehler speculated that what was happening was that sentences were actually stored in their kernel-sentence form together with a mental tag that would trigger the appropriate transformation.

Miller and McKean (1968) continued the investigation of intersentence relationships in an experiment that involved matching pairs of transformationally related sentences. Subjects were presented with a list of sentences and informed that they would be required to find the matching transformation of the same sentence in another list to be presented. They were asked to read the starting list and make the appropriate transformational changes in preparation for the task. However, one of the main points of the investigation was the time it took the subjects to carry out the transformations. As a control metric, subjects were asked to search for sentences that were identical to those on the original list. The idea was that simply subtracting the time necessary for locating identical sentences would provide a measure of the time needed to perform the transformational operations. There were time differences between the transformational types, with negative taking the least amount of time, passive the next, and passive negative the most. The sum of the times for the passive and negative operations alone was similar to the time recorded for sentence matchings that required both operations, passive and negative. However, the results of some later sentence-matching studies did not always jibe with earlier results, so the exact status of the transformational-complexity approach is unclear.

Another experiment using the metric approach was conducted by Savin and Perchonock (1965). However, they used the concept of memory storage space and the metric device of unrelated words memorized after sentences varying in transformational complexity. It was predicted that sentences would differ in processing and interpretation according to their transformational complexity. Consequently the researchers looked for differences in the number of words that could be memorized and recalled together with sentences of differing transformational complexity. One would expect, if the metric assumption is correct, that fewer words would be recalled with sentences having a complex transformational history. The implication is that such transformational operations take up space in the memory, so that the notions of basic sentences and degrees of transformational complexity would seem to be psychologically viable constructs. Thus, subjects were required to memorize a sentence and a list of eight randomized words after the sentence. The number of words recalled after each sentence type was assumed to be indicative of how much space was taken up in the memory storage to memorize the sentence type and how much memory space was left over to accommodate the extra words. The sentence types included passives, negatives, questions, passive negatives, and passive questions. In general, Savin and Perchonock found that transformational complexity was predictive of the number of words recalled; the less complex the transformational history, the more words recalled. Although their notion of metric measurement is congruent with that used in the experiments just discussed, it is interesting to note that the specific results do not exactly overlap. Among other things, whereas in Miller and McKean's study the negative took the least amount of time, in Savin and Perchonock's study the negative took up more storage space than the passive as measured by the number of words recalled. One would have hoped for some overlap in the specific results as well.

In general, it has seemed that passive and negative sentences take longer to deal with than their active counterparts. However, some evidence to the contrary has been presented by Slobin (1966), who found that in cases in which passives were nonreversible, passives were just as easy to understand and remember as their active counterparts. Slobin typed passives as reversible if the grammatical subject and the by-phrase can be interchanged to produce a likely sentence. For example, the sentence *The cat was bitten by the dog* can be reversed to *The dog was bitten by the cat.* But the sentence *The drapes are being drawn by the maid* cannot be reversed to *The maid is being drawn by the drapes.* However, passives like *The patient was examined by the doctor* also seem to fit into the nonreversible group even though they can be reversed to provide a likely and meaningful interpretation. The reason is that *examine* is more likely to go with *doctor* as agentive subject and *patient* as object than the other way around.

Herriot (1969) investigated this aspect of the reversibility–nonreversibility restrictions. The point to be noted here is that although semantic-feature collocations in their grossest sense can be expected to account for the facile evaluation of certain sentences, this factor of collocation in other instances does not answer the pertinent question unless one establishes a hierarchy of priorities for semantic-feature collocations in terms of what features commonly or rarely do go with other features. For example, Herriot found that some passive sentences like *The patient was treated by the doctor* and *The swimmer was rescued by the lifeguard* were treated just as the truly nonreversibles in

Slobin's findings. Although it is possible to reverse these sentences to *The lifeguard was rescued by the swimmer* and *The doctor was treated by the patient,* they are not likely to be reversed. As a result, though not a clear violation of the semantic-feature restrictions, they appear to offer the same facility in processing as active sentences because of the semantic cues implied in their expected semantic interpretations. Herriot did find, moreover, that when he did reverse such passives, facility and accuracy in interpretation dropped; the subjects were obviously paying attention to semantic expectations.

These experiments indicate that meaning plays an important part in the decoding of sentences. Obviously, in many cases semantics supercedes the transformational history of a sentence. There is thus no need to decode a sentence back through its transformational stages if all interpretations but one are short-circuited by the semantic information presented through the normal collocational expectations. Fodor and Garrett (1967) have observed that transformational complexity does not necessarily parallel perceptual complexity. For example, the phrase *the red house* is derived from *the house which is red,* yet the first phrase is a quicker processual clue to the underlying deep-structure proposition *The house is red.* The same appeared to be true for embedded sentences in which adjectives are inserted by extra transformational operations. Although syntactically the insertion of adjectives involves extra operations in the treatment of modification, embedded sentences having them were easier to deal with than those without them. For example, contrast a sentence without adjectives, *The shot the soldier the mosquito bit fired missed,* with the version with the adjectives, *The first shot the tired soldier the mosquito bit fired missed.* The latter sentence is derived from something like *The shot (the shot was first) the soldier (the soldier was tired) the mosquito bit fired missed* and is several transformational steps away from the sentence without any adjectives or relative pronouns. Obviously, this is another instance of many in which perceptual complexity does not match transformational complexity.

Deep Structure and Surface Structure

A major change in N. Chomsky's 1965 elaboration of his linguistic theory has been reflected in experimental psycholinguistic avenues of research. One immediately noticeable change is the lack of further concern over the centrality of kernel sentences and their transformations. Another important factor is the introduction of a semantic component into the grammar and the introduction of the difference between deep structure and surface structure. The syntactic section of the grammar remains as a generative source, indeed the only generative source; the other sections of the grammar, the semantic and the phonological components, are purely interpretative. Here the questions seem fairly obvious. Is there a valid reason to entertain the notion of two such separate levels, surface structure and deep structure? Can they be reduced to one level, or should they perhaps be expanded to three or more levels? What evidence is there for their existence in performance? Moreover, if we accept them, are they related in the way linguistic theory shows them to be?

Some of the experiments already discussed—for example, those by Slobin (1966) and Herriot (1969)—can be viewed in the light of the surface-structure–deep-structure dichotomy. In processing such structures as the nonreversible passives, subjects are likely to use semantic cues to jump directly to the underlying deep structure of the sentences rather than wading through the grammatical operations implicit in their syntactic derivation. Of course, although this interpretation can be used to support the existence of deep structure, it can also be used to support the primacy of semantics.

Some reflection of deep-structure relationships and their effect on surface ambiguity is seen in Fodor, Garrett, and Bever's inquiry (1968) into syntactic determinants of sentence complexity involving multiple verbal relationships. Some verbs enter into one or an extremely limited number of syntactic relationships, while other verbs may enter into many syntactic relationships. One would expect that sentences with such multiple-relationship verbs would be potentially more ambiguous and consequently harder to deal with than sentences with highly restricted verbs. For example, take a highly restricted verb like *elapse*. This verb is only intransitive, taking no object or *that*-phrases, and is, moreover, highly restricted in its noun–subject collocations. One does not expect or find sentences like *The Christmas cookies elapsed, *John elapsed the gray hat, *The time elapsed that John can get on with his work*, and *The time elapsed how to sail*. However, with a multiple-relationship verb like *know*, one does find sentences like *John knows, The poor know their limitations, John knows that Jan can get on with her work*, and *John knows how to sail*. Similarly, a verb like *meet* is more restricted than *know*, though not quite to the extreme that *elapse* is. Accordingly, one is not surprised at the finding that complex sentences containing verbs that can have only one deep-structure relationship are easier to deal with than sentences containing verbs that can have a number of deep-structure relationships. For example, for subjects working out sentences in a syntactic anagram task, building sentences containing *meet* was easier than building sentences containing *know*.

Mehler and Carey (1967) imply some support for the concept of deep structure. They induced a set for a particular deep-structure type by having subjects listen to 11-sentence groups, the first 10 of which were of one deep-structure type and the last of another. The sentence groupings were masked by noise so that they were heard but not clearly and entirely accurately. For example, the first 10 might have been of the type *They are delightful to embrace* and the eleventh of the type *They are hesitant to travel*. Although the two sentences are identical in their surface structure, they differ in their deep-structure origins, with *they* in the first sentence being the object of *embrace* (compare *It is delightful to embrace them*) and *they* in the second sentence being the subject of *travel* (compare *They travel hesitantly*, but not **It is hesitant to travel them*). As a result of the set induced by the preceding sentences, the last exception was harder to perceive and identify correctly under the noise conditions.

Blumenthal (1967) attempted to prompt recall of sentences by using different prompt words drawn from different underlying deep-structure sentence derivations. For example, sentences like the following pair have exactly the same surface-structure relationships but differ in their deep-structure origins: *Gloves were made by tailors* and *Gloves were made by hand*. Both are passive sentences, but the first sentence is simply the passive of the underlying *Tailors make gloves*. The second sentence is a rewrite of an underlying sentence like *Somebody makes gloves by hand*, plus the deletion of the actor word *somebody* in its passive form. When the last noun was used as a prompting aid for recall of the sentences, there was a difference in recall facility for sentences corresponding to the two prompts, *tailors* and *hand*. Prompts like *tailors*, which were actually representative of the original logical subject in the underlying sentence, were better aids for recall than were more extraneous prompts like *hand*.

In a similar experiment (Blumenthal & Boakes, 1967), the logical subject of an underlying sentence was a better prompt for recall than was the word appearing as the object. Once again, a pair of sentences like *John is eager to please* and *John is easy to please* is identical in surface-structure relationships but differs in deep-structure origins. *John* was a better prompt for recalling the first sentence, in which it operates as the logical subject, than the second sentence, in which it operates as the logical object. This finding would seem to imply that a full knowledge of the syntactic relationships within a sentence is necessary to its understanding, storage, and consequent recall. Since the relationships examined here are of a deep-structure nature, the results can be taken as supportive of the notion of deep structure.

The results of an experiment extending the click paradigm (see Bever, Lackner, & Kirk, 1969) indicate that the location of clicks is related to the underlying deep structure of sentences. In sentences in which the surface-structure and deep-structure breaks do not correspond, in some instances speakers will relocate clicks according to the deep-structure alignment rather than the apparent surface-structure ordering. For example, in a sentence like *The corrupt police can't bear criminals to confess very quickly*, a click superimposed on *criminals* may be moved back to the underlying deep-structure boundary between *bear* and *criminals*. On the other hand, with *The corrupt police can't force criminals to confess very quickly*, there is less tendency to move the click back to between *force* and *criminals*.

One of the most powerful arguments in favor of the dichotomy between deep structure and surface structure is the evidence we have seen up to this point calling for the introduction of other than purely surface syntactic factors in the processing and storage of sentences. There were many instances in which semantics played an equal or more prominent part in the understanding and recall of sentences, and this fact must be reflected in whatever theory of language behavior we decide upon. To the degree that two levels are established in linguistic theory, and to the extent that the level of deep structure can account for these facts all the better. The problem, however, is how much of this additional information is in fact adequately answered by the deep-structure commitment; it may be that we need more than what deep structure has yielded to this point. Thus, the very argument in favor of deep structure can also be turned into the question of why there is not more expansion of this level of language theory or, perhaps, more than just this level. Perhaps there are several types of deep structure, or whatever we wish to call it, each of which is providing us with different kinds of vital information. Just this approach to a multilevel analysis of language behavior to account for the various input factors in performance may be necessary. Certainly, approaches in which semantics is seen as primary (see Chafe, 1970) and approaches taking a wholistic view (see Bever, 1970, 1971) of language and other perceptual and behavioral abilities are becoming more common.

Performance Factors in Sentence Understanding and Use

Obviously, although sentence types and transformations all receive the same abstract linguistic evaluation in the description of competence, evaluations in the description of performance may vary. There are two ways of looking at the problem of the circumstantial factors that condition actual sentence production. One is to inquire about which utterances are used in response to or in the description of specific situations—that is, about the origin of certain speech forms from their very beginnings. The other way is related but slightly different. Given two syntactic structures that appear to be largely equivalent, what situational reasons can be uncovered that make one more likely than the other or that may make one probable and the other improbable or perhaps even impossible? The general question covering both approaches is whether there are situational or contextual factors that predict sentence production and syntactic choice.

An ingenious attempt to provide some basis for actual sentence production is offered by Osgood (1971). Not satisfied with the fact that sentences may be novel and unpredictable, Osgood has attempted to provide some answer to the question of where sentences come from. In cleverly employing a limited set of props and activities involving those props, he has been able to demonstrate that there are logical situational priorities reflected in the content of the sentences generated and, more important, that there are apparently priorities to the form that sentences actually take. Osgood suggests that content is decided upon prior to form; meaning is more important than actual syntactic format. He also suggests that situations condition certain perceptual orderings and perhaps even correspond significantly to the syntactic form sentences take. In his experiment, Osgood carefully manipulated the appearance of objects and related activities to create certain perceptual contexts and then had observers describe what they had just seen in simple sentences. By and large, he found that certain linguistic forms were appropriate to these and that certain syntactic structures were appropriate to certain situations given the proper set of variables. For example, he found that the use of definite (*the*) and indefinite (*a*) articles corresponded to the chronological appearance of objects. The first time a ball appeared, it was *a ball*, but in succeeding appearances, it was *the ball*. The definite–indefinite article distinction (like Wason's negatives, discussed later) was tied to the exceptionality of an item in a set, like one blue poker chip amidst a group of white ones. If *a* white chip was taken, it was *a chip*, but if *the* blue chip was taken, it was *the chip*. Differences between actives and passives were also noted in the description of activities employing the same object. When a ball was rolled on the table, the activity was described in an active-verb sentence, but when it was placed on a plate, a significant number of observers employed a passive-verb sentence. Osgood also found that durational verbs, like *hold*, were more likely to be cast in the present or present progressive (*holds, is holding*) than verbs involving a single goal-oriented event, like *put*. These latter verbs usually turned up in the past tense.

The point, of course, is that there are situational factors that must be taken into account in the description of language behavior. Speakers respond to these situational factors in certain ways because of the nature of their perceptual and cognitive abilities, and a description of language like generative grammar is obviously only a description of the system of responses; it does not answer the why and the wherefore of those responses or the question of where sentences come from. As Fillenbaum (1971) has pointed out, the structure and meaning of perceptual events and linguistic signs may have a common representational system and a common set of organizational rules. This common cognitive foundation may be where sentences arise and so must be accounted for in an adequate theory of language. Osgood's point is that generative grammarians to date have not taken this important fact into consideration, have no way of doing so, and apparently have no intention of doing so.

Some interesting experimental results may help us answer the second question, about performance differences for syntactic patterns. An excellent example of this approach is Wason's work with negatives. Wason set out to discover whether there are contexts in which the negative is appropriate, logical, or expected. It does seem that if one has two competing construction types, there is probably a reason for their continuing competition, for if one type will do as nicely as two, why would both survive? Wason (1965) found reasons in the notion of likely or plausible denial. The negative is thus used to correct what is normally expected but is not the case in a particular instance. Let us say that we expected the early train to arrive on time this morning as usual, but it was late. In this instance, the instance of expectation, the information is more appropriately carried by the negative *The train was not on time this morning*. In these instances the negative is just as easy to deal with as the affirmative.

Before discovering this function of negatives, Wason (1961) investigated the possible differences between affirmative and negative sentences by examining the question of whether it is easier to evaluate the truth or falsity of one or the other of these sentence types. He tested four sentence types: affirmatives that are true, affirmatives that are false, negatives that are true, and negatives that are false. In general, he found that negatives took longer to evaluate than affirmatives and were also more subject to error in interpretation. (Surely there must be some moral here for the construction of true–false questions on "objective" tests, if nothing else.) Next, Wason (1965) investigated whether there are instances in which the negative is as easy to deal with as the affirmative. He employed a series of eight items, seven red and one blue. In this instance it is more plausible to say that one of the items is not red than to say that one of the items is not blue. The first would be an instance of plausible denial, the second of implausible denial. In the plausible denial circumstance, the corresponding negative sentence, *That circle is not red*, is just as easy to interpret (takes as long to do so) as an affirmative *That circle is blue*. Thus, at least one important function—perhaps the major one—that the negative fulfills is to underscore something that is contrary to normal expectations or something that is an exception to the rule.

Investigations have also shown that some sentence types may be more appropriate to some contexts than others because they are used to emphasize certain topics rather than others. Turner and Rommetveit (1968) found that the function of the passive in English is to place emphasis on the object of the action rather than on the subject. By using pictures of situations as recall prompts, they found that pictures of objects named in the accompanying sentences would elicit passive sentences (in which, of course, the logical object comes first). On the other hand, pictures of the agentive subject would elicit active sentences, as would pictures in which the entire situation was represented. Thus, when the sentences were prompted for recall by the pictures, differences for children were seen in the matching of passive sentences with pictures that prominently portrayed the object of the action, while active sentences were prompted by pictures showing the agent or the total situation. In support of this finding, Johnson-Laird (1968) suggests that the choice of the passive voice is related to placing emphasis on the underlying object by having it occur first in the sentence, as happens with logical objects in passive frames.

Clark (1965) found that subjects also gave different responses to active and passive sentences when required to fill in missing words in the two sentence types. On the whole, animate nouns figured more importantly in passive sentences in which the grammatical subject (but logical object) was asked for. The number was almost double the number given for active sentences in which the grammatical object (still logical object) was asked for. Similarly, in an experiment on syntactic position and meaning rated according to the semantic differential technique, Johnson (1967) found that subject and object functions in passive sentences were more similar in their semantic differential ratings than the corresponding subject and object functions in active sentences. It has also been found (Olson & Filby, 1972) that there are differences in the comprehension of active and passive sentences under certain circumstances. Although these experiments do not point up exactly what the differences are between performance manifestations and performance evaluations of active and passive sentences, they do graphically illustrate the fact that there **are** differences between the two sentence types.

Some interesting evidence comes from Lackner and Garrett's investigation (1972) of the performance effects of bias in resolving ambiguity. A great deal has been made of ambiguous sentences in arguments for certain aspects of linguistic theory, but the curious thing is that we so rarely falter over them unless they are purposely used, as in puns and evasive answers. It would seem that this is due to the disambiguating context provided by previous stages of the discourse and by the setting. Lackner and Garrett found that when a disambiguating sentence was presented softly, almost unintelligibly, to the other ear, the target ambiguous sentence was always paraphrased in its correct meaning. Thus, potentially ambiguous sentences may be rarely noticed because of disambiguating factors; as soon as one meaning is signaled as the appropriate one, the others are simply completely submerged.

Embedding

One example of the differences between the description of linguistic competence provided for by recursive rules in generative grammar and actual performance comes in the treatment of the various types of embedding. It would appear that not all grammatical sequences allowed for by the description of competence are the same or similar in performance.

Miller (1962) found that speakers could not repeat multiply self-embedded sentences, even in immediate-recall tasks. Although individuals were able to reproduce many of the individual words in the sentence, success in reproducing the original sentence with its original relationships intact was low indeed. For example, read and try to recall word for word the following sentence: *The race that the car that the people whom the obviously not very well-dressed man called sold won was held last summer.* Not surprisingly, similar results were reported by Miller and Isard (1964) for recall of sentences varying in degree of self-embedding. Single self-embedded sentences like *This is the rat that the cat caught* presented no problem. Double self-embedded sentences like *This is the rat the cat the dog chased caught* presented serious difficulties for most, and more than two self-embeddings like *This is the rat the cat the dog the horse bit chased caught* was beyond comprehension for all. Obviously, here competence and performance diverge dramatically. Although the grammar provides for infinite sentence possibilities arising from various sources, among them self-embedding, and may even provide for lengthy self-embedded sentences, a theory of performance tells us that beyond a very limited threshold self-embedded sentences are simply not understandable. We seem to be very limited in dealing with the kind of syntactic interruptions that self-embedding forces upon us.

Schlesinger (1968) reports that self-embedded sentences can, however, be better interpreted if semantic cues in terms of semantic-feature collocations give the direction of the sentence. Thus, although sentences like *The nurse the cook the maid met saw heard the butler* are indeed difficult, if not impossible, to interpret, sentences like *The rat the cat the dog barked at hissed at dug a hole* are easier to interpret because of the semantic cues they contain. The trick, of course, is that the semantic-feature ties between certain noun subjects and certain verb predicates provide immediate cues to which noun phrases go with which verb phrases in such difficult embedded sentences. Dogs normally bark, cats normally hiss, and so forth.

Moreover, it again appears that such semantic cues are at least on a par with and often supercede additional syntactic information. For example, the sentence *The nurse that the cook that the maid met saw heard the butler* is not too much easier than the version without the relative conjunctions separating the phrases. Nor, for that matter, is the sentence *This is the boy, that the man, whom the lady, whom our friend saw, knows, hit* that much easier than *This is the boy the man the lady our friend saw knows hit,* in spite of the clear boundary divisions by punctuation and relative pronouns. In fact, the attraction of the semantic cues in such difficult sentences is so much stronger that they often are predictive of the interpretation of a given string even when they are incorrect in terms of the actual sentence relationships. For example, read the embedded sentence *This is the hole that the rat that the cat that the dog bit made caught.* Chances are it will seem that the rat made the hole, the cat caught the rat, and the dog bit the cat. However, the sentence actually reads that *the hole that the rat caught* and *the rat that the cat made.* Contrast *This is the hole that the rat that the cat that the dog bit caught made.*

As mentioned, Fodor and Garrett (1967) present evidence that embedded sentences with adjectives are also easier to deal with than sentences without. To recall the example, the sentence *The first shot the tired soldier the mosquito bit fired missed* was easier to deal with than *The shot the soldier the mosquito bit fired missed.* Whether this is the same kind of semantic cue discussed here is debatable, but obviously something is operating to make the sentence easier to process, and chances are that it is reflected in underlining the semantic participation of the component phrases. Again, Fodor and Garrett also found that embedded sentences with relative pronouns that provide some minimal break between the phrases are somewhat easier to understand and paraphrase than those without. This is perhaps reflected in the single embedding *The man whom the dog bit died,* which is derived from *The man died* and *The dog bit the man.* The relative pronoun *whom* helps to indicate that *man* is the object of the embedded *whom the dog bit.* The same kind of immediate referencing is not provided in the same sentence minus the relative pronoun—*The man the dog bit died.* Now consider what happens in embedded sentences of greater length. Compare a sentence with such relativizers (*The shot that the soldier whom the mosquito bit fired missed*) with a sentence without them (*The shot the soldier the mosquito bit fired missed*). Embedded sentences containing such relative pronouns are thus somewhat easier to reproduce and paraphrase. This point also underscores the observation that understanding sentences often involves the use of surface-structure cues. It would appear that these cues take precedence over the rules incorporated in the grammar, so that the understanding of sentences is not necessarily a step-by-step decoding of the grammatical operations contained in the finished sentences.

The Independence of Semantics

There has been some dissatisfaction with the adulation paid to syntax, both in terms of the need for expansion of psycholinguistic horizons (see Bever, 1971) and in the types of investigations that characterize more and more of current research (see Johnson-Laird, 1974). More and more attention is being paid to integrating linguistic competence and language behavior with other systems of perception and behavior. Consequently, more studies are focusing on these other contributing systems or the relation of language behavior to them. There is, of course, no objective reason for tying sentences to syntax in their storage and recall. Meaning may be primary. In fact, there is no reason that the way in which information derived from language is stored should in any way parallel or look like the linguistic mechanisms that carry it. We also know from common sense, without benefit of experimental investigation, that content survives much better than verbatim syntactic information. The question, of course, is just how this semantic information is organized, stored, and retrieved when needed. In line with the distinctiveness approach is the suggestion (Begg & Paivio, 1969; Paivio, 1971) that imagery is this distinct nonlinguistic mode of representation and storage. This approach offers a compelling picture in which concrete sentences are best stored as sensory images, while abstract sentences that are less amenable to such translation are stored in a manner reflective of their linguistic shapes.

H. Clark and his colleagues (Clark & Clark, 1968; Clark & Stafford, 1969; Clark & Card, 1969) have also investigated the role of semantics in remembering sentences. Clark assumes that in recalling sentences from long-term memory one attempts to reconstruct sentences on the basis of the information still available. The information will contain semantic features, but with the vagaries of intervening time, these semantic features will be simplified, going from the more complex marked forms to the simpler unmarked forms in the language. The distinction between unmarked and marked forms is an additive one, with the marked form being more complex by one; simple subtraction is what characterizes sentence deterioration in the memory. That extra unit or feature on the marked form is lost, and it is the unmarked form that survives best. In examining sentences with verbs and paying particular attention to the affix differences between those verbs, Clark and Stafford (1969) found that the unmarked forms of the verbs are more prominent in recall. Marking here corresponded to the verbal affixes and their relative relationship; past, perfect, and progressive forms of the verb were considered as marked and their opposite numbers as unmarked. Similarly, in another study (Clark & Card, 1969) subjects commonly reconstructed sentences that were affirmative from original sentences that were negative, and unmarked adjectives (like *tall, deep, good*) from sentences originally containing marked adjectives (like *short, shallow, bad*).

Some attention has been paid to the role of semantic information in the storage and recall of sentences. It is a commonplace that people remember the gist of what was said rather than the exact syntactic shape of the discourse. This is especially true as one moves from the investigation of short-term memory to that of long-term memory. The gist may in fact be quite different from the original in form, but its content may be surprisingly similar. Fillenbaum (1966) has demonstrated that speakers tend to confuse forms that are for all practical purposes synonymous. For example, *dead* and *not alive* are apparently stored in some common fashion dependent upon their near identity semantically. Fillenbaum (1973) has more recently shown that where meaning is much the same, sentences will overlap, so that *If you do that, I'll hit you* later turns out as *Do that and I'll hit you.*

Johnson-Laird and Stevenson (1970) also report that sentences with differing syntactic shapes but similar meaning are recalled in a fashion indicating that speakers store and recall the basic meaning of the sentences rather than their shape. For example, sentences like *John liked the painting and bought it from the duchess* and *The painting pleased John, and the duchess sold it to him* were found to overlap considerably for speakers and were consequently confused. This point is highly reminiscent of the proposal on case grammar in which the actual case relationships are held to be invariant between sentential participants, regardless of sentence shape. Extending the notion in this case, we note that John is the one who took a fancy to the painting, the painting is that to which a fancy was taken, and the duchess is the one from whom it was ultimately parted. A fair amount of such work into basic semantic content has been done in such areas as scientific-abstracts translations, and one can expect to see more of it in psycholinguistics.

Similar results are reported on the nature of inference by Bransford, Barclay, and Franks (1972). There was some obvious overlap in the recall of sentences whose content was such that aspects of one could be transferred to another. For example, sentences like *Three turtles rested on a floating log, and a fish swam beneath* **them** were changed into *Three turtles rested on a floating log, and a fish swam beneath* **it**. Of course, it may just be that knowing the meaning helps to reconstruct the structure of the sentence; one has to admit the performance factors that imply some sentence structures are more common than others in general and some more expected than others in specific instances. In this light, one could expect that knowing the general meaning will give rise to certain sentence structures rather than others, and although one may not be too far from the content of the original, one may also not be so terribly far from the sentence shape as well.

10

Language and Bilingualism

The Definition of Bilingualism

There are several thousand languages, but wherever and whenever two of these languages come into contact, some group of individuals provides a bridge for communication. **Bilingualism,** or the ability to use more than one language, has been a fact of human history since it began to be recorded. With the tremendous increase in population coupled with increasing possibilities for intercultural and international exchange, bilingualism is probably more in evidence today than ever before.

Contrary to popular opinion, one language does not give way to another at national or political boundaries. Languages have lives all their own, separate and distinct from such modern entities as nations and unabridged dictionaries. In fact, if one looks closely, most of the nations of Europe are bilingual, or even multilingual, with two or more different ethnic groups speaking different languages. Nor does one have to look so far for such an example. Canada has a French-speaking population that encompasses nearly one-fifth of the total population of what one often takes to be an "English-speaking" country at a casual glance. If one looks at the history of the United States in terms of all the various ethnic groups who have immigrated since the last century, the picture is one of multiethnic and multilingual activity. If one looks at Asia, Africa, and the Pacific, the story is much the same, with multilingualism being the rule rather than the exception.

Most societies have at least some contact with other communities for reasons of trade, conquest, consultation, and so forth, and as a result they must communicate their needs and desires to one another. Such communication is usually carried out by the group of individuals conversant in the languages of both communities. Bilinguals thus share in the linguistic systems of both speech communities and can be considered members of two cultural communities according to their degree of participation in the two separate spheres of activity.

Bilingual activity is not, of course, an inherent feature of the language itself. Rather, it is a feature of the use of language by individuals who for one reason or another find themselves participants in the linguistic life of two different speech communities. There are obviously reasons for bilingualism—need, desire, experience, or a combination of these—and it is rare to find perfectly bilingual communities whose range and experience in the two languages is entirely coextensive. It is more common to find monolingual communities with bilingual communities of various sizes springing up as the result of contact between the functionally separate monolingual groups.

One can think of bilingualism in Weinreich's (1953) sense of simply the practice of alternatively using two languages. However, bilinguals vary in the degree of ability they exhibit in their second language. Bloomfield's (1933) early portrait of the bilingual as someone with native-like control of the second language is also not necessarily the best characterization. This view of bilingualism is close to the popular notion of bilinguals as individuals with complete proficiency in both languages, but no one of us would assume that we monolinguals have complete control of all language situations in our own language settings. Finding one's way through the intricacies of having certain repair jobs done on the family car and being able to address public meetings on sophisticated themes are just two activities that leave most of us with mixed feelings about our complete control of certain language faculties in our native language. And the bilingual, no matter how fluent, finds himself faced with similar gaps in his lexicon or his stylistic repertoire as a result of a lack of specialized knowledge or faulty experience in a particular area of the second language.

Some, like Haugen (1956), have even viewed bilingualism as best characterized by minimal qualifications rather than maximal qualifications. Haugen views bilinguals as individuals with the ability to produce some complete and meaningful utterances in the second language, and certainly one must admit than an individual who can produce even *Good morning, and how are you today?* in the second language is that much more bilingual than the monolingual, who cannot even produce that. To extend such minimal definitions, a bilingual would be someone who is fluent in English and can read (but not speak) German. So is the individual who is fluent in English and can also speak (but not read) some French, as well as the English-speaking individual who can read, write, speak, and understand Russian. However, there is something unsatisfying about too minimal a qualification on the status of bilingualism, though we can certainly agree with the notion that bilingualism is after all a continuum of abilities, with monolinguals at one end and perfectly fluent and capable native-like bilinguals at the other. Many bilinguals fall somewhere in between, demonstrating various kinds of abilities in the many skills that make up fluency in another language. Some assessment of where the bilingual falls on this continuum is obviously needed if we are to state the degree of bilingualism.

The Measurement of Bilingual Abilities

As Mackey (1962) has pointed out, assessment of a bilingual's degree of ability must take into consideration his mastery of the four skills of oral comprehension, oral production, written comprehension, and written production. Mastery of one area does not automatically mean skill in another area. Many individuals can be considered perfectly bilingual in oral comprehension and production in a language, but through lack of training, they may not have any skills in written comprehension and production. This is often the case with bilinguals who live in countries in which the medium of instruction is different from their native language and who consequently learn to read and write in a language other than their own. Typically, this has been the case for speakers of most Amerindian languages in North America and for speakers of minority languages in a number of countries. It may also be the case with individuals who migrate to other countries at a very young age, as did the large number of immigrants who went to the United States, Canada, and Australia and learned to read and write in English.

There are also examples of passive bilingualism, in which individuals have passive knowledge of the oral-comprehension skills but are completely or relatively unskilled at producing adequate utterances in the language. This is often the case with succeeding generations of immigrant groups in North America. The original immigrant generation may retain its original language, but the next generation may be fluent only in the language of the new country, though passively knowledgeable in the original immigrant language. Or the original immigrant generation may speak the native language as its first language but have some lesser degree of ability in the new language. The second generation may speak English as its native language with native-like ability and may also speak the immigrant language, but with limited ability. A third generation may speak only English but have a passive knowledge of the home language, so that conversations between grandparents and grandchildren are carried out in two languages, with the grandparents speaking in the immigrant language and the grandchildren understanding perfectly but able to respond in English only.

Similarly, one can also expect differences in the abilities shown in the various linguistic levels included in such skills. Although an individual may have native-like control of the phonology, the vocabulary stock available for use in extended conversation may be extremely limited. Or these two areas may be most adequate, but grammatical skills in inflections and sentence structure may be severely limited. It is interesting to speculate on what reactions native speakers may have toward judging the bilingual capabilities of individuals on the basis of limited information along these three dimensions of phonological, grammatical, and lexical competence.

It is obvious, then, that bilinguals exhibit differences in the encoding and decoding skills, as well as in the several abilities through which encoding and decoding processes take place. This complex state of affairs can best be shown by Table 10.1. Speakers of a language that has a writing system typically have two sets of active-production or encoding skills after a certain amount of formal schooling—the skills of speaking and writing. They also have two sets of passive-reception or decoding skills, reading and hearing–understanding. And for each of these skills, one can profitably distinguish between abilities related to the several levels of semantics, syntax, lexicon, and phonology (or graphology in reading and writing).

Studies have typically concentrated on attempting to measure bilinguals' fluency, flexibility, or dominance in the two languages. As Macnamara (1967) has indicated, many such tests are ingeniously designed experimental situations, but it remains to be seen exactly what their status as measurements of bilingualism is. All do seem to be agreed on

Table 10.1 Matrix of Four Aspects of Each of the Four Major Language Skills[a]

Encoding		Decoding	
Speaking	Writing	Listening	Reading
semantics	semantics	semantics	semantics
syntax	syntax	syntax	syntax
lexicon	lexicon	lexicon	lexicon
phonemes	graphemes	phonemes	graphemes

[a] From J. Macnamara, "The Bilingual's Linguistic Performance—A Psychological Overview," 1967. Reprinted by permission of the author and the Society for the Psychological Study of Social Issues.

the variability of skills that bilinguals may exhibit on the several levels of language.

An earlier study by Lambert, Havelka, and Gardner (1959) attempted to group bilinguals as either dominant or balanced on the basis of speed of response as an index of habit strength and automatic behavior. Such a behavioral measure, it was felt, could provide a characterization of the comparative automaticity of the bilinguals' speed of response in the two languages and thus provide a characterization for different types of bilinguals as well. Lambert, Havelka, and Gardner postulate that bilinguals can be typed as dominants—those showing statistically significant differences in speed of response between the two test languages, French and English—or balanced—those showing similar speeds of response in both languages. By extension, one would expect to gain some idea of degree of bilingualism by deviation from balanced ability in one language or the other. Perfectly balanced bilinguals would exhibit little difference in reaction time between the two languages.

Such measurements seem to apply best to those bilinguals who have learned their two languages in the sequence of native and second languages rather than in equivalent time–space settings, with both languages being learned from the earliest acquisition stages on but in different situations. It is difficult to know here whether one is measuring degrees of ability or the settings in which the separate language abilities were learned and are maintained. Tests such as word recognition under tachistoscopic presentation, word-completion tasks, word-detection tasks similar to "Spill-'n'-Spell" games, word response to items having the same orthographic shape in both languages, and facility in reading have all been used as mechanisms for tapping possible differences between bilingual abilities. It has, however, been noted that speed of translation is neither an adequate nor an accurate measure, for bilinguals have exhibited skewed skills in this measurement task. Although one would assume that the speaker would find it easier to translate into the native language, a surprising percentage of speakers in this report were more skilled at translating into the acquired language. It may be that because of specialized training, like school or business practice, this skill has become more developed in one direction than the other. On the other hand, one would not expect such a measurement to be of much consequence in the case of bilinguals who acquired both languages from an early time on. Finally, translation abilities are far more complicated than other mechanical abilities, such as word recognition, and are not as amenable to testing by simple measures.

The point, however, remains that bilinguals can indeed be assessed not only in terms of their differences, as Mackey (1962) has implied, but also by the speed of response with which such abilities are used. There are thus two variables for measurement, the differential abilities in the production of the language skills themselves and the speed of response and automaticity with which such skills are actually put to use in bilingual behavior.

Language Preference, Language Choice, and Language Use

Some assessment of the external function of the two languages in the life of the bilingual must also be made in order to understand completely the nature of bilingualism. The differential uses of the bilingual's two languages may be the result of preference or pressure. He may wish to use the choice between his two languages as an expression of solidarity and perhaps familiarity with the addressee. The same applies to situations, for the bilingual may wish to affirm his status by his choice of language. On the other hand, his choice of language may be the result of pressure from the addressee or the situation. Thus, for political, social, or business reasons, a bilingual may find it expedient or even necessary to speak a particular language in a specific interaction.

Then, too, as Mackey (1966) has pointed out, the use of the two languages may be reflected in their internal functions. Such uses are not communicative but are employed in such autolinguistic activities as thinking, counting, praying, and so forth. More than likely, such activities are carried out in the language in which the particular skill was introduced and mastered. Counting and related mathematical activities are an excellent example of this phenomenon. Having learned a set of verbal labels for the different units and the various operations, individuals simply find it easier to refer back to the original language system in which skill and, perhaps more important, speed were acquired than to acquire the same degree of facility in the other language. This is true only if the setting does not require actual verbalization of such skills. If it does, there may be no choice but to switch language systems, and then the original system may become less adequate through lack of practice.

Thus, as Mackey (1966) has pointed out, a measure of the distribution of the two languages throughout the entire behavior repertoire of the individual may be just as important, if not more important than, a technical definition of bilingualism as such. The assessment of the habitual use of the two languages—when, where, with whom, and to what extent the bilingual uses each of his two languages—is a crucial factor in the complete understanding of bilingual behavior. This position is reminiscent of the kind of concern that has spurred investigations of the relationship between language and society as a crucial issue in the examination of the performance aspects of language. Similarly, with bilingualism it is important not only to understand what kinds of abilities characterize bilingualism but also to understand where the bilingual uses his skills. The one aspect cannot be seen as entirely unrelated to the other.

It is of less consequence to inquire about the bilingual's preferences for using the two languages. What is important is which of the two he does use because there is no other choice, because the social, economic, and perhaps even demographic factors demand it. The use of the bilingual's languages likely depends on the sociolinguistic exigencies of his immediate environment. But this factor also influences the abilities he exhibits in the use of both languages. If the school he attends is conducted in only one language, if the material he reads is available in only one language, and if most technical materials and instructions are forthcoming in only one language, will he not also be expected to have no ability or certainly very little (unless he is a rare and ambitious sort) in the reading and writing skills of the other language? Moreover, stylistic skills that parallel dimensions decreed by the technical areas introduced and maintained in the one language will also be relatively lacking in the other language. And so the situation goes, with sociolinguistic facts of usage to some degree determining not only usage itself but to a large degree the skills themselves.

Such aspects of bilingualism are highly suggestive of the type of sociolinguistic behavior seen in the discussion of the relationships between language and society. Differential use of language varieties or language styles within the same language community communicates sociolinguistic information about the speaker and his attitudes toward the addressee and the setting, just as does the bilingual's use of his two languages. Moreover monolinguals and bilinguals appear to have different sets of values for their respective languages and their judgments of other languages. Obviously, being bilingual involves more than just a set of mechanical language skills. It includes complex social attitudes and motivations and corresponding social postures, some of which may be at odds in the value systems in the two cultures.

Lambert and a number of his colleagues have for some time been involved in assessing the stereotyped reactions of one group toward another group. Typically, a group is asked to make evaluative judgments about personality characteristics of individuals who have recorded short segments of speech on tapes. Ostensibly, the evaluations are made on the basis of voice qualities, but when bilinguals read segments in their two languages, reactions differ. The implication is that something more than just the feature of voice qualities is being assessed. Specifically, when language boundaries are crossed, it would appear that the language serves as the keystone for an entire set of reactions toward the cultural group that the language represents.

An early study (Lambert et al., 1960) had French-speaking and English-speaking students in Montreal evaluate personality characteristics of 10 speakers. Some of the language output was in English and some in French, but unknown to the students, bilinguals were used as speakers in both instances. Evaluational reactions for the same speakers were matched for each of the language guises. These reactions were taken as a measure of the attitudes that French-speaking and English-speaking Canadians had toward the respective language samples and, consequently, one would assume, toward members of the respective communities. The results are not surprising in that English speakers evaluated English guises more favorably than French guises, but it is interesting to note that French speakers also rated the English guises more favorably than the French ones. Moreover, the French speaker's evaluations of French guises were somewhat less favorable than the English speakers' evaluations of them. Some comment is offered by Lambert (1969) to the effect that the tendency to downgrade one's own ethnic group in comparison to the dominant culture is not uncommon in North America according to research done in these areas. However, this may no longer be true in view of the North American emphasis on ethnicity during the past decade.

Another study, by Anisfield and Lambert using a similar approach (1964), had monolingual and bilingual French-Canadian 10-year-olds listen to recordings of children's voices, some speaking in English and some in French. The children were asked to rate the speakers' personalities for 15 traits. One would expect that differences in such ratings might be indicative of the differences in stereotyped notions about French-Canadian and English-Canadian speakers. The results contrasted sharply with those of the preceding study; French-speaking children rated the French-speaking voices more favorably on all but one of the 15 traits, the exception being height. Most striking is the rating given by the bilingual children, for their evaluations of English-speaking and French-speaking voices were more similar. This suggests that bilinguals tend to see fewer dramatic personality differences and are less prone to stereotypic reaction to the two groups as a result of their membership, linguistic and cultural, in both groups. This one factor may in itself be a powerful argument for the advantages of inculating bilingual abilities in one or more other languages. By analogy, it would seem that the more exposure to other linguistic and cultural groups people have, the less prone they are to be misled by biased statements and unfounded stereotypes.

It is clear that certain aspects of the evaluational reactions of the monolingual children contrast with those of the older students in the previous study. Anisfield and Lambert suggest that this may be the result of the young monolingual's limited experience with the world outside his own speech community; it is only as he grows older and becomes acquainted with other groups' characterizations of his own group that he becomes pressured into accepting another, less ethnocentric and, in this instance, less self-satisfying set of evaluational reactions. This method seems to be an interesting means of tapping the various stages that such stereotypes are acquired in and what their consequences are. Moreover, such measurement appears to be amenable to testing over time to assess subtle changes in social perceptions of stereotypic judgments on the basis of language samples. Some attempt to investigate the chronological aspect of evaluational reactions has been reported (Lambert et al., 1966) for female French Canadians between the ages of 9 and 18. Once again the students were required to evaluate the personality traits of (bilingual) English and French voices. Definite preference for the English-speaking guise was apparent at about the age of 12 and continued through the teenage years. At first glance, it would seem that a similar measuring device might be an excellent tool in other bilingual situations in which the possible dimensions of conflict and cooperation are a facet of bilingual behavior in the larger fabric of a multilingual society.

Linguistic Interference

Another question is that of linguistic interference between the bilingual's two systems. Some assessment must be made of the degree to which the two languages may overlap at the various levels—phonological, intonational, morphological, syntactic, and semantic—of the language codes. For example, when one characterizes a speaker as having an accent, all one has done is to have made a judgment that some of the original system of phonological habits in the speaker's native language has carried over into his manipulation of the phonological system of the second language. Obviously, this is the basis for popular conceptions of various accents, and this is how people do characterize Russian, French, Japanese, and German accents in English. All languages, including English, simply exhibit initial characteristic carry-over patterns into other languages. Such carry-over patterns last only as long as the speaker is actually being influenced by his native set of habits; they diminish with his increasing ability to reproduce the habits of the second language. For some, this point may never seem to come, but for the vast majority of learners of a second language, this ability, like bilingualism itself, represents a continuum of abilities.

The point is that an analogy can be made in the bilingual's abilities in the two languages. If the individual is perfectly competent in his two languages, there may be little or no interference in the actual production of the two languages. Or, as is more likely, some interference from one language may carry over into any one of the several levels of the other language system. It may be only a minor feature, such as voice set or an ill-defined but nevertheless recognizable paralinguistic feature, or perhaps some more salient feature, such as phonological overlap or syntactic arrangements that are more reflective of one language than the other. Weinreich (1953) has offered an excellent discussion of this phenomenon and of methods for assessing the type and manner of interference between two languages.

It is amazing that bilinguals are able to keep the two languages as separate as they do, considering that the classes of data they store and retrieve in the two systems are enormous. There may be some tendency for the phonological, syntactical, and lexical systems of one language to intrude into the other. After all, linguistic features are linguistic habits, and the tenacious grasp of habit is likely to result in some interference in the bilingual's use of the second language. Depending on his actual degree of ability in the second language, the degree of interference will be minimal or maximal.

Linguistic interference is a characteristic of the individual's use of language, while borrowing is a characteristic of the language as a system. Lingusitic borrowing is nothing less than elements borrowed from outside the native stock of structural and lexical elements that constitutes the system. If one views a language as a steady historical stream of events, with a particular inventory of grammatical and lexical elements, proceeding in a linear fashion without reference to or contact with any other language, then no such notion of borrowing arises. However, most languages have some contact with other languages during their long history, and they may for one reason or another borrow elements from that second language. Vocabulary words are the most common item borrowed. They fill in vocabulary gaps created when cultural concepts and experiences are borrowed.

Such vocabulary items may prove to be Trojan horses in the manner in which they serve as the carriers of other changes. For example, the surface similarity of Amerindian phonological systems characterized by glottalized consonants on the Northwest Coast may be a result of such borrowing. Borrowing is probably responsible for the existence of retroflex consonants on both sides of the Indo-European and Dravidian language-family line in India. The examples are many and can all be classed as features of the system as system. Monolinguals use them freely and often unwittingly, for once embedded in the system, they are treated like any other item on the same linguistic level. In English, for example, it makes no difference to monolingual speakers that *alcohol* comes from Arabic, *alligator* from Spanish, *skirt* from Scandinavian, *boondocks* from the Philippines, *negligee* from French, and so forth. There is, however, an interesting commentary to be made on the possible carriers of such borrowed elements into the language. Some multiple cases of interference may become standardized in the speech of bilinguals and from there enter the language as system and, consequently, the speech of monolinguals. This is common enough in instances of mass bilingualism—for example, during the period of Middle English in our own language history when French had such a tremendous impact on the structure and vocabulary of English after the Norman Conquest. The point is that borrowing and interference are quite different in substance and effect. Borrowing is the change in language as system; interference is the conflict of competing sets of habit skills, often resulting in a change or disturbance in the bilingual's production or comprehension abilities through the overlap of language habits. However, individual cases of interference repeated in a number of instances are likely to be one major avenue in the origin and transfer of borrowed elements.

The Status of the Two Languages: Dependent or Independent?

Ervin and Osgood (1954) have made some observations about the importance of the language-acquisition context and the interdependent status of the bilingual's two languages. Ervin and Osgood type bilinguals, after Weinreich's (1953) suggestion, as either compound bilinguals or coordinate bilinguals, with the distinction entirely dependent on how they acquired the two languages. Compound bilinguals acquired language in settings in which both languages were used interchangeably. As a result, compound bilinguals attribute identical meanings to words and phrases that correspond in their two language systems. Thus, one can expect a kind of fusion of the two meaning systems as a simple function of the fact that both languages were learned in the same setting. For example, a young second-generation Slovene immigrant in North America might learn *hiša* as the word for his own domicile in Slovene conversations but *house* as the English word for the same object in English conversations.

In fact, the acquisition of a second language in a typical traditional school setting can be classed as a kind of compound bilingual setting. Here the student may learn—and traditionally often has—the second language through the medium of the first. Thus, the first language serves as the indirect carrier of the second, so that in learning school Spanish, the word *casa* invariably is acquired through *house* and as a result takes on the meanings associated with the original English stimulus word. But, the classroom setting has not always provided the rich variation that language in its normal settings does. Even if the second language is presented so as to reproduce or approximate the first language-acquisition setting, the setting is limited and to some degree hampered by already having been assigned a frame of reference by the first and native language.

Coordinate bilinguals, on the other hand, acquired their languages in separate contexts, with the different linguistic settings populated by speakers of only one of the two languages. As a result, the meaning systems of the two languages are somewhat distinct. An example of this type of bilingual is an individual who learned French in France and English in North America, or Cantonese in Hong Kong and English in Hawaii, and maintains both languages as he passes through linguistic adulthood.

There are obviously further implications for the study of bilingualism than merely a typology of bilinguals. For one thing, compound bilinguals exhibit meanings that are more similar as translational equivalents than coordinate bilinguals, for whom the language of each setting may represent an entirely different codification of a world of objects and experiences. Moreover, if the assumptions underlying the classification are correct, then one can expect that members of the two groups will exhibit differences in their various external and internal language-related behaviors.

Lambert, Havelka, and Crosby (1958) similarly classified bilinguals as either fused or separate on the basis of the acquisition of bilingualism in either separated or fused contexts. They postulated that if such classification is correct, continued separation of the two languages in terms of settings and experience would increase the functional separation of the two systems. On the other hand, continued compound experience in mixed contexts should be reflected in a minimal or reduced separation of the two language systems. Lambert and his colleagues tested bilinguals with such differentiated histories of language acquisition in several areas of language behavior. They examined the possibilities of greater semantic distinctiveness in one language as opposed to its translational equivalent in the other, the associative dependence of translational equivalents in the two languages, and the general translational facility. In a review of the results of these studies, Lambert (1969) notes that in general the results support the separate typology. Specifically, they found greater semantic differences in translational equivalents, as measured by semantic rating scales, for the coordinate bilinguals. Compound bilinguals, moreover, appear to have greater dependency relationships between translational equivalents in the two languages, so that rehearsing with the word in one language also to some degree represented rehearsing with the word in the other language on tasks that required and measured such transferability. There was, however, no marked difference between the groups in their translational abilities in general. Both types of bilinguals appear to be equal in speed of translation and general ability to move from one language to the other.

Thus, the assumption that corresponding words in the two languages have separate meanings because of the quite separate contexts in which they were acquired seems justified by these and later results. Each of the linguistic symbols draws images and retains domain ties of a different kind for the coordinate bilingual, for they represent separate contextual settings to him. This may run the gamut of possibilities from the youngster who learns the language of his peer group in another culture abroad and then returns to his home country and another language, to the individual who is bilingual in the same physical environment but experiences one language in contexts like his business life and another in his more relaxed and intimate social life. Another example is the bilingual child who has learned to speak one language with one member, friend, or employee of the family and another with people in his environment. Each of these appears to be a coordinate system of some kind.

Compound bilinguals, on the other hand, appear to have assimilated both languages in essentially the same settings and probably with the same interlocutors. If this is the case, then some degree of fusion will have taken place, with a minimal difference between symbols in the two systems. Essentially, the same environment is labeled by two separate systems, and the two systems bear a fair degree of resemblance to each other in the way in which they were initially constructed. An example of this situation is a bilingual home in which parents and family switch indiscriminately between one language and the other. This situation can be extended to a subcommunity of a larger society in which, for whatever historical, political, and social reasons, the members engage in the same kind of language switching. However, one is hesitant to speculate on an entire culture or community that is entirely bilingual and switches in this manner, for common sense and history both decree that a community in which everyone is completely and perfectly bilingual is very unlikely. If it were so, and two languages were performing the task of one, it would likely not be very long before one language would be doing the previous work of two.

Some interest has also been shown in the possible effects on memory of the variation of the languages used in both learning and recall. Ervin (1961b) notes that bilinguals can be characterized as dominant according to the language in which they exhibit greater facility in naming common objects. If this is true, one would also expect better recall abilities in that language. This expectation is substantiated by Ervin's findings that the optimal condition for recall in certain tasks is the original learning in the dominant language and the recall in that language. Ervin also notes that recall abilities are weakest when learning takes place in the dominant language and recall takes place in the other language. A parallel finding reported by Nott and Lambert (1968) is that bilinguals required to recall lists of words in the two languages recall fewer words from lists in the weaker, or nondominant, language.

A number of studies have concentrated on the coding properties of language for bilinguals as opposed to other kinds of arbitrary coding systems in memory and recall tasks. An excellent example of such work is the investigation carried out by Kolers (1965) on the coding features of language. Kolers assumed that a linguistic system, being a well-learned and familiar code, would exhibit functional properties in memory and recall tasks different from those exhibited by some equally well-constructed but arbitrary code. Kolers presented subjects with word lists that were to be recalled after an appropriate period. On some lists the words were presented in red or black and in others in French or English. Another set of lists was mixed, with words on the color lists appearing as either red or black and on the language lists in either French or English. As was expected, a well-formed coding scheme like language is built into the word's very existence, so that twice as many words were recalled from the mixed-language list as were recalled from the mixed-color list. This finding suggests that arbitrary systems like color do not have the same functional equivalency as more familiar and integral systems like language coding.

Koler's conclusions seem quite obvious, but the implications are somewhat more far-reaching than they seem at first. In remembering words from the mixed-color list, a speaker must remember both the word itself and the color in which it appeared, so that two features of information are required in storage and retrieval. One might also expect that an adult learning the two languages for the first time would have the same problem in remembering words given in French and in English on a mixed list, for he must remember both the shape of the word and the language system from which it comes. Subjects who are bilingual and thus competent in both languages, however, are not faced with this problem on the mixed-language list, for each word is automatically coded as the language, and the bilingual is simply using well-formed rules of the set membership of each word. His only task is to remember as many words on the mixed list as possible; their language membership is automatically marked for him. This is not, however, the case with the mixed-color list, where words are coded according to a system that is complete but arbitrary and, for the subjects, obviously unfamiliar. Such set membership is not an automatic feature for bilingual subjects, as is language membership, so only half as many items form a mixed-color list were recalled.

Later studies by Lambert, Ignatow, and Krauthamer (1968) seem to suggest that although the recall factors of language as a highly coded system and the fact of language dominance are important, some attention must also be paid to semantic-category clustering. In tasks in which word-recall lists have been constructed to test also for such clustering around semantic categories, the clustering influences the bilingual's recall performance. In fact, for bilinguals, organization according to semantic categories may be even more useful for such tasks than language coding. Of course, such observations apply only when both factors are present, but in any event, there is no doubt that both play an important part in recall abilities for bilinguals.

Other researchers, like Kolers (1963, 1968), have also been interested in the interaction between the bilingual's two languages. As Kolers (1968) points out, much can be learned about the mind in general by investigating the operations involved in the acquisition, storage, and retrieval of language information. This is especially true in the case of bilinguals because they have internalized two sets of symbols, two highly coded systems, and one wonders what the outcome is when information is acquired in one language and tested in another. The same question is of interest regarding languages that are mixed in their actual manifestations. In one approach to this problem reported by Kolers, bilinguals read a series of four passages in French alone, in English alone, in mixed French and English favoring English word order, and in mixed English and French favoring French word order. The bilinguals had no difficulty with comprehension tests on the mixed passages. This is contrary to what one would have expected if the bilinguals had actually been translating the mixed passages to themselves. In fact, the comprehension scores on the silent reading of the mixed passages were no different from the scores on the passages in either English alone or French alone.

It is not surprising, however, that significant time differences were shown between the aloud readings of the mixed passages and the unilingual passages. The actual physiological fact of switching apparently takes an observable amount of time, though it may be wise not to make too much of this. In Kolers' experiments perhaps reading the mixed passages took longer because of the need to adjust physically the vocal mechanisms in preparation for the different voice set and corresponding articulation habits in the other language. Kolers and his colleagues determined that the time it took to shift averaged an extra third of a second. Thus, there is little difference in the total comprehension for the following four sequences:

1. *His horse, followed by two hounds. . . .*
2. *Son cheval, suivi de deux bassets. . . .*
3. *His horse, followed de deux bassets. . . .*
4. *Son cheval, suivi by two hounds. . . .*

However, there are apparently time differences in actual reading production between the first two and the last two.

In another approach to the possible interlingual relationships of the bilingual's two languages, Kolers (1966, 1968) took on the frequent comment that bilinguals make about thinking and responding differently to a given emotion or experience in the two languages. In a rather complex word-association study designed to test interlingual word associations, Kolers tried to determine the accuracy of considering bilinguals as having either a single storage capacity or a multiple but unrelated set of storage capacities. The matter of characterization is reminiscent of the coordinate and compound differentiation, but the question at issue is not so much acquisition as how linguistic information is stored. To use his metaphor, does the bilingual have one large tanklike capacity with two taps, corresponding to the two languages? Or does he have two separate storage capacities with two separate taps, corresponding to the two languages? In other words, is linguistic information of such a nature that it is shared or separate in the bilingual's mental and intellectual processes?

Kolers designed an intricate association test to investigate the matter of such storage with German–English, Spanish–English, and Thai–English bilinguals. After testing intralingual associations from English to English and native language to native language, Kolers also examined interlingual associations given by English to native language response and native language to English response. In the last instances, the stimulus appears in one language and the response in the other. His results are most interesting. Approximately a fifth of the responses were the same in both languages, but as much as a fourth of the responses were limited to one language alone. To put it simply, neither assumption, the shared or the separate contention, is entirely validated. It would appear that some information is acquired, coded, maintained, and retrieved only within the confines of the one linguistic system, with all its concomitant nuances and associations. Fairly elusive concepts such as abstract terms and culturally determined concepts and experiences would fit into this latter category. On the other hand, certain objects and physical experiences can be easily coded or equated in both of the languages. Such items are likely to be concrete objects that are manipulated in similar ways by speakers of whatever language and so are not necessarily coded specially in a given language only. Thus, dependent on the kind of information one is speaking of, the information can be stored in systems that make it accessible in other ways—in this case, through several linguistic systems. Some information, however, is of such a nature that it is coded uniquely in terms of one system and can only be retrieved within that system and by reference to all the other component parts of that system.

Other aspects of Kolers' (1968) investigations suggest that information of certain kinds can indeed be stored in a common form. He has noted that equivalent information repeated in different languages may be as well retained as information repeated as many times in a single language. Building on the earlier observation that word-recall ability is proportionately enhanced by the number of times a given word is repeated in a random list, Kolers and his colleagues inquired about what might happen if the items repeated were words in different languages that were direct translational equivalents of one another. For example, if the English *ten* and the French *dix* were repeated in word lists, would they be recalled according to their single appearance as words, or would they be recalled according to some commonality of meaning and reference feature? It would appear that the latter is the case, and repetition of the forms *ten* and *dix* twice apiece has the same effect as presenting either item four times. Apparently, bilinguals store them according to the meaning they share or some similar dimension in a form other than the language in which they appear.

Bilingual Education and Second-Language Acquisition

These observations and aspects of the other investigations discussed that point to commonality of storage by the mind lead to some interesting speculations about the possibility of such things as bilingual education. The question for many countries is, of course, not so much the theoretical question of the measurement of bilingualism and its consequences, but how best to provide facilities for the acquisition of bilingual abilities. Many countries, such as Canada and Ireland, have a national policy that officially recognizes two or more languages; each is used exclusively by a certain percentage of the population. For national purposes, some attempt to make an increasing proportion of the population bilingual has been seen by some as a worthy goal. Other countries, such as Israel, the Phillippines, and India, have rather large populations of various language origins, and the desire here is to inculcate some kind of bilingualism in order to establish a single recognized medium of communication.

Some interesting suggestions have been made about what the nature of bilingual education should be. In most attempts to introduce a second language to younger generations through the medium of the school situation, the second language has been presented as a special subject together with a number of other subjects in the curriculum. The other possibility, of course, is to have students of other native-language backgrounds simply begin their school experience in the target language and continue in it. This is typically what happens in North America with immigrant groups whose succeeding generations are expected simply to surge headlong into the language itself. There would appear to be no choice, and this is probably what accounts for the rapid demise of much of the rich variety of linguistic types seen on this continent on the past century. The question in those countries in which bilingualism is desired for a growing number of children, but in which there is no urgent need for it, is what to do with the school curriculum to achieve this end.

Traditionally, of course, teaching a language as a special subject in the curriculum with the same time and space limitations as mathematics, geography, or history has not been very effective. The language experience is divorced from social reality and is associated with a particular time slot in the daily scholastic schedule. Some have, on the other hand, suggested the possibilities in simply administering large parts or all of the school curriculum in the target language. Thus, all the subjects are taught in the language, and the entire classroom situation is turned into a setting that employs only that language. One would suspect that if the shared hypothesis of bilingual intellectual activity is indeed true for information that need not have domain ties to a particular cultural setting, the approach could prove successful. Thus, a lesson in geography, as Kolers (1968) implies, would be the same in effect whether given in either language. More important, two lessons, one given in each of the two languages, might be the equivalent of both lessons in one language. The nuance to note is that through presentation of material in both languages, the individual is able to recall readily information about the geography topic in both languages and should be able to converse freely, fluently, and knowledgeably about matters geographical in both languages. Conversely, as has been all too evident from previous second-language courses in the regular curriculum, teaching students a language and subject matter like geography separately and in the first language will not guarantee the individual's ability to communicate about geography in that second language. There seems to be little transfer, an ability that seems to require additional training.

The advantages of some form of bilingual education seem rather attractive, providing they come as readily as the preceding suggestion would indicate. Children progress through the regular stages of the curriculum, but they become bilingual with no extra scholastic effort. The school setting is treated as a particular social setting, and everything is carried out in the new medium of communication, the target language. The problem, of course, has been to assess what other tasks the child faces in this situation and whether the situation is really as simple as some make it out to be.

Prior to any discussion of bilingual education, it is wise to distinguish among the many individuals who engage in the acquisition of another language. Large numbers of individuals proceed to learn another language without apparently ever studying it formally. This is in sharp contrast to the equally large numbers of individuals who are taught some aspects of another language without ever learning it. According to Mackey (1967a), it may be instructive to note the characteristics of each situation and the results that derive from the different attitudes in each. Mackey notes that, first of all, the one who ends as a bilingual does not necessarily learn language as an academic exercise but as behavior. The bilingual quickly learns what to say and when to say it as a means of getting things done in real situations. Second, the bilingual learns the language as a form of communication that is geared to results. It is the result that counts, and to the degree that the result is obtained, the goal of language as a communication device has been achieved. Classroom techniques may concentrate heavily on drills and exercises that may to some degree compensate for or reproduce the appropriate behavioral settings, but their stressing of perfection and accuracy may run counter to the actual uses of language. Thus, one learns the important facts of how the language is organized and what its component parts are, but little time may be devoted to actual behavioral patterns of use. Third, in speaking the second language, the bilingual has become a member of a second linguistic community, with all the concomitant privileges and responsibilities. He is identified as one with the members of that society or at least one who is sympathetic with the aims of that society, and he receives the rewards thereof. Obviously, this situation is difficult to reproduce in a formal classroom setting. For the bilingual, the other language becomes a codification of new cultural dimensions, and his expertise in the second language will reflect his restructuring of many cultural experiences. This, too, is difficult to reproduce in a formal situation, in which the student essentially is being requested to restructure his experience without the benefit of actually experiencing the restructuring firsthand. This may be compared to attending class lectures that outline the philosophy of tennis without ever being permitted to go out and swing a racket a few times.

Conversely, it only stands to reason, as Lambert, Gardner, Barik, and Tunstall (1963) have pointed out, that a would-be bilingual with favorable attitudes toward the speakers of the language he is learning will more easily identify with the group and will experience less difficulty in acquiring competence in the language.

In turn, his favorable attitudes will make the group more likely to accept him readily and to reinforce his linguistic and social efforts. The bilingual's linguistic and social behavior will then more closely parallel that of native speakers. Native speakers in turn will see him as increasingly like them and thus one of them. The more he acts and speaks like them, the more he will be rewarded for being one of them, and the entire process speedily contributes to his fullest participation in the language and the culture. Many of the important considerations seen in the previous two decades of work on the questions of attitudes and motivation in second-language learning can be derived from a reading of the recent summarization by Lambert and Gardner (1972).

Similarly, the artificiality of some formal class settings can never reflect the actual innovative behavior that bilinguals are required to master in coping with new situations. The semantic functions inherent in language do not carry the same depth of firsthand experience as they do for the bilingual who has in fact experienced various aspects of them. One is left with the feeling of speech as mere verbal manipulation without any substance to it and without any depth of feeling behind it. This may be why programing machines like computers with some linguistic abilities may be futile until one reprograms the people who deal with them to expect only machine-like speech in turn.

Observations made by Penfield and others (Penfield, 1965; Penfield & Roberts, 1959) on the physiology of the human brain and the child's corresponding linguistic adaptability can also be taken into account in planning for bilingual educational practices. A decade and a half ago, Penfield reckoned that the child's brain is well suited to the learning of languages up to a certain time. Penfield claims that after the age of 9 to 12, the areas of the brain that are related to such activities become less flexible, and the language-learning capacities decrease. Although some have disagreed with Penfield's chronological sequencing, few will disagree with the fact that such abilities appear to peak at puberty and then steadily decline. The result, of course, is that learning another language becomes a difficult, and for many a near-impossible, task. For the child, it is as automatic as growing up, and language-learning tasks are not tasks at all but are simply assimilated as other behaviors to be acquired. The discussion of language acquisition in previous chapters is perfectly congruent with such notions, though not a great deal is said by Lenneberg and others about the nature of language acquisition in two, three, or more contexts resulting in bilingualism and multilingualism. An innate view of language acquisition would suggest, however, that such attempts to learn a second language should be carried out at an early date in the child's development. One would expect that the processes in the acquisition of a first language are the same in the acquisition of the second language from the child's birth. The same may be true in the child's acquisition of another language somewhat later in his maturational development, say, around the age of 5 or 6 or possibly later. By analogy, one would assume that the maturational propensities by which the child acquires his first language are brought to bear in identical or at least similar fashion if exposure to the other language is introduced at a sufficiently early date. At any rate, it would appear from the foregoing discussion that such attempts should be made in a manner that makes language acquisition another form of behavior and not necessarily a formal exercise.

Such observations and the desire for greater distribution of bilingual abilities have led some communities and countries to launch programs directed at this problem. These programs have had varying degrees of success, often inextricably tied up with external social and political factors. For example, the teaching of Hebrew in Israel has been largely successful because of the obvious unifying circumstances. On the other hand, Irish Gaelic in Ireland has remained viable primarily in the poorer and less accessible western reaches of the country and gives no hint of replacing the Hibernian English that has become the native language for most. Not even the practice of offering 10 pounds per year per child has entirely succeeded in making Irish Gaelic the home language for many more young Irishmen, though it has made the assessment of the accuracy of answers to official language-background questionnaires much more difficult (Macnamara, 1967).

Somewhat closer to home, Canada offers an excellent example of the bilingual situation and an illustration of some of the liabilities and assets of the concept of bilingual education. Being officially a bilingual country, Canada has seen some interesting innovations in bilingual programs in recent years. Canada recognizes English and French as the country's official languages, with about two-thirds of the population speaking English only and about one-fifth speaking French only—those able to speak both languages constitute about 12% of the population, according to Lieberson's (1970) figures. Yet English seems to have emerged as the dominant language in several other significant ways. Canada has experienced enormous waves of immigrants over the past century, and they have also affected the relative positions of the two languages. English appears to be more attractive to immigrants, past and present, so they are more likely to learn English than they are to learn French. To use Lieberson's (1970) example, if the home language learned by a child is other than English, chances are one in two that English will also be spoken. On the other hand, only 1 out of 20 persons will learn to speak French if it is not the first language of the home.

Even in the province of Quebec, commercial activities were at times carried out in English, to the exclusion of French. Many of Canada's social and political activities were carried out through the medium of English, much to the dismay of French-speaking Canadians who thought themselves speaking what seemed to be a language with little real influence, though one with official status. This is reflected in the fact that of Canada's bilingual population, an overwhelming majority are from a native Francophone background rather than from a native Anglophone background. Such facts seem to run counter to the fundamental fact of official-language status afforded French constitutionally, or so many French-speaking Canadians have felt, and steps have been taken to right the situation. Legislation dealing with bilingual and bicultural aspects of the country's life has appeared on both the national and the provincial level. Some of this legislation favors the promulgation of bilingual abilities for a larger segment of the population as well as simply ensuring the official status of Canadian French. In some areas the interest in bilingual educational programing has been increasing.

One of the more interesting of these programs has been reported in several places (Lambert & Macnamara, 1969; Lambert, Just, & Segalowitz, 1970; Tucker, Lambert, & d'Anglejean, 1973) and has been summarized by Lambert and Tucker (1972). They describe a long-term project designed to develop bilingual skills in elementary-school children that has been in progress in Montreal since the 1965–1966 school year. What began as a program to promote bilingual abilities through a policy of home-language and school-language switching has proved relatively successful and has been expanded to a full program from kindergarten through Grade 7 at the St. Lambert Elementary School, a primary school in a Montreal suburb that initiated the program in response to requests from English-speaking parents in the community. The approach is a fairly straightforward one and is in fact familiar in many countries. Once the children leave their English-speaking home environment and enter school, the entire curriculum and all the day's activities are conducted in the target language—in this case,

French. The difference, of course, between these English-speaking Montreal children and other children in mixed-language communities is that they are there by choice, or at least by their parents' choice, and this obviously makes for some positive factors in the attitudes the young would-be bilinguals bring into the learning situation.

At the kindergarten level, of course, conducting all curriculum activities in French does not imply the introduction of complex skills, but what is done is done in French and by a direct language approach. French is not introduced as a second language or a foreign language; it is simply the language in which everything is done. By Grade 1, such curriculum activities as reading, writing, and arithmetic are introduced in French. By Grade 2, two periods a day in English Language Arts may be added, but the entire remainder of the day's activities continues in French. Gradually the amount of instruction through the medium of English is increased, and by the end of the elementary-school period in Grade 7, approximately half of the curriculum is taught in English and the other half in French.

Unlike many other such programs, consistent efforts to evaluate the general intellectual development of the children have been carefully matched with control-group classes of French children taught in French and English children taught in English. In general, without giving the particulars of the tests or the exact results, the bilingual program has not resulted in any dramatic deficiency in either native-language skills or in subject-matter skills. Children enrolled in this kind of program appear to read, write, speak, understand and, in general, use English as well as children instructed through the medium of English alone. The incredible advantage, of course, is having similar skills in French at little extra effort. The effort would appear to be on the part of the native French-speaking teachers who must take care to use only the appropriate language of instruction at the desired times. The children acquire skills in French that no foreign-language approach could deliver and, most important, have none of the inhibiting or negative attitudes toward the second language that often develop when it is treated as a "foreign" language.

As Lambert et al. (1972) admit, children who have progressed through this program cannot yet be classified as completely balanced bilinguals in their abilities. Balanced bilinguals, it will be recalled, are those whose proficiency in both languages is excellent and more or less equal in the two languages; dominant bilinguals are those whose abilities in one language exceed their abilities in the other language. It seems clear enough that a school or a school-like situation cannot provide all the possibilities of using the language in realistic settings in which spontaneity is mandatory. Nevertheless, if anyone were ready to continue on into perfectly balanced bilingual activities, children who have been provided with this experience seem to be in a likely position to be able to do so.

Bibliography

Anisfield, E., & Lambert, W. E.   Evaluational reactions of bilingual and monolingual children to spoken languages. *Journal of Abnormal and Social Psychology*, 1964, *69*, 89–97.

Attneave, F.   *Applications of information theory to psychology*. New York: Holt, 1959.

Bach, E., & Harms, R. T. (Eds.)   *Universals in linguistic theory*. New York: Holt, 1968.

Begg, I., & Paivio, A.   Concreteness and imagery in sentence meaning. *Journal of Verbal Learning and Verbal Behavior*, 1968, *8*, 21–27.

Bellugi, U., & Brown, R. (Eds.)   *The acquisition of language. Monographs for the Society of Research in Child Development*, 1964, Vol. 29, No. 1.

Berko, J.   The child's learning of English morphology. *Word*, 1958, *14*, 150–177.

Berlin, B.   A universalist-evolutionary approach in ethnographic semantics. *Bulletin of the American Anthropological Association*, 1970, *3*, 1–17.

Berlin, B., & Kay, P.   *Basic color terms: Their universality and evolution*. Berkeley: Univ. of California Press, 1969.

Bever, T.   The cognitive basis for linguistic structures. In J. R. Hayes (Ed.), *Cognition and the development of language*. New York: Wiley, 1970.

Bever, T.   The integrated study of language. In J. Morton (Ed.), *Biological and social factors in psycholinguistics*. London: Logos Press, 1971.

Bever, T., Lackner, J., & Kirk, R.   The underlying structure of sentences are the primary units of immediate speech processing. *Perception and Psychophysics*, 1969, *5*, 225–234.

Birdwhistell, R. L.   *Introduction to kinesics*. Louisville, Kentucky: Univ. of Louisville Press, 1952.

Birdwhistell, R. L.   Kinesics and communication. In E. Carpenter & M. McLuhan (Eds.), *Explorations in communication*. Boston: Beacon Press, 1960.

Birdwhistell, R. L.   Some relations between American kinesics and spoken American English. In A. G. Smith (Ed.), *Communication and culture*. New York: Holt, 1966.

Birdwhistell, R. L.   Kinesics. In D. Sills (Ed.), *International encyclopedia of the social sciences*. Vol. 8. New York: MacMillan, 1968.

Birdwhistell, R. L.   *Kinesics and context*. Philadelphia: Univ. of Pennsylvania Press, 1970.

Blom, J., & Gumperz, J. J.   Some social determinants of verbal behavior. In J. Gumperz & D. Hymes (Eds.), The ethnography of communication. *American Anthropologist*, 1964, *66*, No. 6, Part 2.

Bloom, L.   *Language development: Form and function in emerging grammars*. Cambridge, Massachusetts: MIT Press, 1970.

Bloomfield, L.   *Language*. New York: Holt, 1933.

Blumenthal, A.   Promoted recall of sentences. *Journal of Verbal Learning and Verbal Behavior*, 1967, *6*, 203–206.

Blumenthal, A.   *Language and psychology*. New York: Wiley, 1970.

Blumenthal, A., & Boakes, R.   Prompted recall of sentences. *Journal of Verbal Learning and Verbal Behavior*, 1967, *6*, 674–676.

Bobren, H., Hill, C., Snider, J., & Osgood, C. E.   A bibliography of literature relevant to the semantic differential technique. In J. Snider & C. E. Osgood (Eds.), *Semantic differential technique: A sourcebook*. Chicago: Aldine, 1968.

Braine, M.   On learning the grammatical order of words. *Psychological Review*, 1963, *70*, 323–348. (a)

Braine, M.   The ontogeny of English phrase structure: The first phase. *Language*, 1963, *39*, 1–13. (b)

Bransford, J., Barclay, J., & Franks, J.   Sentence memory: Constructive vs. interpretive approach. *Cognitive Psychology*, 1972, *3*, 193–209.

Brown, R.   Linguistic determinism and the part of speech. *Journal of Abnormal and Social Psychology*, 1957, *55*, 1–5.

Brown, R.   *Words and things*. Glencoe, Illinois: Free Press, 1958. (a)

Brown, R.   How shall a thing be called? *Psychological Review*, 1958, *65*, 14–21. (b)

Brown, R.   *Psycholinguistics*. New York: Free Press, 1965. (a)

Brown, R.   *Social psychology*. New York: Free Press, 1965. (b)

Brown, R.   *A first language: The early stages*. Cambridge, Massachusetts: Harvard Univ. Press, 1973.

Brown, R., & Bellugi, U.   Three processes in the child's acquisition of syntax. *Harvard Educational Review*, 1964, *34*, 133–151.

Brown, R., & Berko, J.   Word associations and the development of syntax. *Child Development*, 1960, *31*, 1–14.

Brown, R., & Fraser, C.   The acquisition of syntax. In U. Bellugi & R. Brown (Eds.), The acquisition of language. *Monographs of the Society for Research in Child Development*, 1964, *29*, No. 1.

Brown, R. & Ford, M.   Address in American English. *Journal of Abnormal and Social Psychology*, 1961, *62*, 375–385.

Brown, R., & Gilman, A.   The pronouns of power and solidarity. In T. Sebeok (Ed.), *Style in language*. Cambridge, Massachusetts: MIT Press, 1960.

Brown, R., & Lenneberg, E. H.   A study in language and cognition. *Journal of Abnormal and Social Psychology*, 1954, *49*, 454–462.

Brown, R., & McNeill, D.   The "tip of the tongue" phenomenon. *Journal of Verbal Learning and Verbal Behavior*, 1966, *5*, 325–337.

Burling, R. Language development of a Garo and English speaking child. *Word,* 1959, *15,* 45–68.

Burling, R. *Man's many voices: Language in its cultural context.* New York: Holt, 1970.

Byers, P., & H. Byers, Nonverbal communication and the education of children. In C. B. Cazden, V. P. John, & D. Hymes (Eds.), *Functions of language in the classroom.* New York: Teachers College Press, 1972.

Carmichael, L., Hogan, H. P., & Walter, A. A. An experimental study of the effect of language on the reproduction of visually perceived forms. *Journal of Experimental Psychology,* 1932, *15,* 73–86.

Carroll, J. B. *Language and thought.* Englewood Cliffs, New Jersey: Prentice-Hall, 1964.

Carroll, J. B. Language and psychology. In A. A. Hill (ed.), *Linguistics today.* New York: Basic Books, 1969.

Carroll, J. B., & Casagrande, J. The function of language classifications in behavior. In E. E. Maccoby, T. M. Newcomb, and E. L. Hartley (Eds.), *Readings in social psychology,* New York: Holt, 1958.

Cazden, C. B., John, V. P., & Hymes, D. (Eds.), *Functions of language in the classroom.* New York: Teachers College Press, 1972.

Chafe, W. L. *Meaning and the structure of language.* Chicago: Univ. of Chicago Press, 1970.

Cherry, C. *On human communication* (2nd ed.) Cambridge, Massachusetts: MIT Press, 1966.

Chomsky, C. *The acquisition of syntax in children from 5 to 10.* Cambridge, Massachusetts: MIT Press, 1969.

Chomsky, C. Reading, writing, and phonology. *Harvard Educational Review,* 1970, *40,* 287–309.

Chomsky, N. *Syntactic structures.* The Hague: Mouton, 1957.

Chomsky, N. Review of *Verbal Behavior* by B. F. Skinner. *Language,* 1959, *35,* 26–58.

Chomsky, N. *Aspects of the Theory of Syntax.* Cambridge, Massachusetts: MIT Press, 1965.

Chomsky, N. *Topics in the theory of generative grammar.* The Hague: Mouton, 1966.

Chomsky, N. *Language and mind.* New York: Harcourt, 1968.

Chomsky, N. Problems of explanation in linguistics. In R. Borger & F. Cioffi (Eds.), *Explanation in the behavioral sciences.* New York: Cambridge Univ. Press, 1970.

Chomsky, N., & Halle, M. *The sound pattern of English.* New York: Harper, 1968.

Clark, E. On the child's acquisition of antonyms in two semantic fields. *Journal of Verbal Learning and Verbal Behavior,* 11, 1972, 750–758.

Clark, E. What's in a word? On the child's acquisition of semantics in his first language. In T. E. Moore (Ed.), *Cognitive development and the acquisition of language.* New York: Academic Press, 1973.

Clark, H. Some structural properties of simple active and passive sentences. *Journal of Verbal Learning and Verbal Behavior,* 1965, *4,* 365–370.

Clark, H. H. Word associations and linguistic theory. In J. Lyons (Ed.), *New horizons in linguistics.* Baltimore, Maryland: Penguin, 1970.

Clark, H., & Card, S. Role of semantics in remembering comparative sentences. *Journal of Experimental Psychology,* 1969, *82,* 545–553.

Clark, H., & Clark, E. Semantic distinctions and memory for complex sentences. *Quarterly Journal of Experimental Psychology,* 1968, *20,* 129–138.

Clark, H., & Stafford, R. Memory for semantic features in the verb. *Journal of Experimental Psychology,* 1969, *80,* 326–334.

Conklin, H. C. Lexicographical treatment of folk taxonomies. In F. W. Householder & S. Saporta (Eds.), *Problems in lexicography* Publication No. 21 of Indiana Univ.

Research Center in Anthropology, Folklore and Linguistics. Bloomington, Indiana: 1962.

Conklin, H. C. Ethnogenealogical method. In W. H. Goodenough (Ed.), *Explorations in cultural anthropology*. New York: McGraw-Hill, 1964. (a)

Conklin, H. C. Hanunoo color categories. In D. Hymes (Ed.), *Language in culture and society: A reader in linguistics and anthropology*. New York: Harper, 1964. (b)

Curtiss, S., Fromkin, V., Krashen, S., Rigler, D., & Rigler, M. The linguistic development of Genie. *Language*, 1974, *50*, 528–554.

Deese, J. On the structure of associative meaning. *Psychological Review*, 1962, *69*, 161–175.

Deese, J. *The structure of associations in language and thought*. Baltimore, Maryland: Johns Hopkins Press, 1965.

Derwing, B. L. *Transformational grammar as a theory of language acquisition*. New York: Cambridge Univ. Press, 1973.

Donaldson, M. & Balfour, G. Less is more: A study of language comprehension in children. *British Journal of Psychology*, 1968, *59*, 461–472.

Donaldson, M., & Wales, R. On the acquisition of some relational terms. In J. R. Hayes (Ed.), *Cognition and the development of language*. New York: Wiley, 1970.

Ekman, P., & Friesen, W. V. Head and body cues in the judgment of emotion: A reformulation. *Perceptual and Motor Skills*, 1967, *24*, 711–724.

Ekman, P., & Friesen, W. V. Nonverbal behavior in psychotherapy research. In J. Schlien (Ed.), *Research in psychotherapy*, Vol. 3, Washington, D.C.: American Psychological Association, 1968.

Ekman, P., Friesen, W. V., & Tomkins, S. S. Facial affect scoring technique: A first validity study. *Semiotica*, 1971, *3*, 38–58.

Emig, J. A., Fleming, J. T., & Popp, H. M. (Eds.) *Language and learning*. New York: Harcourt, 1966.

Ervin, S. Changes with age in the verbal determinants of word association. *American Journal of Psychology*, 1961, *74*, 361–372. (a)

Ervin, S. Learning and recall in bilinguals. *American Journal of Psychology*, 1961, *74*, 446–451. (b)

Ervin, S. M., & Osgood, C. E. Second language learning and bilingualism. *Journal of Abnormal and Social Psychology*, 1954, *49*, 139–146.

Ervin-Tripp, S. Language development. In L. W. Hoffman & M. L. Hoffman (Eds.), *Review of child development research*, Vol. 2. New York: Russell Sage Foundation, 1966.

Ervin-Tripp, S., & Slobin, D. I. Psycholinguistics. *Annual Review of Psychology*, 1966, *17*, 435–474.

Ferguson, C. F. Diglossia. In D. Hymes (Ed.), *Language in culture and society: A reader in linguistics and anthropology*. New York: Harper, 1964.

Fillenbaum, S. Memory for gist: Some relevant variables. *Language and Speech*, 1966, *9*, 217–227.

Fillenbaum, S. Psycholinguistics. *Annual Review of Psychology*, 1971, *22*, 251–308.

Fillenbaum, S. *Syntactic factors in memory*. The Hague: Mouton, 1973.

Fillmore, C. J. The case for case. In E. Bach & R. T. Harms (Ed.), *Universals in linguistic theory*. New York: Holt, 1968.

Fillmore, C. J. Types of lexical infromation. In D. D. Steinberg & L. A. Jakobovits (Ed.), *Semantics: An interdisciplinary reader in philosophy, linguistics, and psychology*. New York: Cambridge Univ. Press, 1971.

Fillmore, C. J., & Langendoen, D. T. *Studies in linguistic semantics*. New York: Holt, 1971.

Fishman, J. A systematization of the Whorfian hypothesis. *Behavioral Science*, 1960, *5*, 323–329.

Fishman, J. *The sociology of language*. Rowley, Massachusetts: Newbury House, 1972.

Flores D'Arcais, G. B., & Levelt, W. J. M. (Eds.) *Advances in psycholinguistics*. Amsterdam: North-Holland, 1970.

Fodor, J. A. & Bever, T. The psychological reality of linguistic segments. *Journal of Verbal Learning and Verbal Behavior*, 1965, *4*, 414–420.

Fodor, J. A. & Garrett, M. Some syntactic determinants of sentential complexity. *Perception and Psychophysics*, 1967, *2*, 289–296.

Fodor, J. A., Garrett, M., & Bever, T. Some syntactic determinants of sentential complexity, II: Verb structure. *Perception and Psychophysics*, 1968, *3*, 453–461.

Fodor, J. A. & Katz, J. J. (Eds.) *The structure of language: Readings in the philosophy of language*. Englewood Cliffs, New Jersey: Prentice-Hall, 1964.

Frake, C. O. The ethnographic study of cognitive systems. In T. Gladwin & W. C. Sturtevant (Eds.), *Anthropology and human behavior*. Washington D.C.: Anthropological Society of Washington, 1962.

Frake, C. O. How to ask for a drink in subanun. In J. Gumperz & D. Hymes (Eds.), The ethnography of communication. *American Anthropologist*, 1964, *66*, No. 6, Part 2. (a)

Frake, C. O. The diagnosis of disease among the Subanun of Mindanao. In D. Hymes (Ed.), *Language in culture and society: A reader in linguistics and anthropology*. New York: Harper, 1964 (b)

Furth, H. G. *Thinking without language*. New York: Free Press, 1966.

Gardner, R. A., & Gardner, B. Teaching sign language to a chimpanzee. *Science*, 1969, *165*, 664–672.

Gardner, R. A. & Gardner, B. Discussion presented at the American Anthropological Association meetings. Toronto, 1972.

Gardner, R. C., & Lambert, W. E. *Attitudes and motivation in second-language learning*. Rowley, Massachusetts: Newbury House, 1972.

Garrett, M., Bever, T., & Fodor, J. A. The active use of grammar in speech perception. *Perception and Psychophysics*, 1966, *1*, 30–32.

Geertz, C. *The religion of Java*. New York: Free Press, 1960.

Gilman, A., & Brown, R. Emerson and Thoreau: Personality and style in Concord. In M. Simon & T. Parsons (Eds.), *The legacy of transcendentalism*. Ann Arbor: Univ. of Michigan Press, 1966.

Gladwin, T., & Sturtevant, W. C. (Eds.) *Anthropology and human behavior*. Washington, D. C.: Anthropological Society of Washington, 1962.

Gleason, H. A. *An introduction to descriptive linguistics*. (New rev. ed.) New York: Holt, 1961.

Goldman-Eisler, F. Hesitation, information, and levels of speech production. In A. V. S. deReuck & M. O'Connor (Eds.), *Ciba foundation symposium: Disorders of language*, London: Churchill, 1964.

Goldman-Eisler, F. *Psycholinguistics: Experiments in spontaneous speech*. New York: Academic Press, 1968.

Goldman-Eisler, F., Skarbek, A., & Henderson, A. Cognitive and neurochemical determination of sentence structure. *Language and Speech*, 1965, *8*, 86–94.

Goodenough, W. H. Componential analysis and the study of meaning. *Language*, 1956, *32*, 195–216.

Goodenough, W. H. (Ed.) *Explorations in cultural anthropology*. New York: McGraw-Hill, 1964. (a)

Goodenough, W. H. Property and language on Truk: Some methodological considerations. In Hymes (Ed.), *Language in culture and society: A reader in linguistics and anthropology*. New York: Harper, 1964. (b)

Gottschalk, L. A. (Ed.) *Comparative psycholinguistic analysis of two psychotherapeutic interviews*. New York: International Univ. Press, 1961.

Greenberg, J. (Ed.) *Universals of Language.* (2nd ed.) Cambridge, Massachusetts: MIT Press, 1966.

Greenberg, J. *Anthropological linguistics.* New York: Random House, 1968.

Greene, J. *Psycholinguistics: Chomsky and psychology.* Baltimore: Penguin, 1972.

Gumperz, J., & Hymes, D. (Eds.) *The ethnography of communication. American Anthropologist,* (Special Publication), 1964, *66,* No. 6, Part 2.

Gumperz, J., & Hymes, D. (Eds.) *Directions in sociolinguistics.* New York: Holt, 1972.

Hall, E. T. *The silent language.* Garden City, New York: Doubleday, 1959.

Hall, E. T. A system for the notation of proxemic behavior. *American Anthropologist,* 1963, *65,* 1003–26.

Hall, E. T. *The hidden dimension.* Garden City, New York: Doubleday, 1966.

Hall, E. T. Proxemics. *Current Anthropology,* 1968, *9,* 83–108.

Hall, E. T. Silent assumptions in social communication. Reprinted in J. Laver & S. Hutcheson, *Communication in face to face interaction.* Baltimore: Penguin, 1972.

Haugen, E. *Bilingualism in the Americas: A bibliography and research guide.* Univ. of Alabama: American Dialect Society, 1956.

Hayes, C. *The ape in our house.* New York: Harper, 1951.

Hayes, J. R. (Ed.) *Cognition and the development of language.* New York: Wiley, 1970.

Herriot, P. The comprehension of active and passive sentences as a function of pragmatic expectations. *Journal of Verbal Learning and Verbal Behavior,* 1969, *8,* 166–169.

Herskovits, M. J. *Man and his works.* New York: Knopf, 1948.

Hewes, G. W. The anthropology of posture. *Scientific American,* 1957, *196,* 122–132.

Hewes, G. W. Primate communication and the gestural origin of language. *Current Anthropology,* 1973, *14,* 5–24.

Hockett, C. F. *A course in modern linguistics.* New York: MacMillan, 1958.

Hockett, C. F. The origin of speech. *Scientific American,* 1960, *203,* 86–96.

Hockett, C. F. The problem of universals in language. In J. Greenberg (Ed.), *Universals of language.* (2nd ed.) Cambridge, Massachusetts: MIT Press, 1966.

Hockett, C. F., & Ascher, R. The human revolution. *Current Anthropology,* 1964, *5,* 135–168.

Householder, F. W. Review of Z. Harris, *Methods in Structural Linguistics. International Journal of American Linguistics,* 1952, *18,* 260–268.

Householder, F. W. On linguistic primes. In S. Saporta (Ed.), *Psycholinguistics.* New York: Holt, 1961.

Householder, F. W., & Saporta, S. (Eds.) *Problems in Lexicography.* Publication No. 21 of the Indiana Univ. Research Center in Anthropology, Folklore and Linguistics. Bloomington, Indiana, 1962.

Hymes, D. (Ed.) *Language in culture and society: A reader in linguistics and anthropology.* New York: Harper, 1964.

Hymes, D. *Foundations in sociolinguistics: An ethnographic approach.* Philadelphia: Univ. of Pennsylvania Press, 1974.

Irwin, O. C. Infant speech: Vowel and consonant frequency. *Journal of Speech and Hearing Disorders,* 1946, *12,* 123–125.

Irwin, O. C. Infant speech: Consonantal sounds according to place of articulation. *Journal of Speech and Hearing Disorders,* 1947, *12,* 397–401. (a)

Irwin, O. C. Infant speech: Consonantal sounds according to manner of articulation. *Journal of Speech and Hearing Disorders,* 1947, *12,* 402–404. (b)

Irwin, O. C. Infant speech: Development of vowel sounds. *Journal of Speech and Hearing Disorders,* 1948, *13,* 31–34.

Itard, J. M. G. *The wild boy of Averyon.* New York: Appleton, 1962.

Jakobovits, L. A. & Miron, M. S. (Eds.) *Readings in the psychology of language.* Englewood Cliffs, New Jersey: Prentice-Hall, 1967.

Jakobson, R. *Child language, aphasia, and phonological universals,* The Hague: Mouton, 1968.

Jakobson, R., Fant, G., & Halle, M. *Preliminaries to speech analysis: The distinctive features and their correlates.* Cambridge, Massachusetts: MIT Press, 1953.

Jakobson, R., & Halle, M. *Fundamentals of language.* The Hague: Mouton, 1956.

Jenkins, J. J., Russell, W. A., & Suci, G. J. An atlas of semantic profiles for 360 words. *American Journal of Psychology,* 1958, *71,* 688–699.

Johnson, M. G. Syntactic position and rated meaning. In L. A. Jakobovits & M. S. Miron (Eds.), *Readings in the psychology of language.* Englewood Cliffs, New Jersey: Prentice-Hall, 1967.

Johnson, N. F. The psychological reality of phrase structure rules. *Journal of Verbal Learning and Verbal Behavior,* 1965, *4,* 469–475.

Johnson-Laird, P. The choice of the passive voice in a communicative task. *British Journal of Psychology,* 1968, *59,* 7–15.

Johnson-Laird, P. Experimental psycholinguistics. *Annual Review of Psychology,* 1974, *25,* 135–160.

Johnson-Laird, P., & Stevenson, R. Memory for syntax. *Nature,* 1970, *227,* 412–413.

Katz, J. J. *The philosophy of language.* New York: Harper, 1966.

Katz, J. J., & Fodor, J. A. The structure of a semantic theory. *Language,* 1963, *39,* 170–210.

Katz, J. J., & Postal, P. *An integrated theory of linguistic descriptions.* Cambridge, Massachusetts: MIT Press, 1964.

Kolers, P. A. Interlingual word associations. *Journal of Verbal Learning and Verbal Behavior,* 1963, *2,* 291–300

Kolers, P. A. Bilingualism and bicodalism. *Language and Speech,* 1965, *8,* 122–126.

Kolers, P. A. Reading and talking bilingually. *American Journal of Psychology,* 1966, *79,* 357–376.

Kolers, P. A. Bilingualism and information processing. *Scientific American,* 1968, *218,* 78–86.

Kuhn, T. S. *The structure of scientific revolutions.* (2nd ed.) Chicago: Univ. of Chicago Press, 1970.

LaBarre, W. Paralinguistics, kinesics, and cultural anthropology. In T. A. Sebeok, A. S. Hayes, & M. C. Bateson (Eds.), *Approaches to semiotics.* The Hague: Mouton, 1964.

Labov, W. Phonological correlates of social stratification. In J. Gumperz & D. Hymes (Eds.), The ethnography of communication. *American Anthropologist,* 1964, *66,* No. 6, Part 2.

Labov, W. *The social stratification of English in New York City.* Washington, D.C.: Center for Applied Linguistics, 1966.

Labov, W. *Sociolinguistic patterns.* Philadelphia: Univ. of Pennsylvania Press, 1972. (a)

Labov, W. *Language in the Inner City.* Philadelphia: Univ. of Pennsylvania Press, 1972. (b)

Lackner, J. R., & Garrett, M. Resolving ambiguity: Effects of biasing context in the unattended ear. *Cognition,* 1972, *1,* 359–372.

Lambert, W. E. Psychological studies of the interdependencies of the bilingual's two languages. In J. Puhvel (Ed.), *Substance and the structure of language.* Berkeley: Univ. of California Press, 1969.

Lambert, W. E., Frankel, H., & Tucker, G. R. Judging personality through speech: A French-Canadian example. *Journal of Communication,* 1966, *16,* 305–321.

Lambert, W. E., Gardner, R. C., Barik, H. C., & Tunstall, K. Attitudinal and cognitive aspects of intensive study of a second language. *Journal of Abnormal and Social Psychology*, 1963, 66, 358–368.

Lambert, W. E., Havelka, J., & Crosby, C.   The influence of language-acquisition contexts on bilingualism. *Journal of Abnormal and Social Psychology*, 1958, 56, 239–244.

Lambert, W. E., Havelka, J., & Gardner, R. C.   Linguistic manifestations of bilingualism. *American Journal of Psychology*, 1959, 72, 77–82.

Lambert, W. E., Hodgson, R. C., Gardner, R. C., & Fillenbaum, S.   Evaluational reactions to spoken languages. *Journal of Abnormal and Social Psychology*, 1960, 60, 44–51.

Lambert, W. E., Ignatow, M., & Krauthamer, M.   Bilingual organization in free recall. *Journal of Verbal Learning and Verbal Behavior*, 1968, 7, 207–214.

Lambert, W. E., Just, M., & Segalowitz, N.   Some cognitive consequences of following the curricula of grades one and two in a foreign language. *Georgetown Monograph Series on Languages and Linguistics*, 1970, 23, 229–279.

Lambert, W. E., & Macnamara, J.   Some cognitive consequences of following a first-grade curriculum in a second language. *Journal of Educational Psychology*, 1969, 60, 86–96.

Lambert, W. E., & Tucker, G. R.   *The bilingual education of children: The St. Lambert experiment.* Rowley, Massachusetts: Newbury House, 1972.

Lambert, W. E., Tucker, G. R. & d'Anglejean, A.   An innovative approach to second language learning. Mimeo, 1972.

Laver, J., & Hutcheson, S.   *Communication in face to face interaction.* Baltimore, Maryland: Penguin, 1972.

Lenneberg, E. H.   The capacity for language acquisition. In J. A. Fodor & J. J. Katz (Eds.), *The structure of language: Readings in the philosophy of language.* Englewood Cliffs, New Jersey: Prentice-Hall, 1964.

Lenneberg, E. H.   *Biological foundations of language.* New York: Wiley, 1967.

Lenneberg, E. H., & Roberts, J. M.   *The language of experience.* Indiana Univ. Publications in Anthropology and Linguistics, Memoir 13. Baltimore, 1956.

Leopold, W. F.   *Speech development of a bilingual child: A linguist's record.* 4 Vols. Evanston, Illinois: Northwestern Univ. Press, 1947.

Leopold, W. F.   Patterning in children's language learning. In S. Saporta (Ed.), *Psycholinguistics.* New York: Holt, 1961.

Lieberson, S.   Bilingualism in Montreal: A demographic analysis. *American Journal of Sociology*, 1965, 71, 10–25.

Lieberson, S.   *Language and ethnic relations in Canada.* New York: Wiley, 1970.

Lilly, J. C.   *Man and dolphin.* Garden City, New York: Doubleday, 1961.

Lounsbury, F. G.   A semantic analysis of the Pawnee kinship usage. *Language*, 1956, 32, 158–194.

Lounsbury, F. G.   A formal account of the Crow- and Omaha- type kinship terminologies. In W. H. Goodenough (Ed.), *Explorations in cultural anthropology.* New York: McGraw-Hill, 1964.

Lyons, J. (Ed.)   *New horizons in linguistics.* Baltimore, Maryland: Penguin, 1970.

Mackey, W. F.   The description of bilingualism. *Canadian Journal of Linguistics*, 1962, 7, 59–85.

Mackey, W. F.   The measurement of bilingual behavior. *Canadian Psychologist*, 1966, 7, 75–92.

Mackey, W. F.   The lesson to be drawn from bilingualism. *Applied linguistics and the teaching of French.* Montreal: Centre éducatif et culturel, 1967. (a)

Mackey, W. F.   *Bilingualism as a world problem.* Montreal: Harvest House, 1967. (b)

Maclay, H.   Linguistics and psycholinguistics. In B. Kachru (Ed.), *Issues in linguistics: Papers in honor of Henry and Renee Kahane.* Urbana: Univ. of Illinois Press, 1973.

Maclay, H., & Osgood, C. E. Hesitation phenomena in spontaneous English speech. *Word*, 1959, *15*, 19–44.

Macnamara, J. (Ed.) *Problems of bilingualism. Journal of Social Issues*, 1967, *23*, No. 2.

Mahl, G. F. Disturbances and silences in the patient's speech in psychotherapy. *Journal of Abnormal and Social Psychology*, 1956, *53*, 1–15.

Mahl, G. F. Exploring emotional states by content analysis. In I. Pool (Ed.), *Trends in content analysis*. Urbana: Univ. of Illinois Press, 1959.

Mahl, G. F., & Schulze, G. Psychological research in the extralinguistic area. In T. A. Sebeok, A. S. Hayes, & M. C. Bateson (Eds.), *Approaches to semiotics*. The Hague: Mouton, 1964.

Mandelbaum, D. B. (Ed.) *Selected writings of Edward Sapir in language, culture and personality*. Berkeley: Univ. of California Press, 1949.

Marks, L. E. & Miller, G. The role of semantic and syntactic constraints in the memorization of English sentences. *Journal of Verbal Learning and Verbal Behavior*, 1964, *3*, 1–5.

Martin, S. Speech levels in Japan and Korea. In D. Hymes (Ed.), *Language in culture and society: A reader in linguistics and anthropology*. New York: Harper, 1964.

Matarazzo, J. D., Wiens, A. N., Matarazzo, R. G., & Saslow, G. Speech and silence behavior in clincial psychotherapy and its laboratory correlates. In J. Schlien (Ed.), *Research in psychotherapy*. Vol. 3. Washington, D.C.: American Psychological Association, 1968.

Matarazzo, J. D., Wiens, A. N., & Saslow, G. Studies in interview speech behavior. In L. Krasner & L. P. Ullman (Eds.), *Research in behavior modification*. New York: Holt, 1965.

McIntosh, A. Patterns and ranges. *Language*, 1961, *37*, 325–337.

McNeill, D. Developmental psycholinguistics. In F. Smith & G. A. Miller (Eds.), *The genesis of language: A psycholinguistic approach*. Cambridge, Massachusetts: MIT Press, 1966.

McNeill, D. *The acquisition of language*. New York: Harper, 1970.

McQuown, N. A. *The natural history of an interview*. Microfilm Collection of Manuscripts on Middle American Cultural Anthropology, No. 95–98. Univ. of Chicago Library, 1971.

Mehler, J. Some effects of grammatical transformations on the recall of English sentences. *Journal of Verbal Learning and Verbal behavior*, 1963, *2*, 346–351.

Mehler, J., & Carey, P. Role of surface and base structure in the perception of sentences. *Journal of Verbal Learning and Verbal Behavior*, 1967, *6*, 335–338.

Menyuk, P. *The acquisition and development of language*. Englewood Cliffs, New Jersey: Prentice-Hall, 1971.

Miller, G. A. *Language and communication*. New York: McGraw-Hill, 1951.

Miller, G. A. What is information measurement? *American Psychologist*, 1953, *8*, 3–11.

Miller, G. A. Some psychological studies of grammar. *American Journal of Psychology*, 1962, *17*, 748–762.

Miller, G. A. The psycholinguists. *Encounter*, 1964, *23*, 29–37.

Miller, G. A. & Isard, S. Some perceptual consequences of linguistic rules. *Journal of Verbal Learning and Verbal Behavior*, 1963, *2*, 217–228.

Miller, G. A. & Isard, S. Free recall of self-embedded English sentences. *Information and Control*, 1964, *7*, 292–303.

Miller, G. A., & McKean, K. A chronometric study of some relations between sentences. In R. C. Oldfield & J. C. Marshall (Eds.), *Language: Selected readings*. Baltimore, Maryland: Penguin, 1968.

Miller, G. A., & Selfridge, J. A. Verbal context and the recall of meaningful material. *American Journal of Psychology*, 1950, *63*, 176–185.

Miller, W., & Ervin, S. The development of grammar in child language. In U. Bellugi &

R. Brown (Eds.), The acquisition of language. *Monographs of the Society for Research in Child Development,* 1964, *29,* No. 1.

Moore, T. E. (Ed.) *Cognitive development and the acquisition of Language.* New York: Academic Press, 1973.

Morris, C. W. Foundations of the theory of signs. *International encyclopedia of unified science.* Vol. 1, No. 2. Chicago: Univ. of Chicago Press, 1938.

Moskowitz, A. Early phonology acquisition. Paper presented at Linguistic Society of America meetings, 1970.

Moskowitz, A. On the status of vowel shift in English. In T. E. Moore (Ed.), *Cognitive development and the acquisition of language.* New York: Academic Press, 1973.

Mosteller, F., & Wallace, D. L. *Inference and disputed authorship: The Federalist.* Reading, Massachusetts: Addison-Wesley, 1964.

Mowrer, O. H. The psychologist looks at language. *American Journal of Psychology,* 1954, *9,* 660–694.

Neisser, U. *Cognitive psychology.* New York: Appleton, 1967.

Nelson, K. Concept, word, and sentence: Interrelations in acquisition and development. *Psychological Review,* 1974, *81,* 267–285.

Noble, C. An analysis of meaning. *Psychological Review,* 1952, *59,* 421–430.

Noble, C. E. Meaningfulness and familiarity. In C. N. Cofer & B. S. Musgrave (Eds.), *Verbal behavior and learning.* New York: McGraw-Hill, 1963.

Nott, C. R., & Lambert, W. E. Free recall of bilinguals. *Journal of Verbal Learning and Verbal Behavior,* 1968, *7,* 1065–1071.

Oldfield, R. C., & Marshall, J. C. (Eds.) *Language: Selected headings.* Baltimore, Maryland: Penguin, 1968.

Olson, D., & Filby, N. On the comprehension of active and passive sentences. *Cognitive Psychology,* 1972, *3,* 361–381.

Osgood, C. E. *Method and theory in experimental psychology.* New York: Oxford Univ. Press, 1953.

Osgood, C. E. Behavior theory and the social sciences. *Behavioral Sciences,* 1956, *1,* 167–185.

Osgood, C. E. A behavioristic analysis of perception and language as cognitive phenomena. In *Contemporary Approaches to Cognition, A Symposium Held at the University of Colorado.* Cambridge, Massachussets: Harvard Univ. Press, 1957.

Osgood, C, E. On understanding and creating sentences. *American Psychologist,* 1963, *18,* 735–751.

Osgood, C. E. Semantic differential technique in the comparative study of cultures. *American Anthropologist,* 1964, *66,* 171–200.

Osgood, C. E. Universals and psycholinguistics. In J. Greenberg (Ed.), *Universals of language.* (2nd ed.) Cambridge, Massachusetts: MIT Press, 1966.

Osgood, C. E. Where do sentences come from? In D. D. Steinberg & L. A. Jakobovits (Eds.), *Semantics: An interdisciplinary reader in philosophy, linguistics, and psychology.* New York: Cambridge Univ. Press, 1971.

Osgood, C. E., & Luria, Z. A blind analysis of a case of multiple personality using the semantic differential. *Journal of Abnormal and Social Psychology,* 1954, *49,* 579–591.

Osgood, C. E., & Sebeok,T. A. (Eds.) *Psycholinguistics: A survey of theory and research problems.* Indiana Univ. Publications in Anthropology and Linguistics, Memoir 10, 1954.

Osgood, C. E., Suci, G., & Tannenbaum, P. *The measurement of meaning.* Urbana: Univ. of Illinois Press, 1957.

Osgood, C. E., & Walker, E. G. Motivation and language behavior. A content analysis of suicide notes. *Journal of Abnormal and Social Psychology,* 1959, *58,* 58–67.

Paivio, A. *Imagery and verbal processes.* New York: Holt, 1971.

Penfield, W. Conditioning the uncommitted cortex for language learning. *Brain,* 1965, *88,* 787–798.

Penfield, W., & Roberts, L. *Speech and brain-mechanisms.* Princeton, New Jersey: Princeton Univ. Press, 1959.

Piaget, J. *The origins of intelligence in children.* New York: International Univ. Press, 1952.

Piaget, J. *The language and thought of the child.* Cleveland: Meridian Books, 1955.

Piaget, J. *Structuralism.* New York: Basic Books, 1970. (a)

Piaget, J. *Science of education and the psychology of the child.* New York: Orion Press, 1970. (b)

Piaget, J., & Inhelder, B. *The growth of logical thinking from childhood to adolescence.* New York: Basic Books, 1958.

Pike. K. L. *Language in relation to a unified theory of the structure of human behavior.* (2nd rev. ed.) The Hague: Mouton, 1967.

Pittenger, R. E., Hockett, C. F., & Danehy, J. J. *The first five minutes.* Ithaca, New York: Paul Martineau, 1960.

Pool, I. de Sola (Ed.) *Trends in content analysis.* Urbana: Univ. of Illinois Press, 1959.

Premack, A. J., & Premack, D. Teaching language to an ape. *Scientific American,* 1972, *227,* 92–99.

Pride, J. B., & Holmes, J. (Eds.) *Sociolinguistics.* Baltimore, Maryland: Penguin Books, 1972.

Reber, A. S. On psycho-linguistic paradigms. *Journal of Psycholinguistic Research,* 1973, *2,* 289–319.

Romney, A. K., & D'Andrade, R. G. (Eds.) *Transcultural studies in cognition. American Anthropologist,* 1964, *66,* No. 3, Part 2. Special Publication.

Rosenberg, S. (Ed.) *Directions in psycholinguistics.* New York: MacMillan, 1965.

Rosenberg, S. & Jarvella, R. Semantic integration and sentence perception. *Journal of Verbal Learning and Verbal Behavior,* 1970, *9,* 548–553.

Rubenstein, H., & Aborn, M. Psycholinguistics. *Annual Review of Psychology,* 1960, *11,* 129–322.

Rubin, J. *National bilingualism in Paraguay.* The Hague: Mouton, 1968.

Sapir, E. Conceptual categories in primitive languages. *Science,* 1931, *74,* 578.

Saporta, S., & Sebeok, T. A. Linguistics and content analysis. In I. Pool (Ed.), *Trends in content analysis.* Urbana: Univ. of Illinois Press, 1959.

Saporta, S. (Ed.) *Psycholinguistics.* New York: Holt, 1961.

Savin, H., & Perchonock, E. Grammatical structure and the immediate recall of English sentences. *Journal of Verbal Learning and Verbal Behavior,* 1965, *4,* 348–353.

Scheflen, A. E. *How behavior means.* New York: Gordon & Breach, 1973.

Schlesinger, I. *Sentence structure and the reading process.* The Hague: Mouton, 1968.

Searle, J. R. *Speech acts: An essay in the philosophy of language.* New York: Cambridge Univ. Press, 1969.

Sebeok, T., Ed. *Style in language.* Cambridge, Massachusetts: MIT Press, 1960.

Sebeok, T. A., Hayes, A. S., & Bateson, M. C. (Eds.) *Approaches to semiotics.* The Hague: Mouton, 1964.

Shannon, C. E., & Weaver, W. *The mathematical theory of communication.* Urbana: Univ. of Illinois Press, 1949.

Skinner, B. F. *The behavior of organisms: An experimental analysis.* New York: Appleton, 1938.

Skinner, B. F. *Walden II.* New York: MacMillan, 1948.

Skinner. B. F. *Verbal behavior.* New York: Appleton, 1957.

Skinner, B. F. *Beyond freedom and dignity.* New York: Knopf, 1971.

Slobin, D. I. Grammatical transformations in childhood and adulthood. *Journal of Verbal Learning and Verbal Behavior*, 1966, 5, 219–227.

Slobin, D. I. Universals of grammatical development in children. In G. B. Flores d'Arcais & W. J. M. Levelt (Eds.), *Advances in psycholinguistics*. Amsterdam: North Holland, 1970.

Slobin, D. I., Miller, S. H., & Porter, L. W. Forms of address and social relations in a business organization. *Journal of Personality and Social Psychology*, 1968, 8, 289–293.

Smith, A. G. (Ed.) *Communication and culture*. New York: Holt, 1966.

Smith, F., & Miller, G. A. (Eds.) *The genesis of language: A psycholinguistic approach*. Cambridge, Massachusetts: MIT Press, 1966.

Staats, A. W. *Human learning*. New York: Holt, 1964.

Staats, A. W. *Learning, language and cognition*. New York: Holt, 1968.

Staats, A. W. *Child learning, intelligence, and personality*. New York: Harper, 1971.

Steinberg, D. D., & Jakobovits, L. A. (Eds.) *Semantics: An interdisciplinary reader in philosophy, linguistics, and psychology*. New York: Cambridge Univ. Press, 1971.

Steinberg, D. D. Phonology, reading, and Chomsky and Halle's optimal orthography. *Journal of Psycholinguistic Research*, 1973, 2, 239–258.

Terwilliger, R. F. *Meaning and mind: A study in the psychology of language*. New York: Oxford Univ. Press, 1968.

Thigpen, C. H., & H. M. Cleckley, *The three faces of Eve*. New York: McGraw-Hill, 1957.

Thorne, J. P. Generative grammar and stylistic analysis. In J. Lyons (Ed.), *New horizons in linguistics*. Baltimore, Maryland: Penguin, 1970.

Trager, G. L. Paralanguage: A first approximation. *Studies in Linguistics*, 1958, 13, 1–12.

Trager, G. L. The typology of paralanguage. *Anthropological Linguistics*, 1961, 3, 17–21.

Tucker, G. R., Lambert, W. E., & d'Anglejean, A. French immersion programs: A pilot investigation. *Language Sciences*, 1973, 25, 19–26.

Turner, E., & Rommetveit, R. Focus of attention in recall of active and passive sentences. *Journal of Verbal Learning and Verbal Behavior*, 1968, 7, 543–548.

Ullmann, S. *Semantics*. Oxford: Blackwell, 1962.

Velten, H. V. The growth of phonemic and lexical pattern in infant language. *Language*, 1943, 19, 281–292.

von Frisch, K. *Bees: Their vision, chemical senses, and language*. Ithaca, New York: Cornell Univ. Press, 1950.

von Frisch, K. *The dancing bees*. New York: Harcourt, 1955.

Vygotsky, L. S. *Thought and language*. New York: Wiley, 1962.

Wales, R. J., & Campbell, R. On the development of comparison and the comparison of development. In G. B. Flores d'Arcais & W. J. M. Levelt (Eds.), *Advances in psycholinguistics*. Amsterdam: North Holland, 1970.

Wason, P. Response to affirmative and negative binary statements. *British Journal of Psychology*, 1961, 52, 133–142.

Wason, P. The contexts of plausible denial. *Journal of Verbal Learning and Verbal Behavior*, 1965, 4, 7–11.

Watson, J. B. *Psychology from the standpoint of a behaviorist*. Philadelphia: Lippincott, 1919, 1924.

Watson, J. B. *Behaviorism*. New York: C. C. Norton, 1924.

Weinreich, U. *Languages in contact*. Publication of the Linguistic Circle of New York, No. 1. New York, 1953.

Weir, R. H. *Language in the crib*. The Hague: Mouton, 1962.
Weir, R. H. Some questions on the child's learning of phonology. In F. Smith & G. A. Miller (Eds.), *The genesis of language: A psycholinguistic approach*. Cambridge, Massachusetts: MIT Press, 1966.
Whorf, B. L. *Language, thought, and reality*. Cambridge, Massachusetts: MIT Press, 1956.

Index

A

associations, 157–159, 199, 233
bilingual, 233
composition of, 14
mediational model of, 41–42
pronunciation of, 14–15
recall ability, in bilingualism, 234
relational ties between, 155–159

in semantic development, 77–78
transitional error probability and, 199
Writing, 12, 56, 219–221

Z

Zipf's law, 93